This is a timely book. In a climate of overheated and oversimplified religion, Thomas Fudge's essays are a welcome antidote. They are written for reluctant unbelievers but are needed even more urgently by righteously certain Christians. Brought up to "only believe", the author lives by the creed of questioning everything. But he does this out of a faith well examined and deeply grounded in scholarship and history. That lifetime of learning is transparent in these pages. It's quite rare to find an academic who can anchor his insights in contemporary film, literature and everyday experience as easily as the classical texts. We range from Tolkien to Tertullian, from poetry to anecdote with the ease of a storyteller who trusts his memories and images to cut more sharply than ideas and abstractions. And all of this beautifully woven in a tapestry of verbal threads that would make any pulpit proud. Everyone who is even slightly curious about Christianity; anyone who is still wondering, and even some who don't wonder at all, will be enriched by these pages.

+ John Bluck
Anglican Bishop of Waiapu (retired)
New Zealand

Full of rich surprising insights, heart-warming stories and illustrations, *The Empty Box* is a true treasure trove for preachers of a Gospel that enlightens and liberates rather than hardens into righteous certainty. This is indeed a book for reluctant unbelievers: All those for whom God is the constant question, rather than the glib answer of those for whom Christianity is more an ideology than a way of life in love. It challenges institutional practice that masks the Mystery, walls people within legal and dogmatic security, and protects the childish from the trials and doubts required to test and mature the faith. I think it will both give hope to the reluctant unbeliever, and inspire love in those for whom doubt is not the enemy of faith. While sometimes discomforted by its prophetic challenges, I found *The Empty Box* remarkably full.

Father Paul McCabe
Rector, St. Patrick's Seminary (retired)
Manly, NSW Australia

The Empty Box is anything but what the title might suggest. Full and overflowing with rich insights that Thomas Fudge has chronicled over several decades in his faith journey, the book does not so much mark the milestones of his pilgrimage as it does establish landmarks in the evolution of his thought and the distilling and deepening of his faith. Since Thomas has worked both in the academy and in the church, each chapter pulsates with the passion of the pastor undergirded by the robust discipline of reflective thought characteristic of his profession. Although we grew up only an hour apart in our native New Brunswick, Canada, it was not until I had served in pastoral ministry for two decades, and Thomas had become an academic in New Zealand that we first met. His father, the late Rev. James Fudge, whom I am honoured to have called a friend, and, who was both a decorated and distinguished police officer and an ordained minister of the gospel, introduced us. I was captivated as I travelled with Thomas in his faith journey from chapter to chapter in *The Empty Box,* each of which challenged my thinking and beckoned me to a higher and deeper realization of the grace of God, and the majesty and magnitude of His calling upon the lives of we, mere mortals, yet the crowning act of His creation.

Don Carmont
President and Principal, HRXL Associates
Surrey, B.C., Canada

I've not read a book quite like this - which indicates the distinctly unique character of Thomas Fudge's recent book. Those interested in a very special and at times moving blend of biographical, historical, spiritual reflections shot through with good humour and allusions to a broad range of literature, this is your book.

Rainer Behrens
Pastor, Christliche Gemeinschaft (Lutheran)
Hamburg-Altona, Germany

Thomas Fudge has discerned the spiritual mood of our times and offers in this book some helpful words for postmodern pilgrims. In these first decades of the twenty-first century, the global community has been straining to absorb the lessons of the wars, scientific discoveries and civil reconstructions that so radically shifted our view of reality and our sense of personal significance in the previous century. Our spiritual lives have been deeply affected by this discerning moment. Contemporary Christians can relate to the blind man whom Jesus asked: 'Do you believe?' Like us, the man replied: 'Yes, I believe, please help me with my unbelief.' These musings on the spiritual journey contain the help that man was looking for. They will surely resonate with anyone who is longing to define the meaning of faith in a time like ours.

Dan Scott
Senior Pastor, Christ Church (retired)
Nashville, Tennessee

Not since I worked on the problem of the year zero have I been as close to relieving the paradox as I have while reading Thomas Fudge's modest masterpiece *The Empty Box*. I found it liberal and conservative, both evangelical and Anglo-Catholic, deeply oneness and so quintessentially trinitarian. The energetic and compelling prose offers as much useless consolation to those confined to small, dark, subterranean, low-ceiling, one-room apartments as to those dancing to whatever tune is played. It should be required reading for each and every candidate applying for the Donnelley Stool or even those who simply want to see it. *The Empty Box* is a wonderful collection perhaps best understood as *Either/Or and/or Both/And*. This offering is a keen inspiration to all in a Covid-19 world whether this year or next, both, or neither. Personally, I have been much encouraged to never again be discouraged even when I miss an appointment. *The Empty Box* should be heartily endorsed as the best book of any year particularly 1989 or 2026.

Franz Bibfeldt
Honorary Sexton and Verger, Unsinnig Turnverein Church
SMS Groszenkneten

THE EMPTY BOX

THE EMPTY BOX

AND OTHER STORIES FOR RELUCTANT UNBELIEVERS

Thomas A. Fudge

Lone Wolf Books
an imprint of St. John University Press
2022

Published in 2022 by Lone Wolf Books
An imprint of St. John University Press
Vancouver and Collegetown

Library of Congress Cataloguing-in-Publication Data
Fudge, Thomas A., author
        The Empty Box and Other Stories for Reluctant Unbelievers
        Vancouver: Lone Wolf Books, 2022.

ISBN 979-8-9859892-0-5 (hardcover)
ISBN 979-8-9859892-1-2 (electronic)

For Laura Leigh (1967-2019)
who filled so many empty boxes

TABLE OF CONTENTS

ACKNOWLEDGEMENTS

The roads are long, the mountains high and the rivers wide. From time to time there are arid deserts, floodplains, and sheets of ice. There are dark forests and blinding bright fields of snow. There is calm and storm, wind and silence. That is the nature of the journey we call life. I have been fortunate to find along the way other pilgrims, travellers, and companions whose lives and quests have encouraged, enlightened and energized mine. Some remained for quite a long time along many miles while the paths of others crossed with mine only briefly and then our paths diverged. The names are too many to number but some have left deep footprints: Dad, Mom, C.H., Don, April, Jerry, Irv, Peggy, Mandi, Laura, Brenda, Vern, Karyn, Eric, Lynn, Skip, Stuart, Winfred, Phil, Virginia, and of course the many I never met whose books, ideas, and wisdom provided direction, comfort or stimulation. From Canada to Canberra, from Prague to Portland, New Zealand to New Brunswick, Amherst to Australia, Cambridge to Christchurch, Central America to South Africa, and a few hundred places in between, I have joined with others along pilgrim pathways in pursuit of questions and answers, faith and reason, fulfillment and frustration, to see what life was all about, to understand our place in the cosmos, and try to make crooked places a bit straighter.

This book has been many years in the making and there are many who facilitated its development. Joel Bustard provided the cover photograph featuring the hands of my mother and her great-grandson Liam. Trish Wright was terrific, as always, in every dimension of desktop publishing and unfailing support. I am also indebted to the sources and authors of the stories that make up this book, many of whom I cannot identify. I collected and kept all of these tales to remind myself of the stages of my own journey, to signpost progress, as well as to provide a testament of questions and findings from a fellow traveller to those who remain on pilgrimage.

Crack-in-the-ground, Christmas Valley, Oregon

INTRODUCTION

Faith is simple. Believing is more difficult. These are stories for reluctant unbelievers. The idea of reluctant unbelievers is not a concept I ever heard elaborated in church, anywhere, at any time. Somewhere along the line, it gradually occurred to me that these were an unreached, unacknowledged, group of people. It was possible they might even be a silent majority.

Most of these stories-turned essays had their origin in various sermons I preached between 1986 and 2016, many delivered at The Church of Our Redeemer and Cascade Community Church, in Oregon, and at First Covenant Church and Epiphany Lutheran Church in Denver, Colorado. Later, I had occasion to develop new ideas when in 2004 I was twice invited to Minnesota to preach or present in several different venues partly at the behest of my old friend from New Brunswick, Stuart Ward. A few others are texts of sermons I delivered at St. Anne's Episcopal Church in Washington between 2009 and 2012 and at large ecumenical gatherings in Germany and Switzerland in 2015 and 2016. I have had the adventurous opportunity to find engagement in various aspects of church work, broadly speaking, in Canada, the United States, England, Germany, the Czech Republic, New Zealand, and Australia. Some of the essays had their origins in the form of other addresses that I presented at conferences, colleges and universities, especially Warner Pacific College in Portland, Oregon where I taught theology and the history of Christianity prior to taking up an academic appointment in New Zealand and later in Australia.

While on the faculty of WPC I was called upon to teach a required third year interdisciplinary course called "Faith, Living and Learning." This course, taught several times, afforded useful opportunities for sustained reflection on many of the themes considered in this collection. I am grateful to my teachers who ran that course when I was a student: Joyce Quiring Erickson and Arthur Kelly. It is fair to say that a number of my students during those years stimulated my thinking and forced me to give up the tendency of resorting to easy answers. These included Jim Cobb, Kate Foglio, Matthew Plies, Jill Hagen, David Haigh, Lisa Henry, Sandy Masters, Laurie Moore, Mike Greenhalgh, Laurel Noe, Michael Budde, Cynthia Woods, Maria Obas, Nanette Sheetz, Brad Watkins, Jill Christensen, Kandy Morrison, Kate Wade, Laura L. Dillman, Kandace Jones, Melinda Rusaw, Jeff Williams, Ryan Shockey, Rebecca de Young, Cindy McNeely, Tobin Holden, Mary Ann Dawkins, Becky Flaming-Martin, Shane Williamson, Isabel Ramirez, and many others too. I am further indebted to my successor in that teaching role, Dennis Plies, for numerous stimulating (and humorous) exchanges on the themes of the course over quite a number of years. A few other essays were written specifically for other occasions based upon notes, news clippings and various other documents I have kept over the years in a folder in the proverbial bottom drawer. The impetus for transforming these notes and oral presentations into essays must be credited to my long-time friend, April Purtell, and another former student from WPC days, Laura Anderson. Both thought there might be some merit in the effort. In the southern hemisphere winter of 2020 during the Covid-19 pandemic, I read aloud the collection to Trish Wright who enthusiastically declared the stories should be published.

A few of the essays are autobiographical in nature, but I hope that something useful can still be gleaned from their reflections. It is quite impossible to separate oneself from the journey of faith and the search for God and none of us should wish it otherwise. I cannot make my experience normative for others nor am I prepared to accept someone else's experience as appropriate for me. God is larger than human structures, theological systems, churches, denominations, or doctrinal truth claims. That said, there is a chance that in the efforts of men and women to find God others might be able to find some strength for today and perhaps a bit of hope for our uncertain tomorrows. It is part of the historic communion of the faithful.

It has been an interesting exercise pulling out old folders and notes and looking over materials I once gave so much attention to. It has been refreshing to see that much of what I taught and preached as long as thirty five years ago still holds true for me and retains some validity. I am heartened in some ways to see where I have come from and how I arrived where I am now. In other ways, I find it curious that some of my questions back then are still questions today; a few others have resolved themselves into answers of one sort or another. A few things in my notes I now regard as utterly hopeless or entirely wrongheaded and those aspects have been deleted from the following pages. There is no point in perpetuating known errors. There will be enough unconscious ones. In twenty years I may read these essays again and find more to discard but that is the beauty of the journey and the wonder of faith, living and learning and the attraction of living the questions.

The preacher, the poet, and the prophet must have courage to speak truth. It is not easy. I developed two homiletical practices along the way. I usually began my sermons by invoking the name of God. It went something like this: "In the name of God, creator, redeemer, life-giver. Amen." Of course I hoped for divine sanction. Naturally, I wanted to speak a message that reflected aspects of divine grace. I was never so benighted as to imagine that everything I said could be labelled "thus sayeth the Lord." Still, priests and preachers are vicars of Christ. I concluded my sermons with a verbal device I copied from John Bluck who was, in the 1990s and early 2000s, dean of the Anglican Cathedral in Christchurch, New Zealand. He later went on to become the bishop of Waiapu. John was a good preacher and I noted that he finished his homilies by saying: "In the name of the one who … [add a phrase from the homily] …we dare to say these things." Every sermon I have preached since the 1990s has featured that doxology. After all, it is in the name of Christ that the good news is announced and it is by that authority that some things can be said or must be said.

The other observation is about the use of stories and specific real-life references. As a young preacher, deeply committed to scholarship and the life of the mind, I was able to deliver forty-five minute sermons awash in a sea of dense theological concepts chugging along in the rarefied atmosphere of intellectualized discourse. After I was appointed to the pulpit of the Church of Our Redeemer and had to face the same small congregation every Sunday, it soon became apparent to me that this approach would not work. I began to tell stories. It occurred to me that this is exactly how Jesus taught. His parables were pedagogical devices aimed at communicating a message through the vehicle of story. I came to embrace permanently this method after taking a class on preaching with former United Methodist Church bishop James Armstrong (1924-2018) while studying in seminary in the summer of 1990. Armstrong was a great story-teller but it was an exercise he had the class undertake that has stuck in my mind ever since. Chalk in hand, Armstrong asked for titles of books we had read (excluding the required course readings) in the past six months. He wrote these on the board. Then he asked the same question about films we had seen recently. He added those to the board too. Then he asked us to explore titles of pop songs currently playing on the radio. He patiently wrote these down. After a few minutes, Armstrong had filled up the entire blackboard with words and titles offered by the group. Once there was no more space to write he asked us why we thought he had done this. Of course we had no idea what he was up to. He told us these were the things holding the attention of those sitting in church pews on Sundays. We needed to know this. Our sermons needed to be relevant, informed, and accessible to our listeners. Nowadays it's less about books, movies and radio and far more about social media, including Facebook, Twitter, Instagram, Youtube, Tumblr, TikTok, Anchor, internet blogs, all things Wiki, and the ever-present technological gadgetry that many people seem unable to think, function, or live without. In the early 1980s, Neil Postman worried about *Amusing Ourselves to Death* in the age of television. That medium now seems rather quaint in our computerized era wherein the tyranny of technology is almost unavoidable. Still, I believe that telling stories remains a good way to connect. Those who hear sermons recall few of them. Most people like stories and many can remember stories better than obtuse points of doctrine and if the stories are good the listeners might even remember the point or the message carried along by the story.

Many of the ideas, stories and perspectives contained in these pages cannot be claimed as original. Over the years I have been influenced by many thinkers: Martin Luther, Karl Barth, Albert Schweitzer, Dietrich Bonhoeffer, John A.T. Robinson and a host of others. More specifically, when I used to preach regularly, I found much inspiration especially in the essay work of Bruce Larson, Rabbi Harold Kushner, the non-fiction writings of Frederick Buechner and the wit and wisdom in the many, many stories I heard C.H. Yadon tell. At times both their ideas were helpful as well as their avenues of expressing those thoughts. It has been said that imitation is the highest form of flattery. I can only hope that my flattery has not actually encroached into plagiarism. Moreover, I have to say that while some of the stories are mine, there are many whose source I no longer recall.

Finally, the stories, reflections, meditations and essays herein have been prepared for people like myself who sometimes, or perhaps often, find themselves reluctant unbelievers. These stories are not offered for those who understand God, have mastered theology, or have laid hold on "Truth." I can only envy such people and marvel from a distance. Perhaps my audience is more the part-time Christian; the men and women who truly want to believe but just cannot seem to find peace, justification or good reason to do so. Blaise Pascal once remarked: "One would not be looking for God if one had not already found God." I have taken some comfort in those words over the years. I no longer preach with any regularity but my quest for God and for the meaning of life goes on and on, perhaps even more intensely now that I seldom stand in a pulpit. If the struggle for faith seems persistent and unending there is some chance that triumph may emerge like a phoenix from defeat. There is no point in selling out the chance to win the war for the sake of a single battle. As John Diefenbaker, prime minister of Canada from 1957 to 1963, once put it: "The probability of defeat is no justification for surrender to a false principle." The insistence is salutary. Long ago, Albert Schweitzer insisted: "Truth, however disenchanting, is better than falsehood, however comforting." The poet Constantine Cavafy remarked: "No ship will ever take you away from yourself" and while ships normally are safe in harbors that is not what ships were built for. These essays, then, constitute an invitation to sailing on the high seas of examined faith.

It's no use pretending that faith is something that comes easily and is capable of resisting all temptations to assume the worst about God, the world, life, humanity and the future. I have never been able to take hold of that sort of assurance at least for very long. Still, I believe that faith is a gift of God. Why God did not see fit to bestow more of that good gift on me is beyond me. I would like to believe. I really would and I would like to hold to hope now and always. But for the time being I find myself a reluctant unbeliever with infinitely more questions than answers. That is not sad; it's just true and for the moment that is enough at least for me. Is it better to travel than to arrive? Perhaps the road itself is the answer.

This collection makes no pretence at being proper theology and my arguments hopefully have remained mostly undogmatic. I do not claim to possess truth nor am I prepared to adjudicate the finer points of right and wrong. I see little merit in the dialectic of right and wrong on the road to faith. Scholarship is important to me, academic inquiry is what I have devoted much of my adult life to. I do not, however, pretend that this collection is either. I do intend for it somehow to reflect the desire of Teresa of Avila when she sighed: "From silly prayers and sour-faced

Christians, deliver us, good Lord." There are certain bits and pieces in these essays that I am aware are somewhat repetitive. I have elected to leave those bits in since they seem to me to represent important themes in my thought and sometimes, though not always, repetition equals significance. Some references are rather dated but they represent stages of my thought.

If right and wrong have little meaning in this context, truth certainly does and it matters very much. But it is out there, ahead of us, luring us on. I have no idea where the road leads or even where it ends. I am in that sense an agnostic. I am a pilgrim in search of truth, not a prophet proclaiming truth accessed, understood and applied. One should never argue towards a conclusion but ought rather to follow truth wherever it leads. Bilbo Baggins put it well in *The Lord of the Rings*:

> The road goes ever on and on
> Down from the door where it began
> Now far ahead the road goes on
> And I must follow if I can
> Pursuing it with eager feet
> Until it joins some larger way
> Where many paths and errands meet.
> And whither then?
> I cannot say.

Thomas A. Fudge
Armidale, Australia
May 2022

Oregon forest trail

Dog Mountain, Columbia River Gorge, WA

SEVEN MILES TO EMMAUS

Late in his long and distinguished career as a British statesman, Winston Churchill was invited to give the commencement address to the graduating class at Cambridge. Mr Churchill slowly mounted the stairs to the podium and very carefully hung his cane from the corner. He then turned to face the audience. The room was packed to the doors. For a moment he said nothing. His piercing eyes swept the room. Then he spoke three words: "Never give up." Again, he looked to the right and to the left, his eyes taking in the entire room. Again he spoke: "Never give up." With a wave of his hand, his eyes shot from corner to corner and he repeated those three words once more: "Never give up." Then just as deliberately he collected his cane and descended the stairs. The crowd erupted in wild applause.

Churchill aside, sometimes we do give up. At times that giving up is temporary. At other times it is permanent. Either way there is always the Emmaus Road. The Gospel of Luke records the first trip to Emmaus but that road has been travelled millions of times by countless millions. It is not the road that is initially important but rather the story that puts one on that particular road. In the Gospel of Luke two men are walking along a seven mile stretch of road between Jerusalem and Emmaus. Their master was dead. Executed in brutal fashion like a common criminal, he had been hung up between robbers in the blazing sun on a Roman cross and left to die. He did. He was buried in a tomb and that was the end of it. These two men had been fervent followers and believers in the message of Jesus. They expected the in-breaking of the Kingdom of God just as Jesus promised. But now that he was dead and buried that seemed quite unlikely. So they did what most of us do in similar circumstances of duress and trial. They just gave up. They left the city and headed for Emmaus. As strange as it may seem there is not one of us who has not gone to Emmaus with them. Who among us has never faced fear? Who has never experienced loss? Can there be anyone who has not suffered the bitterness of anguish and despair? Grief is like fear and grips one in almost the same fashion. In these moments or hours, the journey of life and faith will round a corner on the road and each of us, in turn, finds ourselves on that seven mile road to Emmaus.

The site of the historical Emmaus is somewhat indefinite. There are four possibilities proposed by archaeologists. There is no scholarly consensus on the question and indeed it does not matter. Frederick Buechner writes that Emmaus is a symbol of that which takes each of us away momentarily from the pain, sorrow, grief, loss and despair. It could be a walk along an ocean beach, a hiking trip into the mountains, going to church, going home, going to a movie. Emmaus is whatever we do or wherever we go to try to make sense of the chaos, where we imagine order within the disorder, love amid lovelessness, peace within the storm. It is the place where hope is possible, however slight. In this sense, each of us has been to Emmaus; each one knows exactly where his or her Emmaus is.

In the film "Hanover Street," Harrison Ford plays a soldier during World War II, who on his free days goes to Hanover Street in London and whiles away the time. On one occasion, during an air raid he meets the lovely Lesley-Anne Down and romance follows. The relationship is impossible and despite the best efforts of the two, their love is simply not meant to be. At the end of the film we see Ford again standing on the corner of Hanover Street. Each one of us has a Hanover Street in our lives whether we care to admit it or not. Hanover Street is the place where we go every now and then, off the beaten track, where we seek love, hope and peace. During the frequent air raids in our lives we seek shelter in these places.

In Luke's gospel, two men are walking along a dusty road when all at once they encounter a stranger. He walks with them and they converse. He seems unaware of what has transpired in the city and never once does he tell the two why he is on the Emmaus Road. Perhaps they have been blinded by grief or fear or both but at any rate they fail to recognize their master. They had been with him in life for perhaps as long as three years. They had listened to his teaching, they had followed him, witnessed the miracles and had in time become disciples. Why did they fail to recognize him now? Was their anguish that great? Perhaps. Was their despair so overwhelming? That is altogether likely. The depths of despair can shape reality. There is some chance that even though they had been with Jesus they had never really known who he was or what he was. Perhaps their image of him died on the cross. Whatever the cause of their inexplicable blindness they cover the seven miles to Emmaus and invite their companion to share a meal with them. He agrees. When he blesses their food they recognize him and he vanishes.

Many times we succumb to the urge to try and make him stay but the effort is always in vain. Luther once said that the Word of God was like a passing thunderstorm that bursts here at one moment and then is gone. It cannot be possessed, it cannot be contained and the Word made flesh likewise cannot be forced to conform to any circumstance or made to remain still. For each one of us at Emmaus there is the opportunity to recognize him. Sometimes we see through the gloom and recognize him for who he is. Other times we remain blinded by sin, despair, sorrow, pain and loneliness and he is just another stranger at the table, another pilgrim on the journey, another figure on the long and winding road that leads nowhere.

It is just seven miles to Emmaus. It is 140 miles from Jerusalem to Damascus. The Acts of the Apostles relates the tale of a man named Saul of Tarsus who took that 140 mile journey with the intention of arresting Christians and putting them behind bars. Along that journey as he breathed out threats and murder against the believers in Christ, Saul was suddenly confronted with an amazing flash of light. He was knocked from his horse to the dusty road and heard a voice that brought him to Emmaus. By the time he got straightened out he stopped calling himself Saul of Tarsus and everyone else down through history has called him the Apostle Paul. The road to Damascus was Paul's Emmaus Road and the fact that he recognized the voice transformed his life and he was never the same again

It is seven miles to Emmaus. It is 140 miles to Damascus and it is about 400 miles from Kraków, Poland to Prague. Among the tales of the Hasidim is one concerning the recurring dream of a rabbi named Eizik the son of Yekel in Kraków. In the dream the impoverished rabbi was bade to go to Prague and dig under the bridge leading to the castle and there he would find treasure. After the third occurrence of the dream Rabbi Eizik made the long trip to Prague. When he found the bridge, however, he was dismayed to find that it was heavily guarded and he did not dare to dig. Each day for several days he went to the bridge and walked about wondering what to do. At length the captain of the guards asked him why he came every day. Rabbi Eizik told him about his dream. The captain laughed heartily and then reproached the rabbi for believing in silly fantasies. The captain related to the rabbi that he too had a recurring dream that urged him to go to Kraków and find a rabbi named Eizik, son of Yekel and dig under his stove. There he would find treasure. The captain laughed again: "Can you imagine how silly that would be? How many rabbis named Eizik would there be in Kraków?" Rabbi Eizik bowed, thanked the captain, travelled home, dug under his own stove and discovered treasure.

The place where the treasure is found is often in the least suspected place. Christ as the stranger comes to us at Emmaus, where we find ourselves most of the time. Somewhere on that seven mile stretch of road there may be a stranger. He may very well come whenever and wherever men and women seek him. Wherever there is faith, he may be there. Whenever he is needed most, he sometimes appears. Along seven mile stretches of road nameless strangers may in fact be recognized as someone rather unexpected.

On the road it is important to listen for him. It is likewise important to listen to him. We may discover that in his presence, even in the midst of sorrow, loss and despair, there is the presence of God. Burning bushes are not the issue. Any bush will do since God only wants to talk to us. If that be true then every bush and indeed the whole world is ablaze with the presence of God. It is in these moments, in the ordinariness of life, that he comes. He does not come in the sermon as much as on the road. He comes less as a saint and more as the unpretentious stranger on the corner of Hanover Street.

It is seven miles to Emmaus. It is 140 miles to Damascus and it is 400 long miles to Prague. It is also just 49 miles from Selma to Montgomery, Alabama. In 1965 there was a march along those 49 miles for human rights. Somewhere along that road trip, a group of courageous people encountered a stranger. Martin Luther King Jr. was among them. The night before he was murdered in Memphis in April 1968, King gave witness to that stranger on the road to transformation: "I have been to the mountaintop and I have seen the promised land. And mine eyes have seen the glory of the coming of the Lord."

On these various trips there are sacred moments, moments of what can be termed nothing other than miraculous and the irony is that such moments are often the moments of everyday. Too often we see only strangers, too frequently we think it is just another meal, just another trip, just another day. It could be the Emmaus Road, it could very well be the one we long thought was dead and gone. Like those two men in Luke's gospel we are on a journey. For us on Hanover Street and on the Emmaus Road trip the stranger who confronts us with sacramental presence is God who was once a child and who is also on a journey; a journey of redemption and reconciliation, a mission to unite estranged humanity with Godself. Without that stranger on the way to Emmaus, and our recognition and acceptance of him, everything else we do in a religious sense – preaching, worship, singing, liturgy, prayer – is entirely superfluous.

It is seven miles to Emmaus, 49 miles to Montgomery, 140 miles to Damascus, 400 miles to Prague and an infinitely long journey to faith, love and God. Yet, it is only a few steps to the table of the Lord for one can receive his body and blood, the medicine of immortality as Ignatius of Antioch called it 1,900 years ago. The two men reached Emmaus and as they broke bread they recognized the stranger as Christ. There is a good chance that as we break bread again today the stranger among us will be recognized. After the cold, long Christmas-less winter, the land of Narnia was freed at last from the curse of the wicked white witch. "'Creatures, I give you yourselves,' said the strong happy voice of Aslan. 'I give you forever this land of Narnia. I give you the woods, the fruits, the rivers, I give you the stars, and I give you myself.'"

God has given Godself to us in the stranger on the seven-mile road to Emmaus. So on your trip to Emmaus this week, listen carefully, break the bread thoughtfully and take note of that stranger hurrying down the road toward you. You could be nearer to Emmaus than ever before; nearer than you've ever imagined; nearer than you've ever hoped.

In the name of the one who meets the traveller on all the roads leading to every Emmaus, we dare to say these things. Amen.

Misunderstandings and Miracles

Life is filled with misunderstandings, or getting it wrong. Four stories illustrate this poignant point. In the first, a teacher once gave a class an examination on human anatomy. Everyone passed the exam with one exception. That one student completely misunderstood the subject. He wrote that the body was composed of three parts: the brainium, the borax and abominable cavity. The brainium contained the brain; the borax held the heart, lungs, liver and other "living things" while the abominable cavity was made up of the bowels of which there were five: A, E, I, O, and U. Poor soul. The second, is a delightful story told by Bruce Larson of a little boy who began his prayers before going to bed in this fashion: "Dear Harold, bless Mommy and Daddy and…" His mother interjected and with much surprise and wonder asked: "Who is Harold?" "Oh," the little fellow solemnly replied, "that's God's name." The stunned mother asked: "Where in the world did you get the idea that God's name is Harold?" The little boy replied: "They taught us in Sunday School to pray, our father who art in heaven, Harold be your name." So, God's name is Harold? Interesting. In the third story, a little girl asked her grandmother: "Grandma, just how old are you?" The grandma replied: "I've gotten to that stage when you don't tell your age anymore." Later the grandmother noted the little girl going through her purse then suddenly announcing: "Grandma, you are 86 years old!" "That's right," replied the grandmother, "but how do you know that?" Said the little girl: "Oh, I just subtracted today's date from your birth date on your driver's license." There was a short pause and then the little girl spoke again: "I also know you got an "F" in sex!" Lastly, a small boy stood in the foyer of a church staring at a large plaque. The pastor asked him how he was doing but the boy wanted to know about the plaque covered with names and adorned with American flags. The pastor told the young fellow these were the names of young men and women who had died in the service. After a long pause, the boy asked in a very low voice: "Which service? The 9:45 or the 11:15?"

Misunderstandings! They're easy, they're understandable, sometimes quite unavoidable. These stories help illustrate our human capacity for misunderstanding. Three of the set readings from the lectionary underscore this problem. When it comes to God, it is all the more likely we get it wrong. As St. Augustine reminds us: "If you understand it, it's not God. If it is God, you do not understand it."

In the narrative from I Kings, we find the prophet Elijah spending a night in a mountain cave. He is told that he should go outside the cave for God is about to pass by. What happened next was a series of impressive events. A wind so strong it split mountains and broke rocks into pieces. God was not in the wind. Then an earthquake. God was not in the seismic activity, even when it reached 8.6 on the prehistoric Richter scale. Then a fire broke out. But God was not in the fire. After these impressive and extraordinary phenomena, a "still small voice." This is the traditional rendering, but the literal Hebrew words imply "a sound of gentle stillness" or a "sound of sheer silence." In that stillness, in that silence, God. Last month, while on holiday, I heard the second-hand comment: "Dr. Fudge belongs to a dead church." The reference was to the wider Anglican communion. It's not really that offensive. Anglicans sometimes refer to themselves as the frozen chosen. The man who made that statement attends a church where one might see during a service people dancing, running, jumping, shouting, great displays of emotion, and so on. Admittedly, it is difficult to imagine any of that in a typical Anglican church. So while there may be plenty of wind, and shaking and heat, there may well be an absence of the stillness and silence. Sometimes there is far too much noise. Sometimes there is too much attention paid to this, that, and the other thing, and insufficient attention given to the stillness, the sheer silence. It may be an example of sound versus substance. And there are those who cannot abide the silence. It is too disconcerting. Once I stayed at a Cistercian monastery and the following morning one of my colleagues complained that he had been unable to sleep on account of the fact that it was too quiet! We are not told what Elijah was thinking while on that mountain. But it is possible that like many of us he assumed that in the wind, God would be heard. It is not unlikely that in the ground-shaking tremors of the earthquake he imagined he would be confronted with the presence of God. It is possible that the heat of the flames caused him to imagine God was about to be manifested. I wonder if there was not a moment of total bewilderment before he was enveloped by the sheer silence. It is altogether too easy to be distracted by roaring winds, shattering earthquakes, and wild fires. Our lives are sometimes filled with these things. That said, the writer of I Kings insists that God was not present where perhaps God was expected or predicted. These were distractions, potential misunderstandings, not the real thing.

In 1884 Guy de Maupassant published a short story called *La Parure* ("The Necklace") in the French newspaper *Le Gaulois*. The tale tells of a young married couple living in a new home in the suburbs of a large city. Nothing extraordinary about them. He had an ordinary job but she wanted to live the "good life." One day, they were invited to her husband's company banquet. All of the executives would be there. The young wife saw this as a chance to be in high society. She went and bought a fancy dress and borrowed a very elegant diamond necklace from one of her friends. She was a hit at the party! She looked gorgeous and everyone seemed to want to be around her and talk to her. The evening was a smashing success. But when they arrived home, to their dismay they discovered the necklace was missing. Immediately they retraced their steps. They searched everywhere without success. The necklace was gone. The young couple decided to tell their friend that one of the links in the necklace had broken and was being fixed and would soon be returned. Meanwhile, they went around town to several jewelry stores and finally they discovered another necklace that looked exactly like the lost one. It cost 36,000 francs. The husband took out loans from several banks and purchased the diamond necklace which they gave to their friend who was none the wiser.

Soon, of course, it was time to start paying off the loans. They were forced to give up the house and move into a cheap room in the inner city. They sold their car and started using the bus. Both of them were working several jobs, odd jobs, dirty jobs, anything at all to earn money to pay off the loans. It took ten long years of struggle and hard work but finally the loans were all paid off. Who could have imagined that one evening in the "good life" would cost them 36,000 francs and ten years of their lives? Shortly after this, the wife ran into her old friend, the one who'd owned the original necklace, in a park. They had not seen each other in years. The friend noticed that the wife looked different. She was no longer as pretty as she once was. Her hair was streaked with gray, there were wrinkles on her face and she just seemed old and tired. The friend asked what had happened. Why had their friendship just stopped? As they talked, the wife broke down and told her old friend the whole sad story. Her friend was shocked and dismayed: "Why didn't you tell me about this at the time? That necklace was just a clever imitation. It was worth only about 500 francs."

Earthquakes, fires, and storms may impress and be ever so dramatic but they are not necessarily what is truly important. We must discriminate between the immediate and the important. They are not necessarily the same.

Turning to the Gospel reading, we encounter another storm, this time on a lake and another misunderstanding. Like Elijah, Jesus has gone up into a mountain. His friends have taken a boat and are attempting to cross to the other side. A great storm blows up and there is a ferocious gale preventing them from making land. Life is also like this from time to time for many people. Battered by waves, far from safety, the winds of the world against them. They begin to see ghosts and fear seizes them. In the midst of such a scenario, we must give credit to Peter. His courage cannot be denied. Even the naysayers who condemn his lack of faith do so from the relative safety and security of the boat! No. Peter is to be admired. The story is well known. Jesus appears walking on the water. Peter decides he'd like to take a stroll upon the water too. Jesus summons Peter. Alas! Peter is distracted by the storm, the towering waves, the howling wind, perhaps on how far he is from shore, and he takes his eyes off Jesus and losing his footing on the slippery surf, starts to sink. It is easy to criticize Peter. It is foolish to imagine that our own lives are not beset with storms. It does make me wonder though about the man or woman for whom there is no miracle. When Peter began to sink, there was a miraculous hand to take hold of. There are those for whom there seems to be no miracle. But here's the point. As soon as Jesus and the soggy Peter got into the boat, the storm ceased. The disciples were ever so impressed and worshiped Jesus as the son of God. The disciples were absolutely impressed by what seemed to them to be rather exceptional. But walking on water and calming meteorological disturbances was not the mission of Jesus at all. Like many of us they were awed by the "miracles" of water-walking and storm control. These things (real or imagined) had nothing to do with the mission of Jesus. The disciples misunderstood. In the work of Jesus, "miracles" were sometimes exceptions to natural law but the greater miracles came when any event or experience brought greater reality into the core of human existence. The "miracle" is the light that shines in the dark places, in the midst of storms, and brings the pilgrim to the shores of safety.

The miracle of light can change everything. Two boys went off fishing one day and they fished all day but only caught four small fish. Disappointed, tired and hungry they decided they had better head for home before the sun went down. They decided to take a shortcut via the railway tracks. They had never gone that way before. All they knew was that it was supposed to be shorter and that the tracks crossed three trestles before reaching town. They reached the first trestle. It was very high. The trees and the river far below looked like miniature toys. The sun was sinking fast. They hurried on. They reached the second trestle. It too seemed fearfully high. By now they were moving as fast as they could. By the time they reached the third trestle it was totally dark. All at once a light gleamed up ahead and they heard the whistle of an approaching train. It was impossible to tell how far it was to the other side of the trestle. They had no choice but to hang off the side of the trestle and let the train pass. It roared by throwing dirt and grime into their faces and bruising their whitened knuckles. The train seemed so very long. It took almost eternity to pass. By the time it was gone the two youngsters did not have the strength to pull themselves back up. One of the boys said: "We'll have to let go and fall into the river. You go first." The other fellow replied: "No, you go first." Neither could get the image of that long, long, fall from the trestle out of their minds. In desperation they began to scream for help. Just as their strength came to an end and they were about to fall, they heard a still, small voice in their ears and a man's face appeared at eye level. He was holding a lantern: "What do you guys think you're doing?" The two boys looked down and in the glow of the lantern saw that their feet were dangling about ten inches off the ground.

They had been distracted by previous visions, their own fears, and assumptions. It is easy to be distracted by earthquakes, hurricane-velocity winds, fires, and storms. Sometimes our experiences create misunderstanding. There are plenty of these in the world of church and religion. There was clear factionalism in the early Church. Some Jews thought they were privileged and there are Christians even today who assume they possess Truth and somehow are the guardians of the sacred mysteries. Others imagine they must gain salvation through their own efforts. It is the classic conflict between law and gospel that marks a good part of the Protestant Reformations of the sixteenth century. Over against the arguments, Paul offers a different perspective: Being in a right relationship with God has nothing at all to do with rules and regulations. It is not about the storms, or earthquakes, or winds, or fires. It has more to do with the sheer silence of faith. There is no difference between Jews and Greeks. I cannot believe that God takes any note of denominational superiority. Make all the claims you want. Christ may be the center, but Christianity cannot be the limit. There is an element of universalism in Paul's declarations that rule out policies of exclusion. All religion is directed towards an end which is beyond itself. In Hinduism, the goal is union with Brahman, the universal principle. In Buddhism, it is nirvana. In Judaism and Christianity, it is a concept of heaven while in Islam it is paradise. In each case, it is a form of existence beyond the storms, embraced in the sheer silence of God or a greater reality. But in the meanwhile, misunderstandings. So what can be said? The solution is in the primary essence of God. But we should not leave God so high up and so far away as to be of little practical value in our lives.

One of the great literary works of the twentieth century is Thornton Wilder's *The Bridge of San Luis Rey*. It begins: "On Friday noon, July the twentieth, 1714, the finest bridge in all Peru broke and precipitated five travellers into the gulf below." By chance a monk witnesses the tragedy. Brother Juniper spends six years researching and writing a book in a quest to determine the meaning of the event. His quest leads to his own death. The book ends with this observation: "But soon we shall all die and all memory of those five will have left the earth, and we ourselves shall be loved for a while and forgotten. But the love will have been enough; all those impulses of love return to the love that made them. Even memory is not necessary for love. There is a land of the living and a land of the dead and the bridge is love."

The crucial question is this: Where does the true love come from? The Psalmist says: Listen to what the Lord is saying now. God speaks peace. Salvation is near. Mercy (or love since in the Hebrew it is the same root) and truth meet. Righteousness and peace kiss. When these things occur the storms abate, the earthquakes end, the winds die down, the fires go out, and the restlessness of the human heart finds rest in the stillness and sheer silence of God. That is truly the miracle that transcends all misunderstandings.

In the name of the one who comes in the stillness and in the silence, we dare to say these things. Amen.

Mathematical Bridge, Cambridge, England

Roads, Journeys and Maps

"I went to the woods because I wished to live deliberately, to front only the essential facts of life, and see if I could learn what it had to teach, and not, when I came to die, discover that I had not lived. I did not wish to live what was not life, living is so dear; nor did I wish to practice resignation, unless it was quite necessary. I wanted to live deep and suck out all the marrow of life." Thus wrote Henry David Thoreau in 1845.

People of faith and reluctant unbelievers must go into the woods to examine our faith deliberately, or our lack of faith equally deliberately; to examine our lives deliberately, to examine anew our learning in a deliberate fashion. The "woods" Thoreau spoke of were indeed a forest of trees near Walden Pond in Massachusetts. The woods we all need to enter may well be in a forest but the truly necessary "wood" is the place of conflict, solitude, community, of questioning. It is the place where we practice honesty and integrity, where we get serious with ourselves and with life and where we dare to ask the important and tough questions. In these woods we must ask the essential questions of God, of ourselves, of life, to truly see what life has to teach. Only in this way can we avoid arriving at death and making the awful discovery that we have not lived. That would be a tragedy of the highest magnitude. Applying Thoreau in the religious or spiritual context means going to the woods and laying our faith on the line actively. Only in this way can we truly live deep, have an informed faith, know and understand.

J.R.R. Tolkien's massive *Lord of the Rings* trilogy now popularized by a series of major motion pictures speaks also of this aspect of life. Bilbo Baggins puts it thus:

The road goes ever on and on
Down from the door where it began
Now far ahead the road has gone
And I must follow if I can
Pursuing it with eager feet
Until it joins some larger way
Where many paths and errands meet
And whither then?
I cannot say.

Going to the woods does involve great risk. Setting out on the road to enlightenment and discovery and examined faith is taking a chance. However, it is only in the woods and on the road where faith, living and learning can truly be apprehended. The church father of the second century Tertullian once asked the question: "What has Athens to do with Jerusalem?" He meant to ask, what relationship is there between knowledge or learning and faith or formal religion? The assumption underlying the question is flawed. There need be no binary distinction between faith and learning. One does not get an education, education gets you. The light of knowledge is an instrument of power, but also of destruction, and the glow of creativity. The intersection of faith, living and learning is a business to be taken with the utmost seriousness. Our journeys into the "woods" and "down the road that goes ever on and on" should stretch us and plant within us the seeds of curiosity about faith, life, learning, ourselves, God, and all manner of things.

Charles Hodge once remarked with much pride that in his fifty years at Princeton University there had never been broached a new or original idea in terms of Biblical theology. The statement is a shocking disgrace to the creative work of the Holy Spirit. Men and women of faith ought stridently to oppose it. Education and real faith does not teach us what to think and it certainly does not tell us what to believe. Instead, it spurs us on through the risks of exploring new worlds, of going deep into the "woods," of thinking deliberately and intentionally taking new roads. There are some Christians who preach long and loud about accepting Jesus into your heart. That may be all fine and well. But have you accepted Jesus into your mind? Authentic faith should instil in all of us a desire for understanding and for truth – not half-truths, not socially acceptable truths, not just comfortable truths, not even ecclesiastically sanctioned truths – the truth that is out there, luring us on, challenging us, challenging our ways of thinking, our pre-conceptions and our biases.

Truth is rarely as simple as neat slogans and clever phrases. Truth is much bigger than books, institutions, creeds, formulas and doctrinal statements. Faith is not ivory tower speculation, instead it is practiced, attained and understood in real life encounters. The Greek philosopher Plutarch once observed: "The mind is not a vessel to be filled but a fire to be lit." So it must be for all of us.

Too often we travel in great haste through the world of our lives and often we travel the same way along the byways of faith. Flying in air planes at 30,000 or 40, 000 feet in the air allows one to see things unseen on the ground like the patchwork of crop fields and meandering rivers. But while the perspective is significant one is detached and becomes an observer rather than a participant. Thousands of automobiles rush here and there. Taking the time to get out and walk in order to know more fully would have significant advantages. One may drive past the ocean and the experience can be truly wonderful. Walking on the beach, hearing the crashing of the breakers, feeling the sand under your feet, the wind in your hair and the taste of salt on your lips is an altogether different adventure. Getting out of the car adds a whole new dimension. By remaining in the car one misses the nearness of the waves, the sensation of the sand, the relief of the breeze and the taste of salt. Rather than driving from point A to point B, charging ahead for the destination, especially in terms of faith, living and learning, one should stop along the way, see the flowers, touch the trees, explore the lava flows, observe the wild life and allow the silence and the spirit to speak.

In the same vein, we would all do well to tear up some of our old faith, living and learning maps and strike out on our own, make new maps, get off beaten trails and see just what life and faith has to teach. There is something worthwhile in getting off the trails followed by the mass of humanity, trails that are sometimes erring and aimless, that tend to follow the way of least resistance, the pathways of the majority. Too many of our old maps are out of date. Some are inaccurate or lead down dead end roads to washed-out bridges or do not include new roads more recently built. These maps may well have served Mom and Dad or past generations but their "use-by" date has long expired. It is counter-productive to faith being passively resigned to conformity to unchallenged traditions. We must not be satisfied with pat answers, shallow questions and comfortable convenient truths. Instead, we must deliberately take to the roads, to the woods. We must deliberately set out on our many journeys. We must deliberately set about making new maps.

Having said all of this, it is important to note that there have always been many, and will always be just as many, who will discourage, forbid and threaten this way of thinking and this approach to faith. There is only one reply to such opinion: Behold the turtle. The only way for the turtle to make progress is to stick its neck out. I like the philosophy of the turtle. Still, there is a cost to this way and that cost might include turning your world completely upside down. Albert Schweitzer put not too fine a point on it when he remarked: "If thought is to set out on its journey without hindrance, it must be prepared for anything, even for arrival at intellectual agnosticism." That is pretty serious. It is also pretty real. There is a danger on the roads and on the journeys that I think we all must take. There are risks in the woods. And what about those maps? The maker of an early map of America wrote across unknown and unexplored regions frightful comments including: "Here there are fiery scorpions," or "here there are dragons."

None of this can be made light of. Are you prepared for the challenges? Are you prepared for the emotional and spiritual turmoil that may very well follow? Are we truly prepared for the examined life, for the growing pains and for the challenges at the fibre of our being? Such journeys in faith, living and learning sometimes constitute dangerous and desperate business. On the other hand, do we simply intend to help perpetuate the problems, errors and shortcomings of the various systems we are involved in? Dag Hammarskjöld once penned these salutary words: "Never for the sake of peace and quiet deny your own experience and conviction." Silence is not always golden! Surely not. According to Joseph Goebbels, Adolf Hitler's propaganda chief: "If you repeat a lie a thousand times it becomes truth." Do we dare to live, believe and learn deliberately? Are we courageous enough to suck the marrow out of life?

"The road goes ever on and on, and whither then? I cannot say." All that is certain is that the roads leading onward will take us on a wonderfully and frightening journey of discovery deep into truth, hope, meaning, understanding, reality and enlightenment. And it will last a lifetime. Faith, living, and learning. Roads, journeys and maps. It is all related. Some people are content to live their lives. Others create theirs. Some will embrace the dead faith of traditionalism. Others will take hold of the living faith of a living tradition in search of life.

In the name of the one who makes our journeys more interesting, we dare to say these things. Amen.

Jump Creek Canyon, Idaho

Cathedral Rock, NSW, Australia

THE STEADFAST WARRIOR AND
THE STRONGEST FAITH

At the Last Supper, Jesus warned Peter that the Devil wanted to have him. Christ said he had prayed for Peter and hoped that his faith would not waver and that when he had turned again, he might strengthen his brethren (Luke 22:31-2). Peter, of course, a man strong in speech and will, faltered, and betrayed Jesus, declaring he did not know him. Jerome of Prague, a scholar who lived 600 years ago, also stood strong for a time, confident, outspoken, and bold, but he too, betrayed his own conscience, agreed that in 1415 Jan Hus had been justly condemned and perhaps like Peter wept bitterly in the darkness and silence of a medieval prison tower. That was not the end of the story either for Peter or Jerome.

Liturgical compositions from the fifteenth and early sixteenth centuries, suggest Jerome was a holy man. Some of those texts declared that he recanted under enormous duress because he feared death but also because he desired to escape from the clutches of his enemies. If Jan Hus has been characterized as a Christ figure, then his colleague Jerome of Prague is perhaps characterized best as Peter. If we think about the blustering impetuous man whom Jesus called Simon, it may seem odd to speak about Jerome in terms of the strongest faith. But there is much that is salutary in the life and thought of this shadowy, largely unknown and forgotten, man who lived so long ago.

In January 1409, Jerome delivered a lecture at Charles University in Prague. It was called a "Recommendation of the Liberal Arts." In this stirring academic address, Jerome laid the groundwork for an argument that the strongest faith is the examined faith. He noted: "Is it not known to everyone that half-educated priests have blathered sermons in the common language in this town claiming there are many heretics, whom they call Wyclifites? As far as I am concerned, I declare before all of you that I have read and examined the books of Master John Wyclif, just as I have the books of other teachers, and I admit that I have learned much good from them. But God forbid, I do not wish to be so foolish and espouse everything as faith that I have read in his books or in the books of any another Church teacher. I will be obedient only to the Gospel. If the Gospel says that it is so, then it is truth."

From this we learn that Jerome believed that truth and a foundation for faith can be found even in sources deemed dangerous or inappropriate by the church. He went further demanding to know: "Why should we not read the books of Wyclif, when they have contained within them many holy truths, even if they agitate both arrogant priests and the laity?" Jerome was not to be dissuaded. What is there to hide? What do the authorities not want the common people to know? What is there to fear? Jerome plunged ahead impetuously like Peter. In the second century Tertullian asked: "What has Athens to do with Jerusalem?" In other words, what relation is there between reason and faith? Jerome considered the question uninformed and infantile.

Ignoring the statutory criminalizing of John Wyclif that had occurred in Prague, and openly scorning the dictates of the archbishop, Jerome appealed to the university students: "Young men, who can prevent you from learning and recognizing truth in Wyclif's books? As far as I am concerned, I encourage you all with great urgency to often read and diligently study his books. If you find in them something that you are unable to understand properly, postpone it until you are older. If there is something in them that appears to disagree with the faith, do not defend it, and do not profess it, but instead be obedient to the faith."

This approach often sends nervous shudders through the corridors of conformity and produces heartburn in those who exercise a command

and control policy. The church replies: Is there not a legitimate duty of care to shield believers from reckless thinking, from pathways that might imperil faith, and warn against forays that lead outside the ark of safety? Any sensible person would say of course there is. But Jerome seems less interested in these considerations.

So far as Jerome was concerned: "No falsehood or heresy, no matter how large, can corrupt even a small truth, because truth is firm and a mere lie cannot corrupt it. The truth never gives way and will not give way for a lie, because the truth triumphs over everything. Therefore, in the future, never give way, as deceitful people wish, from the many glorious truths contained in the aforementioned books and do not ever be afraid to study these same books. Never in the future hand over books of the aforementioned master to people who do not understand them at all, who ridicule the truths before they can understand at least their parts." In other words, the strongest faith is the examined faith.

What should we then do? Jerome advised that everyone should study diligently and follow truth to the end and not become frightened and retreat. He suggested it was much better not to recognize truth than to abandon truth on account of narrow-mindedness and fear. He warned against entangling students in anything other than an honest pursuit of truth and the examined faith.

The proposed pathway that led the pilgrim across the landscape of late medieval Europe was fraught with danger. Some of the observers at the Council of Constance believed the judges in the trial of Jerome were unfair, noting that many people throughout history had been unjustly condemned, including people like the Greek Socrates, Boethius, Elijah, St. Jerome, Daniel, brave Susannah, numerous prophets from the biblical narratives, and many others. Jerome, too, would eventually join that misunderstood and persecuted number but he had already made the point in his 1409 lecture: "Suffering asks everyone if they really love God." Trial, tumult, and tribulation forces each of us to examine what exactly it is we believe and, even more important, why we cling to such commitments. The safest form of faith is to believe uncritically what one is told. The secure faith is to blindly follow orders or surrender to the tyranny of the majority. The surest path to a leisurely retirement in old age is to submit to the command and control policies of those who wield power. But the strongest faith continues to be the examined faith. It is admittedly, as Jerome would learn, the more difficult path.

Shouting posthumously through his controversial big, black, bushy, beard, Jerome reminds posterity of this sobering point: "Haven't you heard and haven't you read about Job, covered with sores from the soles of his feet to the crown of his head? Have you not learned that in the end he was cured and restored? Are you not aware that the honorable man who directed the University debates was the subject of slander and reproach not that long ago? Now he has been returned to his original condition and completely purified. Do you not know from holy biblical events that Joseph, the son of Rachel, was handed over by his brothers to the people of Ishmael and dragged off to Egypt, and that he was tormented by various tribulations? Even though he was innocent, was he not arrested by the other sons of his own mother and turned over to foreigners?" In an age of softness, Jerome's strong voice can still be heard urging believers to take ownership for their own faith. What does this mean? The ancient Greek aphorism "know thyself" is one of the Delphic maxims that apparently was inscribed in the outer court of the Temple of Apollo at Delphi dating to the fourth century BCE. Jerome's approach to faith, living, and learning is an approach that calls for self-examination. During his trial on charges of impiety and corrupting the youth of Athens in 399 BCE, Plato tells us that Socrates declared that the unexamined life was not worth living. If the unexamined life was unworthy of living in antiquity, then surely the unexamined faith is not worth holding in postmodernity. Jerome's life is a vivid testament to the medieval church and to Christians today that reason and faith belong together.

In Jerome, Scripture and philosophy are intentionally joined together. There is no blind, mindless, easy-believism. Jerome holds to a position that Scripture is indeed infallible, and that what Scripture asserts is true. However, this cannot be reduced to the insipid mantra: "God said it, I believe it, and that settles it." While Jerome is convinced that his views are in harmony with Scripture, he also believes that one must actively pursue truth because truth is not always simple or obvious. Hence, in his debates in Prague, Jerome noted that it was essential to search for the proper understanding of truth. Hence, he draws upon Augustine, Wyclif, and others. Jerome urges fidelity to "discovered truth," arguing that education is essential for the Christian mind, and that the strongest faith is the examined faith. Jerome took the view that the life of the mind did not consist in the croaking of frogs and toads in medieval swamps (as Richard Fitzralph had so mischievously quipped in the fourteenth century) but instead was a vitally serious grappling with both traditional answers and new questions.

In his famous debates, that stretch from Paris to Poland, and Kraków to Constance, Jerome boldly drew parallels between biblical writers and philosophers. For example, he declares that Sirach is an "old Hebrew philosopher." John the Evangelist is surely an "authoritative heavenly metaphysician." St Paul is assuredly a "heavenly philosopher." The Old Testament lawgiver Moses is clearly the "wisest and most extraordinary Hebrew philosopher." The gospel writer Luke is also a "philosopher." In other words, Jerome sees the biblical writers as thinkers, seeking after hidden truth, and striving for the strongest faith. By extension, Scripture is also an examined repository of hidden truth as well as "Christian philosophy." Athens and Jerusalem have everything in common.

The liturgical remembrance of Hus and Jerome has vivid testimony in the Czech lands. One text asserts: "Two lamps arose…and through bitter martyrdom crossed over into heaven." While the Council of the wicked in Constance crowned Jerome with flames, the army of heaven interceded to transport the righteous man to heaven. One line in this song implores God to: "Grant that the merits of Hus and Jerome might benefit us by means of our heavenly songs." Jerome and Hus are added to the historic and noble army of apostles and martyrs, and when compared to the men and women who had previously laid down their lives in the cause of Christ, they are given the highest accolades. They are: "The steadfast warriors, firm adherents of the law of Christ, zealous until death. O happy Constance to whom with excellent parts as well the Czech nation grant grace for the benefit of the Church and for our comfort. Having suffered many things for the name of Christ, having washed their robes in blood they possess the joy of eternal life in the court of heaven." So, Jerome is both a lamp of truth and an inspiration who becomes, by means of suffering, an intercessor for all the faithful on earth and an heir of eternal life. Jerome came to occupy a central place in the memory of all faithful Czechs who had suffered for Christ because he strove for the strongest faith.

Some medieval writers esteemed "the excellent man" Jerome as a prophetic figure. Just as Elijah had been transported in a chariot of fire from doubt to the joy of paradise, so now Jerome, "fearless and zealous for the truth of the gospel" on account of his faith and martyrdom, had been transformed into "an example and mirror of perseverance" in witness of the power of truth. Jerome was considered a figure of apocalyptic significance at the apex of history. In the book of Revelation (11:4), the two witnesses are called olive trees and lamp stands who had been ordained of God to bear light. The English martyrologist John Foxe offered a striking interpretation of that passage. He wrote that Hus and Jerome were left in "a difficult place, on the dunghill, in mourning, in darkness, in the harshest fetters, cruelly separated and in need of everything. These are the two olive trees and the two candlesticks." Like Elijah, Jerome's words burned like a torch. Both men left this world in fire having set their worlds ablaze.

When his faith failed and he gave in to weakness, the Galilean fisherman Peter betrayed Jesus. But he later turned and, when he did, he became the chief apostle. He then strengthened his brethren and reinforced the Christian community. He is not remembered as a cursing and fearful coward. Instead, history remembers him as a disciple, an apostle, and as a martyr. Famously and strikingly, he is now routinely called St. Peter. Jerome of Prague, too, failed and signed a recantation, renouncing his faith, his views, his convictions. He denounced Jan Hus and affixed his hand in support of the medieval church. But like Peter, he too regained his composure. He turned again. He strengthened the Czech Christian community. Eventually, at least in some quarters, he was remembered as an excellent man, a lamp of truth, a popular saint, and a steadfast warrior.

Jerome's approach to faith exhibits a firm commitment to examination. It exemplifies a relentless search for the truth. From one end of Europe to the other, he fought the good fight of insisting upon reason in faith. By means of these commitments, Jerome of Prague laid hold of eternal life having arrived at the strongest faith which is always the examined faith.

Lake Constance

Lion's head, Table Mountain, Cape Town, South Africa

Two roads diverging in Moravia

At Home in the Darkness

We spend all of our lives with ourselves. We spend considerable time at home wherever and whatever that might be. As pilgrims on a journey we call life there are pathways intersecting at every turn. Robert Frost might have spoken eloquently of two roads diverging in the forest but in truth I often wish there were only two roads. That way I could have a fifty percent chance of choosing the right road though I might forever remain frozen in thought trying to figure out what exactly "right" is. I have been in this forest all of my life and there is a jumble of pathways through thickets to left and right and the notion of going back to reconsider a previous choice is wishful thinking at best. With Frost I can but sigh. I could not retrace my footsteps back to a former crossroads not even if my life depended on it. Standing still is not an option either. It is altogether too frightening. The weird shadows slant sometimes threateningly. The wind rises ominously from time to time and I seek shelter by hurrying on beneath great trees, along pathways both well-worn in places but elsewhere overgrown almost to the point where the trail fails to qualify as a path by any reasonable definition.

Over the years staggering from one pathway to another and lurching through the seasons of life itself I came to realize that for all the bravado of self-confidence, self-assertion, education, influence and affluence, most of my life was lived less in the light of general illumination and more in the shadows here and there in my life and encountered now and then with unpredicted predictability. Sometimes I found myself living in utter darkness and after a time I became rather accustomed to the dimness of existence. As I grew older, I came to accept the truth that after all our struggles and protests to the contrary we are confined to our own lives, to these shadows and to the darkness. There is no escape from the shadows for any of us so perhaps the question is this: What is there to discover in the shadows, in the grim darkness? What goodness resides along the edges of the darkness that sometimes we deny so vociferously? Are there any traces of grace in the sadness of our living?

Growing up on a church bench upon which I heard much chatter of being saved and considerable blubbering of finding the right path leading to the eternal kingdom, I soon found the terminology of "being saved" in my mind and on my lips and I suppose impressed upon my psyche. I remember a pathetic little tune I heard a few times as a boy that ran something like this: "Above all else I must be saved, whatever you [God] have to do to me don't let me be lost for eternity, above all else, I must be saved." Over the years I began to process that sentiment and came to wonder what justification there might possibly be for placing myself at the center of the universe and insisting that before anything else and everything else I must be saved. Implicitly we were also singing, above everyone else, perhaps before everyone else, I must have what I want. Pick me! Eventually I concluded that the arrogance and self-importance implied in the insipid little ditty was altogether unwarranted. After all, perhaps my life was not worth the effort of asserting my own salvation and maybe, just maybe, I might well be sacrificed for a greater good. Why do we find that suggestion so offensive, so terrifying? Is it because secretly we are devoted to the pursuit of our personal significance and prepared to do anything, or everything, to achieve that significance?

Dylan Thomas once wrote of the urge to rage against the dying of the light and to not go gently into that good night. One might say that Thomas himself did rage and steadfastly refused to go quietly into that good night but went nevertheless at age 39 in New York City after an unbelievable drinking binge somewhat like the character played by Nicholas Cage in the film *Leaving Las Vegas*. All the raging and the fury cannot hold back the night and avoiding the darkness is downright difficult, if not futile. Bathing oneself in blazing spotlights might hold back the creeping darkness that comes each night at set of sun but does nothing to dispel the real darkness for that blackness is within and all the light that ever was cannot hold back that night. Rage, rage, if you must, strut and fret your whole hour long upon the stage of life if you will, but when the hour is up the shadow does fall fast for life itself is a shadow between our fantasies and reality. Walk on.

All the rhetoric I heard over and over as a young boy sitting hour after interminable hour on the wooden benches of the church about being saved took on new meaning once I contemplated this expectation of dramatic cosmic redemption and the apparent divine search and rescue operation. I discovered a useful analogy in the remembrances of my childhood. I grew up on the banks of a waterway holding the distinction for having the greatest differential in water levels between high tide and low tide anywhere in the world. As long ago as the sixteenth century the Portuguese referred to it as "rio fundo" or the "deep river." The name appears on maps as early as 1544 and the Portuguese explorer João Álvares Fagundes may have sailed its tides more than twenty years earlier. There is considerable darkness in the deep river and my own peregrinations over more than five decades of life have taken me deep into the deep river and into the inky darkness of that world in the deep river where light is seldom seen. More than fifty years ago (May 1968) a diver by the name of Clyde Carter when down into the "deep river" and never returned. No one ever again saw hide nor hair of Carter. He had vanished into the thinnest of air out of sight in the fathomless deep river. As a small boy I remember hearing my parents talk about Carter and how the darkness had swallowed him up. He made the front page of the local city newspaper. I saw his photograph somewhere but his disappearance was the talk of the town for a few days. No one ever saw him again. His body was never recovered. No one to this day knows what happened to Carter. All I knew for certain was that the darkness took him far, far away and took him so fully and kept him so completely that not even his flippers turned up. It was as though he had never lived so complete was his disappearance.

As more time went by, I learned that it was not necessary to slip beneath the tantalizing surface of the deep river to be immersed in the darkness. I discovered that darkness lurked within. Being saved was not just getting Carter before he ran out of oxygen or if he did use up all his air hauling his wet, limp, body up on the shore before the darkness took permanent possession of him. Being saved meant rescue from myself and finding safety from the gathering shadows within. Still I came to identify a problem. Getting saved was not nearly quite as simple as the corpulent red-faced preachers claimed. Trapped in a burning building one might be pulled to safety through the ingenuity or heroism of the firefighters. That sort of salvation was understandable. Drowning in a swimming pool one might be plucked from the watery grave by the prowess of the lifeguard on duty. I could grasp that type of rescue as well. But who, or what, can rescue us from the fires and the floods that burn and billow within? A fellow by the name of Saul of Tarsus (a city in what today is the nation of Turkey) who lived two millennia ago lamented the same dilemma in a surviving letter that he wrote to a religious community in Rome nineteen and a half centuries ago. This man Saul admitted he was of the flesh (which seems sensible enough to say) but on that account had been handed over to the slavery of sin and could not even understand his own actions. I found the admission intriguing. In fact he admitted that he did not do what he wanted to do but instead engaged in that which he found reprehensible. I began to identify with this man Saul. Like Frost sighing in the forest, Saul went on to say that it really was not he, Saul of Tarsus, committing these deeds but rather the awful sin that resided inside of him. Reading his confession 2,000 years after the fact sent a cold chill down my spine. Perhaps I was not as unique in my darkness as I had suspected. Then he put the point across rather firmly saying he really wanted to do what was right but found himself unable to actually do it. Instead, he did the evil that he sincerely did not wish to do but he blamed his failure on the sin flourishing inside of him claiming that it really was not Saul of Tarsus who ultimately should be held accountable. Then looking at the dire situation carefully, this ancient author detected a war being waged inside himself on the battlefield people called Saul of Tarsus. Forces of evil combat forces of good and the poor man finally burst out in quivering frustration claiming he had been taken into captivity and made a prisoner of war: "I am a wretched man! Who will rescue me?"

I did not literally follow Carter's flipper prints across the mud flats until they filled up with water and then disappeared into the deep river. I never saw the point. The deep river was far too murky for an interesting dive and far too cold to be of any true joy and why bother with these northern waters anyways when one might plumb the more inviting depths of the Caribbean or the enchanting marine world of the Great Barrier Reef. I avoided those sad flipper prints and steered right clear of the deep river but I went down, alright, into the bottomless sea of darkness just as surely as Carter did and no one knows, least of all me, whether in the end there shall be any trace of me, flippers, hide or hair. I could not help but go down since my goings, regardless of where they took me, meant journeys in the darkness. Like Saul from ancient Tarsus, wherever I went, the darkness went too and in some strange way I took some comfort there and whatever efforts I may have made to avoid the shadows of the deep river in the end I embraced the darkness, or did the darkness embrace me? Or is it possible to say which laid hold upon which? Perhaps I am the darkness and the darkness is me. Are we one and the same? I cannot say for sure except to say that my fitful struggles of raging against the night became rather like the frantic efforts of helpless victims caught in quicksand where the more one thrashes about the deeper becomes the plight. I have never had the misfortune to stumble onto quicksand but I can relate to the Brer Foxes and the Brer Rabbits of the world. It is rather easy to get caught up in the self-centeredness of living to such an extent that I become the very focus of the universe and actually think that the most important thing is me and my salvation. "Above all else." That seems to be in some sense the way of the Brer Rabbits of the world. Swaggering, arrogant, self-centered, boisterous, incorrigible. There are others who do not swagger quite as much (unless they are three sheets to the wind), are less arrogant, but who seem to have become full-time workers of iniquity, "lewd fellows of the baser sort," given over to cunning, waywardness and general-all-round tomfoolery. These are features of the Brer Foxes of the world. Both must contend with the problem of Tar Baby.

In the nineteenth century, Joel Chandler Harris published the stories of Brer Rabbit and his antagonists Brer Fox and Brer Bear. The rabbit's encounter with Tar Baby is a tale of extraordinary defeat and stunning, unexpected triumph. Irritated by the behavior of Brer Rabbit, Brer Fox hatches a shrewd plan to snare that rascally rabbit once and for all. He manufactures a crude critter out of tar and turpentine and his own evil imaginings, pushes a straw hat down on its head and sits it on the road in the general vicinity of where he expects Brer Rabbit to pass. When Brer Rabbit appears he hails Tar Baby with a bombastic greeting but gets no response. Perplexed the highfalutin bunny goes to some lengths to engage Tar Baby in a conversation. Completely frustrated by the non-responsiveness he knocks Tar Baby's hat off. At length, after duly warning the mute creature, Brer Rabbit smacks Tar Baby and discovers his paw is stuck fast. In an effort to free himself he slugs Tar Baby with his other paw only to make his situation even more dire. Now enraged and raving all the while he kicks Tar Baby with one foot, then the other, and finally head-butts his adversary only to find out that he is now good and helpless. Brer Fox who has been watching all the while now appears and after recovering from a sustained fit of laughter intends to kill the rabbit. The story ends with Brer Rabbit tricking Brer Fox into thinking that what he fears most of all is the nearby briar patch. Brer Fox begins congratulating himself a tad too soon and thus heaves the rabbit into the dreaded briar patch where the tricky bunny makes good his escape to the consternation of the outsmarted fox.

Somewhere back inside the forest many years ago I ran smack into my own Tar Baby. God alone knows why I bothered to stop and address the oozing, disgusting thing. It was not very attractive, it smelled, and the straw hat it wore looked ridiculous. Perhaps it was the straw hat that caught my attention. It is hard to say. I parlayed too long with Tar Baby and soon my right hand was stuck in the oozing matter of its form. I was not too concerned until I tried to free myself and found both hands locked in a mystifying grasp. Had I remembered Brer Rabbit I might have avoided further difficulty but I became single-minded to a fault. The more I stumbled along the forest pathways the nearer I came to the deep river. After I furiously, but quite unsuccessfully, head-butted my nemesis I could no longer clearly see the pathway I was on. Neither was I able to determine how dangerously close I had now veered to the treacherous banks above the deep river. Unfortunately I was not Brer Rabbit and the deep river was no briar patch. Once I plunged into the murky waters the straw hat floated away. Tar Baby, however, did not dissolve and drift away nor was I released from its deadly grip. The more I struggled the deeper our embrace became. As I sank it soon became impossible to determine where Tar Baby ended and I began and in the darkness we two became as one. The tale is true but not factual for I never found Tar Baby along a forest way. Instead, I found Tar Baby inside of me, the presence of darkness. In the week prior to impulsively writing this piece, I experienced without any warning at all a sustained floundering around in the darkness and there was less light in that week than one might expect to find while spelunking in Dead Horse Cave beneath Mt. Adams in Washington state. The darkness was so palpable that I suspect that had someone ventured into those same shadows in search of me they would have found neither hide nor hair of me. For all intents and purposes I was Saul of Tarsus in the last week and I knew again exactly what he meant. Avoidably, all theology is to some extent autobiographical whether we are speaking of St. Paul, St. Augustine, Aquinas, Luther or Karl Barth. My ruminations about the darkness are rooted within my own experiences rather than in hypothesis or wishful thinking.

The snail and the turtle carry their homes with them. Recently, I had occasion to observe the journey of a giant tortoise. It is often a painful process watching these creatures move about so slowly and with so much labor. But home is always with them and they never have to worry about getting home before dark or being late for dinner for home is wherever they are, whenever they are. On the night a Galilean rabbi sat to eat a meal with his closest friends one of them plotted to betray him into the hands of his enemies. One ancient text tells us that the enemy within finished dinner and then slipped out and it was night. Judas Iscariot did his deed under the cover of night in the darkness. He may well have stepped from the light into the night but in truth the darkness was already inside of him just as the darkness always is. Just as the darkness is inside each of us sometimes so deep one can feel it. The problem with being saved is that half the time we don't even want to be rescued. Half the time we feel no need to be saved. This is possibly because we feel comfortable in the darkness. It is home. It is familiar and for a moment every now and then we take comfort in that familiarity. Indeed, who wants to be rescued from themselves? Does the turtle long to be saved from his shell? It is possible that we reach a stage in our wanderings where we find ourselves at home in the darkness.

Along the dark forest trails of life and in the grip of the deep river the possibility of salvation always comes as a happy thought. But it means surrender. It implies leaving home and giving up the comforts one has become so accustomed to. Those comforts might be manipulative, destructive, unsavory, or downright repulsive. Still, they help us find our way through the darkness and there is a measure of security therein even if the tradeoff is humiliation, degradation, and a loss of authentic identity. Henry David Thoreau once truthfully observed that the mass of humanity lead lives of quiet desperation. In the comfort of the night it is easy to give in to that impulse. The fact that the desperation is quiet makes it all the easier. If the desperation was frantic or violent one might perhaps be more inclined to put up a better struggle and mount a proper resistance. Quiet desperation is soothing. Peaceful perversions are so much more palatable than those that attract lots of attention and are shouted from rooftops. There are woods here and there in life so calm and so delightful that one might wander for hours on end before coming to the realization they are helplessly and hopelessly lost. An apocryphal tale about Daniel Boone relates how the eighteenth-century American frontiersman was once asked if he'd ever been lost in the woods. Boone said no but added that once he had been confused for three days. Quiet desperation recognizes neither lostness nor confusion.

The Hebrew Bible tells a long story about an affluent man named Job who lived in the curiously named land of Uz, an uncertain place in the ancient near east. Job ran into an awful streak of bad luck and before all was said and done wound up losing his wealth, health and family. We are told that Job was a righteous man and that he asked God why these troubles had come upon him? Why had the darkness descended so quickly and with such devastating force? All's well that ends end, or so they say, because in the end Job got it all back again with interest. But it is noteworthy that Job never got an answer from God about the plight he found himself in. Sometimes life is like that. Explaining the darkness is impossible and where attempts are piously made the results are often unsatisfactory.

"Make yourself at home" are words we not infrequently say to guests and friends when they come around to visit. Often it is just cliché, words without reflection, words we've heard so often they come naturally. That being the case we hardly expect visitors to open the refrigerator and eat whatever they want whenever they want. Moreover, we would be startled if they started cleaning house and tossing out items they deemed no longer useful. No visitor in someone else's house can truly and literally feel at home. Home is where you do what you want to do when you want how you want and where you want. The darkness that pervades our living and our lives allows for us to behave as we wish and therefore it is the only place one can truly make oneself at home. This makes being saved from such environment difficult. It means ultimate surrender and that word carries with it connotations few of us eagerly embrace. We take some comfort in choosing which path to follow through which thicket or beneath which tree in the yellow woods of life.

There is a sense of freedom in the flow of the deep river and we think we know best how to deal with the Tar Babies we encounter here and there along our journeys. Besides, there are benefits in having home with us all the time like the turtle and the snail. Yet what are we missing in our quiet desperation as we stumble through the darkness? Hamlet said: "There are more things in heaven and earth, Horatio, than are dreamt of in your philosophy."

Can one speak prophetically in the darkness to those in darkness? The first-century Jewish rabbi who needed no enemies on account of the friends he had was later announced as the one whose life was the light of humankind. The light shines in the darkness and the darkness cannot overpower it. Early Christian tradition asserts there was a man sent from God whose name was John Baptist. This strange man came particularly to bear witness to the light so that everyone might take note of it. John Baptist went to some lengths to make clear that he was not the light but he insisted the true light that would provide illumination to all people was on the way. Stories began to circulate claiming that people who lived in darkness saw a great light shining on them and their darknesses – every last one of them whatever their specific natures – were dispelled. It is a happy thought, but does it recur?

Who knows all the details behind the World Trade Center disaster on September 11, 2001. What is clear is that two airliners crashed into those skyscrapers and the towers collapsed. By the time the rubble was scoured, more than 2,600 people had lost their lives in the darkness. The idea of God is useless in a moment such as this. The fact of the matter is that God does not prevent such acts from occurring and does not save lives from fires and collapsing buildings. God does not hold back the darkness and does not make life good and right for all people, at all times, in all places. God does not even act that way for Christians. History itself is a stark reminder of this reality and more than sufficient evidence to confound the nay-sayers. There is suffering, there is pain, there is death. Even Jesus Christ experienced all three and he too was shrouded in the darkness in the middle of the day no less. Christianity claims he was the Son of God. If the Son of God could not escape the darkness why do any of us think we might be spared? Are we that truly wedded to that tired refrain, "Above all else, I...?" The idea of God is useless when we pause at the crossroads deep in the forests of life. God will not beckon you down one path or the other. The idea of God was of no help to Carter as he spiraled downwards in the murky darkness of the deep river. Perhaps he cried out to God. No one can say. Perhaps he prayed for deliverance. None can know for sure. All that seems likely is that Carter went down into the darkness, and disappearance and death became his deliverance. The idea of God is useless when we find our hands and feet and head stuck fast to one Tar Baby or the other. Struggle on. It is your fight. Not God's. It is unlikely that a hand will appear, like the one reported on the wall during Belshazzar's palace party, to release us from the pickles we get ourselves into. "Make yourself at home." Many Christians committed to the notion of divine intervention and providential action in the affairs of humankind protest that such claims are heresy. Perhaps. Still, it is possible they are at home with their own unseen version of darkness. Nevertheless, to say that the idea of God at such times is useless may seem like an awful thing to say. Since the thought does not originate with me I feel free to say it seems to me a brave thing to confess. The more I reflect upon it the more I find it a true thing to say and there is a chance that maybe, just maybe, the truth will set us free even from darkness. And what a wonderful thought that is.

Truthfully, I do not expect to emerge from the woods even if I live to be as old as my Great-Aunt Jenny who made it to her 112th year before pulling her feet up into the bed and turning her head to the wall. I have a feeling I must struggle against the rising tide in the deep river for as long as I live. I do not believe the road ahead will ever be cleared of Tar Baby and his cousins and there is a good chance that sooner or later, here and there, one hand or the other, or both, may get stuck in the smelly oozing mass. Have I resigned myself to quiet desperation? I hope not. With Saul of Tarsus so long ago I may be a prisoner of war but I continue to rage against the grim night. What can one discover in the darkness? It is possible that in the night one comes to the realization that he or she is not alone that even Jesus languished in a darkness that not even he could dispel. Yet he was not lost irretrievably. Is there goodness anywhere in the long dark night of the soul that John of the Cross spoke of more than four centuries ago? The goodness that may be found in that darkness is not eternal or even absolute. Here and there amid the shadows, traces of goodness and proof of Presence may be found. In the beginning, back before any one was around or knew anything about goodness or God, darkness covered the face of all that was. In the midst of darkness and everlasting night – which was the only home there ever was – the Presence of God infiltrated the darkness and God said: "Let there be light." Astonishingly, there was light.

In the cosmos in which we live there is both day and night and each appears with unhesitating regularity and mechanical prediction. In our inner lives there is also darkness and light but these resist our control and come and go without precision, invitation or even expectation. God says: "Let there be light" and we can only hope that light will come and that light is God's Presence and God's grace. Will that Presence save us from the perils of the forest or pluck us from the dangers of the deep river? Not likely. But that Presence goes with us, not all the time but some of the time, and every now and then through the gloom we see the face of God, here and there, in the faces of those who pass us by, in the forests, in the water, in the light itself that comes from God. An early Christian text, possibly predating the canonical gospels, invites the reader to realize the extent of the Presence of God: "Split a piece of wood: I am there. Lift up a stone, and you will find me there." If there is any truth whatever in that assertion then there is cause to believe that God is there also in the darkness of my life and in the darknesses of yours.

Back on the same wooden benches above the "rio fundo" I learned another song that emphasized the words "this little light of mine, I'm going to let it shine." It is a theological axiom that humankind carry within themselves, somewhere in some sense, the image of God. Can darkness swallow up that image utterly and forever? Does our fumbling in the night work to obliterate God's image? Or is it the image of God that keeps us from succumbing entirely to the forces of the deep river? Is it this abiding image that keeps us from being lost forever? "This little light of mine" is not mine at all but a gift from God to guide us in the night and to comfort us in the darkness. God says: "Let there be light." Let it shine. It is cliché to be sure but still a kernel of truth remains in the saying: "It is better to light a candle than to curse the darkness." Stop cursing then and "let there be light." There was light in creation. There was light in redemption. There is the hope of light in the darkness I live in. There is light somewhere at the end of even the longest, darkest tunnels.

Consider Judas. This man Iscariot, whose name is so obscure that no one knows what it means, is the arch-villain of Christian history. This is the scoundrel who betrayed his friend Jesus and sold him to his enemies for thirty pieces of silver. Jesus wound up getting crucified. Judas felt so badly about his actions that he killed himself and was sent off to hell forthwith and everyone said "Amen." Good riddance, they all cried aloud in their hallelujah voices, after all he's not one of us for none of us would ever do such a wicked, dirty deed. Really? How can we be so cocksure? A medieval legend tells the tale that suffering in the darkness of his hell Judas repented and earnestly desired to make amends. It seems he was confined at the bottom of a dark and dank well. In the darkness Judas tried to climb out but could only get so high before he would fall back and be forced to start again. This went on for centuries. Judas became rather like poor old Sisyphus whom the Greek gods sentenced to roll a large rock up a steep hill but every time he neared the top he lost control of the rock and had to do it all over again in perpetuity. Finally, at long last, Judas managed to struggle his way to the top of the dreary well in which darkness he had languished for what seemed like an eternity. Frail, withered and pale, Judas stumbled from the damp edge of the well into a brilliant light. Blinded by the light and blinking uncontrollably trying to gain some focus, Judas staggered into an upper room where he found twelve men sitting around a table. The man at the head greeted him in a most familiar voice saying: "Welcome back Judas, we've been waiting for you. We couldn't start without you." Is there light, and hope and grace for Judas Iscariot in his darkness? If not, why not? If there is light for him, then there is light for all.

Whether one is lost in the forest, sinking in the deep river, or blinded by the darkness that comes overpoweringly from within, "let there be light." At home in the darkness, the good news of the one who came to shine light in all the dark places of life and death may come. In what seems like everlasting night may that light enable each of us to let our lights shine to point the way through the darkness, through the forest, through the deep river, through each and every season of life. Is there salvation for Carter lost in the darkness without visible evidence of hide, hair or flippers? Surely there is. And what of Brer Rabbit trapped in the inky lather of yet another mess? Lift up your eyes and look for the briar patch. Will the darkness end for Judas, for you and for me? For one moment we might do well to read the last line of the lament penned so long ago by that man Saul of Tarsus. At the end of the day, in the depth of night, beneath a cloak so dark that none can see the light, Saul put it thus: Thanks be to God for Christ the light. The experience of the darkness within is an opportunity for light to shine. "Make yourself at home" and fight not the night but fight for the light. For in that fighting is all the being saved that has ever been or ever will be for you and me, for Carter, the arrogant rabbit and Judas, too, upon the tree. All sit in darkness, upon all shall great light shine. In the Quaker tradition there is a saying: "I will hold you in the light." I believe it is possible even for those of us who dwell in the darkness to do just that. At least we can hope. So at home in the darkness, "let there be light." That hope makes bearable the darkness.

The Skipper and the Table

He was a regular fixture in the Cathedral. He always sat in the front row, on the right. He came early to make sure no one else got his seat. I called him the Skipper on account of the fact that he always had with him a sailor's cap which he placed carefully on the chair next to him. He had the odd habit of joining the recessional. I first glimpsed him during my early days in the old Cathedral when I used to sit near the rear. I was watching the choristers, the choir members, the acolytes, the liturgical assistants, the lay canons and then the priests coming down the center aisle. Behind the dean of the cathedral, who always brought up the rear of the recessional, was this small, short, little old man wearing a sailor's cap. I wondered who he was and what his particular function was. It was only later that I realized he had no function at all and really had no business leaving church when he did. But as the dean passed his chair the Skipper stepped out into the aisle, flopped his cap down on his bald head and headed for the exit, smacking his lips all the while.

I found out from the dean that the old man's name was Eric. He had the habit of chomping throughout the service, a sort of silent smacking of his lips together that was less of an aural distraction than a visual one. I remember especially his habit, during the sharing of the peace with others. He would turn to those near him, pump their hand and say: "The peace of the Lord Jesus Christ be with you." He often consulted his watch during the sermon, on average about every three to five minutes as though impatient. He never came with anyone and never left with anyone. I sat behind him for perhaps two or three years on Sunday mornings. Once, during the liturgy, when the congregation was to say: "It is right to give him thanks and praise," followed by the celebrating minister saying: "It is indeed right" the Skipper loudly intoned: "IT IS

RIGHT" at precisely the wrong time. The presiding priest was knocked completely off balance. Even now, at that point in the liturgy I lean over to the monk and whisper: "It is right."

The Skipper was at least 80 years old and was thought by some to be just plain nuts. He once told the dean (who told me) that his particular ministry was blessing children and regularly reported to the dean that during the past week he had blessed seventy-four kids or some other such figure depending on the week. That was his thing. He lived in the south city at Nazareth House, an old people's home run by Catholics.

In November 1994, Sir Charles Upham died. Upham had been a well-decorated World War II hero. Twice he was singled out for highest bravery. He fought in Greece, on Crete and later in North Africa and for his gallantry was awarded a double Victorian Cross status. Upham's funeral was held in the Christchurch Cathedral and Bishop David Coles took the service. At the conclusion of the service an Honor Guard stretched halfway out into the square as the casket was carried out to the waiting hearse. The usual recessional occurred and sure enough, the Skipper stepped into line, cap in place, right behind the bishop. Near the door, the bishop turned and saw the Skipper and the old man indicated he had something to say to the bishop: "Well, nice to see you too Eric, but this is really not the time or the place for us to talk." The Skipper was of another mind and told the bishop: "Just because you have become the bishop does not mean you are now so high and mighty that you don't have to talk to me." Right there, at the entrance to the cathedral, in front of the honor guard, during a state funeral, with the guard waiting for the signal to move off, the Skipper gave the bishop a good dressing down. Once finished, the Skipper shuffled off and the ceremony continued.

I always paid close attention to the Skipper when it came time for communion. Since he sat in the front row on the center aisle side he was always the first to approach the altar to receive communion. He always crossed himself as the priest approached and received the elements prayfully and thoughtfully and then returned to his seat smacking his lips.

Inasmuch as I too sat upfront, I began to observe the people coming and going from the table of the Lord. The Skipper was always first, but there were more people, Cathedral regulars and strangers too. Children came with parents. One woman confined to a wheelchair, with a wonderful countenance, always came to the table from the south transept and I often wondered what had happened to her and what this Christian ritual called the eucharist meant to her. Derelicts from the street wandered into the Cathedral and stumbled to the table of the Lord. I often sat and watched them. They were reverent and sober as they stretched out grimy hands to receive the body and blood of Christ as the choir sang the *Agnus Dei* – "Lamb of God, you take away the sin of the world." The young came forward as well as the old. Some of the more elderly had to be assisted. Others hobbled on bad legs. Little retarded Dorothy who always sat across from me never failed to partake of Christ. The same might be said of "big-little" Dorothy, who was also retarded, who liked to wave the host in the sign of the cross before dipping it in the chalice and finally placing it in her mouth. A little girl with a face like a cat, a bald-headed man, who stood as stiff as a soldier without moving a muscle, only his eyes moved, darting back and forth, whom we called "the Parrot," a chap who looked like Monty Python's Eric Idle, a woman who wore the same clothes week after week, Mrs. Lennox, a near-sighted old man, and an Asian woman who always wore some strange head piece were among the regulars coming to the table. "Sweatyhead" never missed. He was an odd, middle-aged, guy who was always doing something rather silly with his hair. One experiment made him look as though he'd just rushed in from the gym. The monk gave him the name and it stuck. "The old goat," another distinctive chap, regularly shuffled up as did an elderly violin player who always wore shorts and had the skinniest legs imaginable. Prokop the dog led his blind master to the table each Sunday and impatiently gave his harness a shake as he paused at the rail. There were long beards, funny hats, well-dressed professional people, spiked hair, people with body piercings, men and women wearing clerical collars, people like you, people like me. Why did they come? What were they thinking? What, if anything, did they receive? People just like these have been coming to the Lord's table for over two millennia. All kinds of people.

I elbowed the monk and nodded my head over to the left. The monk's brow furrowed over a long hard stare. Yes, it was a guy in a dress coming to the table. I shook my head slightly. He was not even convincing. It was eleven o'clock in the morning and already he had a five o'clock shadow. The wig was of poor quality, the makeup and jewellery almost ludicrous. She walked like a man. She wore a name-tag that read "Helen." I had neither seen Helen before nor since. I was a little disgusted. How could someone like that just walk into the Cathedral and come straight to the altar? I rolled my eyes at the monk and tried to think of something clever and sarcastic to say. Almost immediately, I felt condemned. Yes, who did Helen think she was? But who was I? I had just gone to the table, stood beside the Skipper, and heard the priest say: "Thomas, the body of Christ given for you." Then: "Thomas, the blood of Christ shed for you." Who was I to receive such worthy gifts? Okay, I wasn't wearing a dress but did that make me any different than Helen? I watched her, or him, listen to the same words that I too had just heard a few moments earlier. I saw her eyes close as she received the body and blood of Christ. In spite of myself, I began to think about grace.

St. Paul had been pretty clear that the cup we receive is a participation in the blood of Christ. Likewise, the bread we eat is fellowship in the body of Christ. In other words, the activity around the table of the Lord was sacramental. That is to say, grace is active and the eucharistic event is a channel of that grace and unites God and humankind. If that be true, God had just been joined to Helen. Could that be true? In this very moment those streaming forward to the table were participating in the continuing power of past redemptive activity. Christ is truly present and in this moment the Word dwells richly. The elements of bread and wine are not necessarily sacred, but the event is. His presence is true, not just symbol. It is real, not imaginative. Why did Christ instruct those with him to eat and drink rather than simply observe and remember? Quite possibly he deliberately planned a giving and a receiving of his presence. The blood of the eucharist is for the remission of sins and it allows one to share in the redeeming activity of God.

Too frequently we are so concerned with being worthy. I remember as a boy whenever we had Holy Communion (which was not very often) that the minister would call for a period of silence during which each one was enjoined to search their hearts, for, as he explained it, to eat and drink unworthily meant eating and drinking damnation. That sounded pretty serious to me and I always kept my eyes tightly shut and prayed that I would not eat and drink damnation. In those moments of silence I could never think of any reason why I was worthy. The exercise proved fruitless. Too often we spend our time wondering if we are worthy to the point of being neglectful of what he has already designed to accomplish. In the celebration of the eucharist, at the table of the Lord, we find ourselves confronted again with the presence of Christ. As we receive the elements we encounter in dramatic fashion the actual presence of his body and his life. At this magnificent moment we are apprehended by him and the Word again becomes flesh and God is with us. In other words, the eucharist is an extension of the Incarnation.

The New Testament scholar C.H. Dodd wrote that in the eucharist, we are there. We are there in the night when he was betrayed. We are there in the garden. We are there at Golgotha. We are there before the tomb on Easter Day. We are there in the upper room when he again appeared. We are there and he is here. Here for you, for me, for the Skipper, for Helen, for all who come in faith.

I stood transformed as the chancel organ played and the choir sang: "Jesu, joy of man's desiring." I watched the lines of people pressing forward to the table, under the sign of the cross. The ambiance of the Gothic cathedral with all its symbolism and atmosphere brought home to me the powerful realization that millions of men and women throughout Christian history have come to the table, just like this and in faith have been fed with the body and blood of Christ. It was not mere ritual. It was not just part of the traditionalism of the church. It was a living and dynamic component of the faith. As Jaroslav Pelikan put it: "Traditionalism is the dead faith of the living. Tradition is the living faith of the dead." This was part of the latter.

I felt tears in the corners of my eyes as I thought of the great cloud of witnesses gathered all around me; witnesses who were recipients of God's grace; witnesses of divine redemptive activity in the world; eye-witnesses of God's majesty. None of us were worthy, but God counted us worthy enough to go to the cross. The eucharist was not about me, or you, or the Skipper, or Helen, or Dorothy, or the old "Parrot" or "Sweatyhead," or anybody else. It was about what God had done and is now doing among men and women everywhere. In that realization, I experienced divine grace.

The table was empty. The Skipper collected his papers and, as the dean passed his chair, stepped out into the aisle to join the recessional, placing his battered sailor's cap on his bald head. Who knows who the Skipper really is, but one thing is certain, he had been to the table and had eaten and drunk of life, resurrection, grace, and the "medicine of immortality."

THE EMPTY BOX

A long time ago a man whose name time has forgotten punished his three year old daughter for wasting a roll of beautiful gold wrapping paper. The family did not have very much money and the father became angry when he saw his little daughter using the paper to wrap a box to put under the Christmas tree. There were not many gifts under the tree and the tree itself was pretty scrawny and all in all it was a fairly meagre Christmas in terms of gifts and trimmings. The next morning the father became greatly embarrassed when the little girl brought him the box in the golden wrapping and sweetly said "Daddy, this is for you." But when he opened the box he discovered there was nothing in it. It was just an empty box. He exploded in rage and his fury knew no bounds. He stormed about the room yelling at his little daughter who stood quaking with fear trying to say something, but her father roared on. Finally, stooping down in front of her with his face in hers, he berated her with the sarcastic question: "Don't you know little girl that when you give someone a gift you don't just give them an empty box? You're supposed to put something in it." Sneers, jeers and leers abounded.

The little girl looked up at her father and with little tears running down her little face she said: "O, Daddy, the box is not empty. I blew lots of kisses into the box and all of them were just for you." The father was crushed. He threw his arms around his little daughter and with big tears running down his big cheeks he begged her forgiveness. The story goes on that the man kept that golden box by his bedside for many years and even as an old man whenever he felt discouraged, unhappy, lonely or sad, he would open up the empty box, given to him all those years ago, and would take out one of the imaginary kisses and remember with gratitude the love of the little girl who had put it there so long ago and even in the autumn years of his life he was able to warm himself by the fire that continued to glow inside the golden wrapping of the empty box.

Kisses are a wonderful thing. When one is kissed by someone who loves you and someone you love in return the feeling of closeness and warmness is unbelievably satisfying. Many of us had grandmothers we grew up around. Grandmothers always seem to want to kiss their grandchildren. My paternal grandmother had perfected the proverbial grandmother kiss. In fact I seriously doubt that any woman can be a real grandmother until she learns how to kiss like a grandmother. You know what I mean. One of those wet kisses that usually landed, without warning, on one's cheek like a slimy fish and that inevitably smacked loudly like a suction lid letting go ever so slowly alerting everyone in the immediate vicinity to what had just happened. Kids, especially boys, normally just hate Grandmother's kisses. But still, you knew she loved you without condition and the kiss was the price to be paid for a piece of apple pie or a half dozen cookies. Mothers and fathers who kiss their children are saying, perhaps silently: "I love you and I care very much for you."

As one gets older, it becomes more apparent that there is something quite intimate about kissing. Lips are soft and responsive parts of our bodies. Pressing four firm lips together can be a rather exhilarating experience especially when you are 16 or 17 and – if you are a young fellow and you find that special young lady – you get to do it to someone you just happen to think is mighty special. I was 15 years old and had just met a rather wonderful girl from Cherryfield, Maine. I had never really kissed girls before. At 15 one is generally still quite immune from all that sort of thing. She being a couple of years older than I announced one evening that she would teach me to kiss. Indeed she did. What a strange and rather wonderful experience. A few years later, I remember standing on a rain-drenched beach on the Oregon coast under the cover of night sharing the shelter of a wide-brimmed black umbrella with a virtual angel. I was old enough to know better but still young enough to want to do it again. It was no surprise that our lips touched briefly and in that moment I was electrified and had I but closed my eyes I am sure I would have gone straight to paradise. There was another girl once, years ago, who gave me a kiss goodbye as she was leaving my house. It lasted over an hour. I later wrote a poem about it. It was unbelievably wonderful. It was wild. I must have been out of my mind. The first time that special one kissed me I became hopelessly addicted and there were about two million repeats after that. She likes to kiss and I have been learning to like being kissed. The world is admirably arranged. In Bach's "Peasant Cantata" the bass sings: "How good a bit of smooching tastes."

Writing from Oxford to his friend Faustus Anderlin in Paris, the famous Renaissance humanist and scholar Erasmus put it thus: "The English girls are divinely pretty. They have one custom which cannot be too admired. When you go anywhere on a visit the girls all kiss you. They kiss you when you arrive. They kiss you when you go away; and they kiss you again when you return. Go where you will, it is all kisses; and my dear Faustus, if you had once tasted how soft and fragrant those lips are, you would wish to spend your life here."

Kissing is rather like the sun. It brings warmth to the cold and lonely; it melts the ice of grief and pain, it cheers the weary wanderer, it lights the way onward and it says: "No matter how rough the road is, no matter how tough the trial is, I'm right here with you and I care deeply about you." Who among us would say we don't want that kind of energy? Life is full of shattered hopes and dreams. Life is strewn with the remains of days long gone. Life is a series of fragments; some of which are lovely gifts, some of which are sources of strength for today and hope for tomorrow. It is always good to pause in the rush of life and summon up remembrances of things past, whether they be kisses in the rain or gifts you can hold onto.

For Christmas 1980 Kris gave me a gold pocket watch that I still have and whenever I look at it or whenever I open it to check the time, or when I wind it up once more, I think of her and those days filled with the flush of youth that can never ever be repeated. I have in a briefcase a note from another friend written in haste after a friendship that bloomed one winter in such a wonderful and mysterious way. It would be valueless to cite the passage written therein for it has secret, hidden meanings which none would understand save me, but through the years I have often taken it out, unfolded it carefully and read it over again and felt deep thanks each time welling up within for the good things now past. When I finished my first PhD at Cambridge and flew from London to the United States to take up my first academic appointment, I had a three hour layover in Los Angeles. One of my old teachers and mentors, somewhat surprisingly, was waiting for me as I wearily emerged into the terminal. He spent those three hours with me. We reminisced about the past. We discussed our lives. We expressed hope for the road ahead. He asked some fellow sitting nearby to take a photograph of the two of us. I never thought much of it. Three years later my old teacher was dead. One day an envelop post-marked Los Angeles appeared in my mailbox in New Zealand. I opened it and found inside the photograph of Don Fisher and me. A moment captured in time, never to be lived again. Impossible to repeat.

In 1997, after a very long silence, I received a lengthy email from my Cambridge doctoral supervisor. He had gone to Harvard but shortly thereafter fell ill. He had written to apologise for his lack of attention to his correspondence. He brought up several items of interest and asked me to stay in touch promising he too would do his best. The next thing I heard about Bob came a few weeks later. It was an invitation to come back to Cambridge to take part in his memorial service. Bob Scribner had lost the fight against cancer. I put the printed email inside a copy of his great book (which he had also given me and signed) and once in a while I take it out and think of poor old Bob.

Among the most meaningful gifts I have ever received was a candle, presented to me as a gift for Christmas one week before I moved to New Zealand. It was from one of the dearest people I have ever known. Wrapped up with the thick candle was a page on which she had drawn the likeness of the candle in purple, green and pink, the same colors as the candle itself, with a perfectly formed yellow flame, and below it, written in purple, this message.

> More than a candle will shine when you light this; its light symbolizes my love which will continue to glow brightly even across continents. When you smell its sweetness, think of me, as I will often be thinking of you, my friend. This Christmas, met with sweetness and sorrow, is best spent together! I do love you so very much! May God be with you always. Shalom.

Of course I brought that candle to New Zealand. Its fragrance was extraordinary. As I sat night after night by the light of the candle and smelled the aroma that filled my apartment I remembered the love, the light, the laughter, the life I had known which was indeed a fire and a scent I would never forget. The symbolism of the light it cast truly reflected a love unequalled. The sweetness of its scent caused me always to think of a sweetness that continued to linger strongly even across the largest ocean in our world. And whenever the flame burned and the aroma wafted through the air, I could think of nothing other than the one who gave the gift. The candle is now long gone. I enjoyed it to the very end. I have kept the page and always will. The drawing of the candle thereon was perfect and exact and whenever I look at the wonderful drawing I recall the candle itself as it looked when it burned with a flame that warmed my soul for many years. Its shape, its color, its scent and, most importantly, its meaning, lives on and I am all the better for it.

Sometimes the best things in life are the simple things, the notes, the photographs, the candles. A glance, a touch, a kiss. Sometimes life is best known and best appreciated through an empty box. Truly, many of us have been given a gold wrapped box which at first glance might seem rather curiously empty but upon closer inspection we find that it has been filled with unconditional love and many, many kisses from our children, our friends, our family and also from God. It is doubtful that anyone could possibly have a more precious possession than an empty box filled with the kisses of love.

Somerset West, South Africa

Thomas Didymus and the Forgiveness of Sins

I have always been somewhat of a skeptic, a doubter and a questioner. The spirit of questioning descended upon me quite early and I have been afflicted with it ever since. Strangely I have always found it easier to ask the hard questions than accept the sometime easy answers. I value less the bliss of the ignorant than the anxiety of the one struggling to arrive at the empirical pragmatic data: "Unless I see with my own eyes, unless I touch with these hands, I shall not believe." It is these words that have made my namesake so endearing to me. My parents named me well. Friends and acquaintances used to call me "Tom" with some regularity. As I have grown older I have become reinvented as "Thomas." Perhaps it is less re-invention as returning to my roots. I don't like being called "Tom" much anymore and where I now live no one ever calls me that. I am Thomas and to be called thus reflects more accurately my person, my conviction and my true identity. I cannot imagine that the trifling and lazy "Tom" was ever applied to the disciple of Christ.

In a sense I am a latter-day Thomas Didymus. My creed is simple: "Question everything! Accept nothing at face value until all the relevant queries have been addressed and the existing data analysed." The song I learnt as a child — "Only Believe" — ought to be outlawed and declared unfit for use in churches today, especially in their Sunday School departments. It teaches children the wrong approach altogether and accounts for deep and serious problems among "believers" later in life. This is the attitude of Thomas Didymus. I applaud his philosophy and move for his canonization. St. Thomas Didymus indeed. Patron of skeptics, humble, honest agnostics and unbelievers. So there you have it, the both of us doubting our way through the passages of faith as reluctant unbelievers. But then, as it were, a funny thing happened on the way to the library. Except this happening to this Thomas, and to the other Thomas as well, did not occur in the reading room, it happened quite by accident in the chancel.

One night, while I was a PhD student at the University of Cambridge, I slipped down a dark passage in the central university town to The Parish Church of St. Edward King and Martyr to join a small gathering for the Sunday Evensong. I half expected Thomas Didymus to show up as well and in this expectation I was not to be disappointed. At the end of the alleyway the trees in the church yard were standing starkly against the last streaks of daylight in the English skies. The church's tower thrusting heavenward above the damp fens guided silently a few weary pilgrims to rest within earshot of the faintly rising melodies of the chancel organ. I paused briefly in the lengthening shadows to take note of the church sign. Near the bottom of the red painted rustic sign in gold letters I learned that on this site the worshipping community of St. Edward had been meeting for over 800 years. The next line told me that within these same stone walls Hugh Latimer and Thomas Bilney and others of the venerable reformers of the sixteenth century had preached the gospel. Of course Bilney became a relapsed heretic. Hugh Latimer called him "little Bilney, that blessed martyr of God" who suffered for his faith in August 1531 at Norwich. Poor old Hugh Latimer fared no better. He crumbled into ashes at the feet of Nicholas Ridley in Oxford in 1555 after admonishing his colleague to stand firm and help him light "such a candle." I had long studied the European reformations and had years before rediscovered my own spiritual roots in that milieu. I felt awed to be worshipping in a building featuring such a "great cloud of witnesses" tradition. I began to think of "little Bilney" and poor old Latimer and thought to linger longer but the yellow light bathing the cobblestones through the narrow door urged me to my seat.

In the coolness of that medieval stone church I listened to the music (something Bilney could not abide), sang the hymns and heard the reading of the Scripture lessons. Somewhere in the order of worship Thomas Didymus slipped into the pew behind me. He incited me, as he always does and together we began to analyse the liturgy in our attempt to come toward some rational and reasonable understanding of the theology contained therein. Along about seven o'clock a trivial, yet utterly profound, thing happened. Evidently I had become so caught up in my deliberations with Thomas Didymus that I missed a cue in the liturgy and before I could find my proper place, the congregation had joined in a reading of the Apostles' Creed. On account of my basic unfamiliarity with the older *Book of Common Prayer* I was unable to immediately locate the text of the creed. Since my frantic fumbling through the Prayer Book failed to turn up the relevant page, I was either forced to remain silent, and thus appear to be a heathen, or to recite the words from memory. I choose the latter and did entirely satisfactory, so pleased was I with myself that my voice was strong and enthusiastic, until near the end when I heard myself say: "I believe in the forgiveness of sins..." twice! The first utterance was in striking dissonance with everyone else while the second time was in perfect harmony. I felt embarrassment at my loud verbal blunder and then it seemed there was an awkward silence, though upon reflection I am certain it was only my imagination. Before me the aged vicar peered disdainfully over his glasses, and behind me the usually talkative Thomas Didymus had fallen strangely silent, the consistent chatter of his racketation army for once overpowered by the silence. Extraordinary. Then, like a blast of cold wind from the crypt, it hit me. The essence of it all — the meaning of the entire Evensong — indeed the heart of the Christian gospel was contained in that very short phrase: "The forgiveness of sins." Thomas Didymus and I had been doing quite well up until that point. Then we had simply been obliterated by the unspeakable profundity of the mystery. I had even exacerbated the conundrum by repeating the phrase inadvertently. Now I could not explain it at all and it seemed as though, in the hour of greatest need, my constant companion Thomas

Didymus, decided to call it a night and slipped quietly through the side
door to the blackness beyond the walls of St. Edward and I was left alone
with that phrase thundering in my brain.

"I believe in the forgiveness of sins." That statement above all others is
the one that utterly defies all logical explanation. How can such a
statement possibly make sense? It contains no sense at all from a human
perspective. Therefore it is non-sense. But what about "little Bilney"?
He couldn't stand the music, but he believed the gospel, preached it in
the very pulpit before me and embraced the faggots at Norwich. Could
he have been a misguided enthusiast? He was barely 35 when he died.
What about Latimer? Same story. He didn't seem to mind the music,
believed the gospel, recited the very same words I had just mouthed,
preached in that same pulpit and cheerfully challenged Ridley to "play
the man." He was past 70. Both were Cambridge men. I was about to be
made a proper Cambridge man. Oxford aside, going up to Cambridge
and coming down again successfully with a PhD behind your name is
no mean accomplishment. Surely Bilney, Latimer and I were not
complete fools. Or were we? Notwithstanding that, how can such a
preposterous statement be accepted? How does it make sense? I was
reminded then of Calvin's powerful exposition in *The Institutes of the
Christian Religion* on that statement made by another medieval
"hopeless fool" Bernard of Clairvaux: When I am overcome with
despair and driven to the end of my resources, then I call to
remembrance the wounds of the Lord. To believe in the forgiveness of
sins is to have hope. Another Cambridge man, John A. T. Robinson,
once put it thus when he remarked that a Christian takes his or her stand
not on optimism but on hope. In spite of our sins and our sinning we
are always brought into association with the forgiveness of sins. If we do
not believe in this article of faith then we are left without hope, as men
and women most miserable, in the hell of unforgiveness. It is this great
hymn of the church that reminds us constantly of our salvation.

The church's one foundation is Jesus Christ her Lord
She is the new creation by water and the word
From heav'n he came and sought her to be his holy bride.
With his own blood he bought her and for her life he died.

Yet she on earth has union with God the Three in One
and mystic sweet communion with those whose rest is won.
O blessed heavenly chorus, Lord save us by your grace
that we like saints before us may see you face to face.

"I believe in the forgiveness of sins." My sin, not in part but the whole, has been nailed to the cross and nothing here or hereafter shall separate me from the love of God in Christ. Not my propensity to sin; not my debauched nature or desire; not even those times of failure and sin can separate me from the love of God for "I believe in the forgiveness of sins." No, I could not possibly explain it at all. Neither apparently could Thomas Didymus. That is where grace comes in. I guess that is what the reformers meant when they preached a message of human justification by faith alone. *Sola fide.* One has simply to throw oneself upon the mercies of Christ and forego trying to package it up neatly in a basket of explanation. There is little else to do save to simply accept the fact that we are accepted by God in Christ. Our sins are forgiven without our assistance and in spite of our sinfulness. The power of that "joyous exchange" (as Luther called it) wherein Christ takes our sins and gives us his righteousness, is inexpressible mystery and profound reality. This knowledge, however, allows no room for vain boasting. The words of William Wilberforce on his death-bed are worth remembering: "I am in a very distressed state." "Yes," came the answer of one nearby, "but you have your feet on the Rock." To this Wilberforce replied: "I do not venture to speak so positively. But I hope I have." Somewhere in the early morning hours of 29 July 1833 he knew.

In the chilly sanctuary of St. Edward I knew in part for my hope is in "the forgiveness of sins." The moment was coming to an end but along with Wesley I could say that my heart had been "strangely warmed." I could join heartily in the words of conclusion for the Evensong: "The grace of our Lord Jesus Christ, and the love of God, and the fellowship of the Holy Ghost, be with us all evermore. Amen." Indeed, it was true for the forgiveness of sins had become reality.

Outside I ran into Thomas Didymus. He was standing quietly in the shadows of the spire, his hands nervously twisting his cap. We had a moment of silence together. It was sacramental, cathartic as well as an epiphany. Neither of us even hinted at the old "I told you so" cliché. Our eyes met briefly and I think for a moment we understood the limits of our relentless questioning. Together we fell on our knees symbolically and cried out: "My Lord and my God. I do believe in the forgiveness of sins." We paused only a moment longer in the venerable church yard where the spirits of Bilney and Latimer once moved and where the Holy Spirit now comes ever and again, sometimes so quickly. Then we made our way slowly up the same dark passage to the city lights beyond. At the corner we parted company with the resolve to accept simply our acceptance without questions concerning the forgiveness of sins, but to resolve our questions without acceptance on all the rest. As I walked through the gate to King's College I suddenly realized that Thomas Didymus and I had just discovered salvation again for the first time.

In the name of the one who forgives all our sins, we dare to say these things. Amen.

To Kill a Preacher

The proclamation of the gospel is designed to invoke a response and a decision. More often than not that response has either been to accept the good news of Christ or to simply walk away in rejection of that. It is not often that the gospel provokes one to murder. But on a particular Sabbath, immediately following the sermon, the meeting place was filled with riot and, quite literally, all hell broke loose. The response was anything but nonchalant. It was murderous and its focus was to kill a preacher. The story is told with verve in the Gospel of Luke.

In his home town of Nazareth, Jesus went to the synagogue and read from the prophet Isaiah:

> The Spirit of the Lord is upon me.
> Because he has anointed me to preach good news to the poor
> He has sent me to proclaim release to the captives
> and recovering of sight to the blind
> To set at liberty those who are oppressed
> To proclaim the acceptable year of the Lord.

When he had finished he sat down. Isaiah 61 is generally regarded as a messianic pronouncement. The year of the Lord's favor surely refers to a new era, the kingdom of God. Then Jesus says: "Today this scripture has been fulfilled in your hearing." It is of note to see that later Jesus tells the disciples of John Baptist to tell John, the blind receive sight, the lame walk, the lepers are healed, the deaf hear, the poor have heard the preaching of the good news (7:22). Back in the synagogue, those gathered together spoke well of Jesus. Then they wondered. Then, all at once, they doubted. Someone in the back of the synagogue leaned over to the fellow next to him and whispered: "Hey, isn't that guy Joseph's son?" This is the key turning point. "Who does he think he is?" perhaps another whispered. "What does he mean today the scripture is fulfilled? You don't suppose he really thinks that he..." This question about Jesus being the son of a local carpenter indicates that the people are responding to Jesus in terms of his humanity, in terms of the obvious, rather than in terms of his divine mission. When this motive is known, it is apparent that this congregation will not take Jesus seriously enough to truly hear what he has to say. The surprise in the synagogue begins to turn to indignation but before anyone really got out of hand Jesus began to expound on the Isaiah passage and the low rumbling of murmuring voices died down.

Jesus interprets the prophecy in terms of two proverbial sayings and in the light of two historical events. The *Gospel of Thomas* notes that "no prophet is accepted in his own village and no physician heals those who know him." Jesus refers to both statements as if he anticipates the eventual reaction of the synagogue congregation. Then he refers first to the story of the prophet Elijah in Zarephath situated in the land of Sidon, today on the Mediterranean coast in Lebanon. The story is recorded in I Kings 17. The tale is simple enough. The prophet lives in the wilderness beside a brook. Birds bring him food to eat. Eventually the brook dries up. God tells Elijah to go to Zarephath and there a widow will feed him. At first the woman objects saying that if she feeds the prophet there will be insufficient for her and her son. The prophet persuades her by saying: "Feed me first and thereafter you will have plenty." The widow obeys and during the long famine her food supply, meagre though it was, never ran out.

It would be clear to his hearers as well as to the readers of the historical event that a woman living in Zarephath would be Syrophenician by race, hence an outsider; a foreigner! Many women and children in Israel died during the famine but this outsider survived. Elijah went to her rather than to his own Israelite people. Jesus even hammers the point home by saying bluntly: "There were many widows in Israel and Elijah was sent to none of them." Before anyone could say a word, Jesus moves to his second illustration that involves the prophet Elisha and the Syrian military commander Naaman. Naaman was a leper and had done everything he could to find a cure. At length he sent for the prophet from Israel who came and following a bit of an argument about the treatment, the man was miraculously healed. The story can be read in context in II Kings 5. There were many lepers in Israel who died without healing, but a foreigner was healed. And he was not just an ordinary foreigner. He was a military commander of all things. Now that he was well again, what guarantee was there that he would not turn his guns on Israel? Again Jesus rams the point home just in case anyone in the synagogue had nodded off and was not paying full attention: "There were many lepers in Israel, none of them were healed except Naaman the Syrian." It seems very clear that Jesus is saying that the prophecy he has just read, from the sacred literature of the Hebrew religion, spoken by a Hebrew prophet, is not intended for his hearers in the synagogue. Why?

In the first instance, there is the possibility that the hearers of Jesus thought they controlled God in some way or that they had a special claim on God. The history of Israel reveals the assumption that they are the chosen ones. But the truth is, no one, no religion, no church, has a corner on God. That includes the Jews too. The congregation in the synagogue did not like the implication that they were poor and needy. Their response was: "We are the chosen, we are the people of God." The religiously upright assume that all outsiders would surely be cast aside as well as the less devout of the chosen. But the presence of Christ involves the very Spirit of God, the good news, divine grace and the proclamation of salvation. That presence can neither be restricted nor controlled.

In the second place, the congregation in the synagogue was selfish. It reminds one of the cartoon tale when Bugs Bunny and Yosemite Sam are on an air plane together which starts to go down. There is only one parachute. Since Bugs is but a stupid rabbit, Sam insists that he shall have the parachute and after hitting Bugs over the head, to avoid any argument or rebuttal to his proposal, puts on the parachute and jumps out to what he thinks will be salvation. Regrettably for Yosemite Sam, the stupidity of the rabbit was exceeded only by his own and in his haste to escape from the doomed jet he slipped into a mere backpack. There is a proclivity in many religious circles toward sectarianism. The hearers of Jesus in the synagogue became outraged at his interpretation of the Elijah-Elisha narratives. They wanted God all to themselves. They wanted only the miracles, the spectacular. They could not tolerate his ministry yet they found it impossible to allow him to go to others. Their selfishness began to consume them and they sought to destroy him. There is a human tendency to want to possess that which intrigues us and if we cannot lay hold upon it personally we want to make sure no one else can either.

Once there were two men, seriously ill, who shared a room in a large hospital. One man was Mr. Wilson, the other Mr. Thompson. In the room were two beds, two small tables, a door leading to the hall and one small window. Mr. Wilson was allowed to sit up once a day for an hour in order to drain fluid from his lungs. He had the bed by the window. Mr. Thompson was not permitted to move. They talked for hours for there was little else they could do. They talked about everything, their wives, children, jobs, hobbies, travels, and all those sorts of things. Each day when Mr. Wilson was sitting up he would tell Mr. Thompson what he could see through the small window. Mr. Thompson began to live for that one hour. The window overlooked a park and Wilson told him about the pond, the ducks, the model sail boats that the small boys had. He described the flowers, the baseball games, the people walking and talking, how pretty the girls were in their summer dresses and behind it all the view of the city skyline. Mr. Thompson could almost see as Mr. Wilson talked.

One day the thought occurred to Mr. Thompson: Why should Wilson always be the one to see out the window. Why couldn't he? At first he felt ashamed but the feelings persisted. He began to resent Wilson and became convinced that he should be by the window. His condition worsened and the doctors could not understand why. One night as he lay awake staring at the ceiling, Mr. Wilson suddenly woke up, coughing and choking. His hands fumbled for the call button to alert the nurse. Mr. Thompson watched without moving. All of a sudden Mr. Wilson stopped. His breathing stopped. Thompson continue to stare at the ceiling. The next day the body of Mr. Wilson was removed.

After a few days when it seemed decent to do so, Thompson asked if he could be moved into the other bed by the window. The nurses moved him and made him as comfortable as possible. As soon as they left the room and the door had closed behind them, Mr. Thompson propped himself up on one elbow and with great pain and effort raised himself up to the window and looked out. It faced a blank wall. The stories had ended and there was no view.

Intolerance caused the same sort of thing to happen to St. Paul, as it had to Jesus, when he took some Greeks into the temple in Jerusalem. The pious folks there concluded that such a nuisance as Paul ought not to be allowed to live. They roared and raved, waved their clothes in the air and threw dirt around. Jealousy and exclusivity often seem to generate pattern responses.

Thirdly, the congregation in the synagogue flatly refused to take Jesus seriously. After all, he was only Joseph's son. Jesus was right in saying a prophet is without honor in his own country. A physician does not cure his friends for they won't believe it. They began to cry out for signs of confirmation to be done in their midst. They could not believe the mere words of this Jesus, son of Joseph the carpenter. There was no way he could possibly be a prophet. He was an amateur carpenter. Initially, the congregation had spoken well of Jesus but by the time Jesus finished his homily on the Isaiah text "all in the synagogue were filled with wrath." They became so inflamed with anger, hatred, jealousy and bruised egos that in one accord they rose up against him – in the religious house, if you will, on their holy day – and they attempted to kill a preacher. They grabbed Jesus and hustled him out of their holy precincts. They pushed him out of town and up a hill with the intention of throwing him off the cliff. Had they been brought before a court of law they would have been convicted of attempted murder.

What was the response of Jesus to this turn of events and all this ruckus? His response is quite powerfully recorded by Luke in chapter 4 verse 30 "But passing through the midst of them he went away." He went away! That response is of profound significance. He had been rejected, he accepted that rejection, for he had never made it policy or practice to force the work of God, so he just went away. With him went the Spirit of God. With him went the good news. With him went the proclamation of liberty. With him went recovery of sight for the blind. With him went the kingdom of God. He just passed quietly through the midst of the crowd and went away, leaving the congregation from the synagogue gathered at the edge of the cliff wondering what to do next. It reminds me of an old farmer in Idaho who once ordered a great bunch of fresh strawberries. After he placed the order he realized he could never use all of them so he invited friends and neighbors from far and near to come to his farm the next Saturday for a big strawberry feed. The day arrived and everyone came. But the strawberries failed to show. So they had prunes. The people of Nazareth had the chance to enjoy fresh delicious strawberries but their inability to discern left them instead with a bowl of prunes.

What does this mean for us today? We must have the courage to accept the truth whatever it is, no matter how difficult it is to hear. What price must the church pay to have an inclusive message? There is always a price to be paid. Will the church pay that price? Will you pay the cost? Will I pay the price? Perhaps the church needs to find the courage to cut off a theological leg or a theological arm that binds it fast in the face of certain disaster. Will we allow the gospel to run a free course, or will we try to monitor it like the congregation who listened to Jesus that sabbath in the synagogue in Nazareth? It would be better to be missing an arm or a leg in authentic ministry than to be whole in the *rigor mortis* of irrelevancy. We must not make the same blunder as the Nazareth congregation did. Truth and God may come in various ways and in odd fashions. We must recognize them as such and move our fences in order to receive what God wants to do in our own time.

Familiarity may make us deaf to some divine message that might come to us every day from someone close to us. We must beware of the tendency to resent outsiders for God refuses to be boxed in. To kill the preacher, to murder the messenger, is to run the risk of silencing God and if that happens, Christ just goes away.

Gostwyck Chapel, Uralla, Australia

Getting out… one way or the other

Prune Hill, Washington

GETTING OUT OF THIS PLACE

Friday night. Late autumn. The last leaves were losing their battle with forces they had no chance of ever defeating. The warmth of the sun had faded, surprisingly fast, and darkness stealthily crept up the streets and wrapped itself around the buildings. A cold descended and embraced the city and all its dwellers. I watched the faces as they came and went through the glazed automatic sliding glass doors. This was just another nondescript hamburger joint just off Cathedral Square in the heart of the city. I paid little attention to the low background music until a precocious girl standing in front of me began singing along: "We've got to get out of this place, if it's the last thing we ever do." The song had been recorded first in 1965 by the English R&B and Rock band "The Animals." The girl was performing for her boyfriend somewhere behind me. She didn't notice me notice. She kept on singing. I began to think of the words.

We have all come to this place and as sure as the sun will rise in the east tomorrow we are all going somewhere. We will get out of this place. We'll go somewhere. But where? Outside groups of teenagers bunched together on the sidewalk. Cars lined up at red lights. Skate boarders rattled past on the uneven pavement. All going somewhere — caught up in the drama of life, carried along by the force of movement in the stream of what some sarcastically call the "rat race." One thing is certain: We are all getting out of this place. Some go quickly, others take much longer. Jack London was only 40 years old by the time he had used himself up. During his short life he smoked up to 60 Russian Imperiale cigarettes a day. He drank so much that by the time he was 35 his kidneys had begun to fail. Whenever possible, he ate two whole barely cooked ducks for dinner. He was addicted to morphine. When the end came on November 22, 1916 he was the total inversion of his own image and that of his fictional characters; images that had made him famous. His was a very public life ending quickly. An old codger in the ancient literature of the Hebrews lingered on for almost an entire millennium. We know infinitely more about Jack London's 40 years than we do about Methuselah's 969 years. Some go quickly into that good night. Others defy all prognosticators and hang around seemingly indefinitely. King Charles II of England, before his death on 6 February 1685, offered his subjects his embarrassed apology for having taken such an unconscionable long time to die. Near or far, early or late, we are all getting out of this place. And it will surely be the last thing we ever do.

A derelict from the streets wandered into the brightly lit burger joint, stumbled up to the white counter and flung his coins down before the waitress. I had seen him before. Same filthy clothes, smeared, bleared, coated with the stains and the grime of the place he'd lain the night before. Untrimmed beard, uncombed hair, unkempt appearance. These features framed his vacant stare. He bought an ice-cream cone with his filthy, filthy lucre and lurched into a chair behind the pop machine. And the music played on: "We've got to get out of this place, if it's the last thing we ever do." He was getting vanilla ice-cream all over his matted beard. He pulled his legs up on the chair beside him and pressed himself up against the wall. His eyes registered nothing. The music played. His feet, jammed into worn and soiled tennis-shoes, began slowly, almost imperceptibly, to tap out the hypnotic beat. I watched. He ate. The song continued and his feet kept time.

I had seen our ice-cream-eating bum before. He was always around; an inner-city fixture. Yet his eyes suggested he was elsewhere. He muttered to himself as he walked — probably asking himself questions and just as likely getting answers. He always hurried when he walked as though he had somewhere to be. He never did. I had observed him enough to know he merely hurried in circles around the city. He slept in alleys, doorways, parks, down by the river, under the bridge. It didn't matter much. But on this night he tapped his foot to the music and bobbed his head, ever so slightly, to the tune of getting out of this place. I took a long hard look at him as I shoved my spent wrappers into the rubbish container. He just stared ahead — ice-cream in his beard — foot tapping about the last thing he would ever do.

I could have been him, or maybe you could be him. Give us enough time and I might be hurrying about town aimlessly, neglecting to bathe, or you might be muttering to yourself. I wondered where he had come from and more importantly where was he going? I winked at the girl who sold me my hamburger. I never wink at strangers, especially young girls. But this time I did. It looked like it was time for her to get off work and go home. Maybe she too was singing: "I've got to get out of this place, if it's the last thing I ever do." I'll never know for sure. I stepped past the tapping foot into the night.

At the crosswalk I caught up with the girl who had been singing the song in the café while the bum put ice-cream in his beard. She was walking with her boyfriend. Out of the night shuffled another lost soul, silly looking jacket, trousers way too short, head down. He brushed into the girl without a word. She turned and called after him in a gentle voice: "Excuse me." He never turned, never raised his head or uttered a word. Apparently, the only thing on his mind was getting out of this place.

Off to the right was the millennium clock counting down the days, hours, minutes and seconds remaining in the year, the decade, the century and the entire millennium. Father Time would spare no one. Gratefully, eager and willing, or kicking and screaming, we are all getting out of this place as the seconds were swallowing up the minutes which in turn consumed the hours which devoured day after day with mute, but ruthless efficiency. And before I could cross the square I was even closer to getting out of this place than ever before, closer than I'd ever imagined. As the Yukon poet said so long ago: "The clock is always slow. It is later than you think."

"We've got to get out of this place, if it's the last thing we ever do." But where are we going? There wasn't time to avoid him. I had spent far too much time staring at the millennium clock and he had spotted an easy target. He did not say a word, but offered me a tract. I do not like religious proselytizers. I find most of them offensive, insensitive and full of their own propaganda. Besides I was already a Christian, thank you very much, so I did not need the speech. He offered none. I took the tract without breaking stride. For a moment I crumpled it in my self-righteous fist, but then took a peek. After all, I could spare but a moment in my haste to get out of this place and I ought to know exactly what it was I intended to deposit in the trash can up ahead. It read:

> A man was walking past a gravestone when he noticed this inscription. "Pause!! Stranger as you pass me by, as you are now so once was I. As I am now so you will be, so prepare for death and follow me." But he also noticed someone had inscribed a reply on the tombstone that read: "To follow you I'm not content, until I know which way you went." Don't get caught dead without Jesus Christ. "I am the resurrection and the life" (John 11:25). So do you know where you are going?

All I knew at that moment was that we were all getting out of this place. But it made me think and I saw the square in a new light beneath the rising crescent moon.

Huddled up against the south wall of the Gothic cathedral, mere steps from the tract-man, was a group of nameless and faceless people — the squalor of the night — faces partially concealed by plastic bags. Glue-sniffers. Lost souls. Wastelands of human flesh. Did they know anything at all about the resurrection and the life that emanated through the gray stones of the cathedral against which they were crowded? Where had they been and where were they going? It seemed certain they were most eager to get out of this place, if it was the last thing they ever did. The deadly fumes of their paint thinners and aerosol cans deadened their senses, bleared their eyes, reddened their cheeks and perhaps made them feel like there was a resurrection and a life. But did that toxic euphoria have any relation to reality? They were preparing to join that legion who had gone on before. Just steps away was someone with a message — a message about resurrection and life. Within literal reach was a "house of God" where every day the gospel can be heard and the community within the walls speaks by its very existence of resurrection and life.

In a darkened alleyway I could see others, trying desperately to get out of this place, as if it were the last thing they would ever do. A prostitute had her skirt hiked up to her hips while her customer's trousers were down around his ankles. Did they have any notional concept of the resurrection and the life? Was there the faintest hint of a cognitive construct about where they were going once their urgent business was concluded? Or were they utterly consumed with just getting out of this place?

Across the street in a red telephone box were two girls. They had just placed a call into the night. Who was it for? Parents? Boyfriends? A taxi? No one knows. No one cares. No one paid attention. Why should they? Maybe the girls just wanted to get out of city, out of this place as quickly as they could. In the midst of their conversation did they consider the possibility of resurrection and life? I glanced again at my crumpled tract and thought about getting out of this place myself.

Through the great pane-glass windows I could see that the bar was crowded. Businessmen and varsity girls chumming it up, whiling away the time as the booze flowed deep and wide from the never-ending reservoirs. There was music and laughter, the tinkle of glasses and the blur of countless others coming and going through the smoke-filled air, hurrying here, hurrying there, anxious to get out of this place, or into that place, as though it were the last thing they would ever have time to do. Perhaps they came here every Friday night — the regular and usual crowd shuffling in and out — gathering to drink a toast to getting out of this place. Who were these people? They looked very much like me. Perhaps some of them were you. I wondered if they ever had a drink in remembrance of resurrection and life?

Crossing the bridge over the gently flowing river, it struck me that I was just like the Avon River. It was silently but inexorably going somewhere. Across its even back, the bright lights of the city glittered. I, too, was enamoured with the beckoning glow reflecting in my eyes. But the lights of the city and the light of the world were two entirely different sources of illumination. The high society crowd was streaming out of the Town Hall, smug, pleased with the performance, congratulating themselves on the fact that a good time was had by all; money well spent. Designer dresses and tailored tuxedos could not detract from the fact that these people too were just trying to get out of this place. Their cultural evening had obviously been a smashing success, but where were they off to now and were they aware in their going of the resurrection and the life?

I walked on in silence. I took another look: "I am the resurrection." Cars passed. Asian tourists gaped at the sights. Everyone seemed bent on getting to another place. Somewhere in the city lights, I surmised that vanilla ice-cream was hardening in a shaggy beard and that a dirty old tennis shoe hanging off the end of a chair was still tapping to the beat of "we've got to get out of this place, if it's the last thing we ever do." The tract was pretty well wrinkled up now. But in the light of a street lamp I read more. "I am the life." The words were a clarion call to the masses rushing headlong in their several attempts to get out of this place.

At the corner I waited for a break in the traffic and for the little green man to indicate it was safe to proceed. A block away two provocative women, waved at passing cars. The faint orange light of their cigarettes pierced the darkness; the glow like wandering, weary fireflies. Part of me felt compelled — the other part repelled. Lust and loathing. Glee and guilt. Two contradictory emotions competing for attention, waged in an implacable war. Powers of light and powers of darkness. Where were the women going? Obviously they hoped for a ride, a ride that would take them from here to there — a ride to help them more easily and more quickly to get out of this place. Was there resurrection and life for them? When solemn morning broke across the weary world would they have gotten out of this place to resurrection and life, or would they come back tomorrow night, stand on the corner, and make another bid to get out of this place?

The back of the tract made a simple point: "Dear Lord Jesus, I know that I don't meet your standards and I need your forgiveness. I believe that you died for me." That was a novel thought. On his way to getting out of the place he was in, Christ took the time to die for the world. St. Paul had reflected on it thus: "Why, one will hardly die for a righteous man—though perhaps for a good man one will dare even to die. But God shows his love for us in that while we were yet sinners Christ died for us." (Romans 5:7-8) In dying he became resurrection and life. It was true, for every one of us, "we've got to get out of this place, if it's the last thing we ever do." Blind, erring, and aimless, or seeing, perceiving and focused, the fact remains we are all going to the same end: Ashes to ashes, dust to dust, the good, the bad, the ugly; we shall all get out of this place, one way or the other. It will be the last thing we manage, in spite of ourselves, perhaps because of ourselves.

Christ died for us. Christ died for all of us. Christ died for all of them: For Jack London, the girl singing in the café, the foot-tapping outcast, the glue-sniffers pressed along cathedral walls, Christ died for them. It seems absurd, but it is precisely here where the scandal of Christianity finds its center. Christ died for the religious zealot in the square, the whore in the alley as well as her "John." For the crowd at the bar, the girls on the phone, he is resurrection and life. Christ died so that everyone in the city and beyond might have resurrection and life as we do that last thing, as we get ourselves out of this place. Resurrection and life for me. Resurrection and life for you. For him. For her. For the cigarette-smoking prostitute, the dapper businessman. For the gawking Asian tourists. For Charles II. Resurrection and life for that old woman there, that spiked-haired punk rocker, that damned fool. Christ died for them all, without exception, without qualification, without regret.

As the millennium clock ticks off the seconds and minutes and hours and days and the people in the city come and go there is hope on the edges of the city — hope that presses eagerly in around, hope that may apprehend us as we're getting out of this place. A hope that comes to the places where we are that speaks of resurrection and life to all people in the city wherever they are, whatever they're doing, whoever they are. Christ died for us in order that this place might become his place and that the darkness of night might be overwhelmed with his resurrection and his life. In that hope, and for that reason, "we've got to get out of this place, if it's the last thing we ever do."

STEALING COOKIES

It was just another day in the city. Just another afternoon of shopping in the glitzy downtown shopping esplanades. She was a very proper and refined woman; one who made all the right moves, knew all the right people; had everything a proper and prominent woman could possibly need. As the afternoon wore on she decided to go into a tea shop for afternoon tea. She sat in a window seat for two and ordered a pot of tea and planned to have a quiet few minutes drinking the hot tea, reading her newspaper and eating some cookies she had in her bag. Soon the shop filled up with other men and women and eventually all the seats were filled except the one at her table. Pretty soon a man came in. He was obviously not a proper fellow at all. There was stain on his shirt near the left collar, a button was missing from his jacket and his hair was somewhat in disarray. He sat across the table from the very proper woman who was reading her paper and sipping her tea. The man also ordered tea. The proper lady tried to ignore her unwelcomed table partner. As she turned the page and took another sip of tea she took a cookie from the package. Out of the corner of her eye she noted that the man also took a cookie. Of all the nerve, she fumed, he sits here beside me which is bad enough and then he helps himself to my cookies. His action upset her considerably and caused great annoyance. However, being a proper woman she just ignored it and went on reading. A few minutes later she took another cookie. To her absolute disgust he did too. This time she was unable to refrain and she gave the fellow a good hard glare. He smiled back at her and reached for the fifth and final cookie. Still smiling, while she still glared, he broke the last cookie in half and offered her the smaller piece. She was outraged. Without even bothering to decline the offer, she got up, stormed across the room, paid her bill and stomped out of the tea shop in a manner rather unbefitting proper ladies. She was quite incensed at his presumptuousness. Her indignation would not allow her to even do more shopping. So she marched straight across the street to the bus stop. The bus pulled up and the lady reached into her bag to get a coin for the ride. To her dismay she found her package of cookies still unopened.

I related easily to that lady. I really do not like it when strangers sit down with me at a restaurant. It rarely happens in America but in Europe it happens all the time. I hate it when I have settled comfortably into my seat on the city bus and someone plunks down beside me when there are several other empty seats available. It's bad enough when they sit right behind or right in front of me when they could easily have left an empty row between us. The monk loves to sit next to strangers and talk for hours. On our frequent flights across the Pacific I am absolutely delighted when the seat next to me is vacant. The monk isn't. Anyone will do; anyone to while away the hours with talking about whatever happens to come up. I have often wondered why I dislike the intrusion. More than that, why do we hate so much to share? Lord Acton once said: "Power corrupts and absolute power corrupts absolutely." Power and control is one thing we really do not like to share. It is as though we profoundly distrust each other and would much rather keep everything under wraps.

Our proper lady in the urban tea room honestly thought, though quite wrongly as we now know, that the man was stealing *her* cookies. How dare he? Her reaction was typical. We assume that whatever is there is ours and therefore off limits to everyone else. When it comes to faith we often take the same view. It's our church. How dare those people – who are quite different than we are – come in here and act like they belong? It's our God and God will defend us and take up our cause and protect us. God will provide us with cookies and if anyone takes even one of them our God will surely deal with them. Sometimes we just can't help ourselves. Even when we know that sharing cookies is okay and might even be better than getting bent out of shape over someone taking ours, we storm off in a huff breathing out threats. We just can't help it.

Sometimes we yield to temptation, to lust, to desire, to whatever seems natural, even when we know full well that the consequences will be very serious. Do we steal cookies or just get mad at those we think are stealing our cookies? Are the cookies really ours in the first place? Why are we so reluctant to share cookies? Why do we often become annoyed when things do not go as planned, or when someone disagrees with our views? Several blind men were brought out to "see" an elephant. They were led to the beast and then asked later how they would describe an elephant. The first blind man grasped hold of the tail. Then he said: "An elephant is long, slender and wiggles about a lot, kind of like a snake." The second blind man touched the side of the elephant: "Oh no," he said: "The elephant is very large and rough and you cannot move it at all." The third blind man took hold of the ear: "You are both wrong," he said: "The elephant is thin and flaps back and forth and is very soft." The last blind man felt the tusk: "The three of you are crazy," he said: "An elephant is hard and smooth and pointed." All four became indignant at each other and pretty soon a fight ensued about what an elephant really was. Do we know what the cookies are that we think someone else is stealing? Jesus said he had come to bring life so that people might have life to the full. It is hard to live life fully and honestly when we confine ourselves to tea rooms cursing the people we think are stealing our cookies.

At the age of 85 Homer Dodge was still doing white-water canoeing. He was also the president emeritus of Norwich University in Vermont. He had started canoeing when he was only five years old. By the time he was ten, he was paddling the St. Lawrence River. At 69 he became the first person since the early fur traders to run the dangerous Long Salt Rapids before the St. Lawrence Seaway removed them forever. He was once asked about the secret of his long and fulfilling life and he had this to say: "If you want to have interesting experiences, you've got to put yourself where they can happen." You cannot step in the same river twice but there is no reason not to place oneself in the stream of opportunity. It's not a leap. Just a step. So it is with faith and God. Are the cookies really that important?

Byron Bay lighthouse, Australia

San Francisco Bay and the Golden Gate Bridge

TWO FLOODS AND ONE HOPE

St. Augustine once wrote long ago: "You have made us for yourself and our hearts are restless until they find rest in you." The winds of life at times carry us far away from our place of beginning. In the chaos of the world there is but one means to the rest that Augustine spoke of and that is through a singular hope.

The first book in the Bible tells a tale of a great flood in which the world was destroyed. A chap named Noah built a large boat, called an ark, but the only ones who boarded with him was his wife, three sons and their wives. He also took on board male and female species of all birds and animals he could get his hands on. When the waters receded, everyone was gone except for those in the ark. It must be admitted that neither our contemporary world nor the world of Noah fosters a true concept of hope. In many respects our world is life-negating and hope-negating. Now, as then, the earth is corrupt, filled with violence and humankind seem to have corrupted their way in almost every way imaginable. Back in Noah's time, God got fed up with the whole mess and decided to wipe out the inhabitants of earth and start over.

Hope began in that context when Noah took out a contract with God to build what can only be described as an experimental floating zoo in the middle of a desert. The idea was one thing; the location was absurd. Noah was getting on. At the time he was somewhere in his 500s. This was his biggest building project yet: 450 feet by 75 feet by 45 feet and weighed in at more than 43,000 tons. One can only imagine how silly the whole thing looked. An old man building what appeared to be a functionless monstrosity out in the arid middle of nowhere. One can imagine that hecklers came out to the building site everyday just to see what was going on. It seems doubtful indeed that they would have simply looked on in silence: "Hey Noah, how long are you gonna keep workin' on that THING?" "Noah, don't you think this is getting a bit ridiculous?" "Haven't you got anything else to do?" "Noah, my wife told me there is a new psychotherapist in town. Maybe you ought to make an appointment." "C'mon Noah, the weather's fine, live it up, let's have a drink. It's Miller time, Noah!"

Right about that time, old Noah's radio stopped playing music and a voice was heard: "This is Deuteronomy, son of Gath, with the weather report. A ridge of high pressure continues to build in our region and this brings with it more clear, warm days and nights. Our extended forecast is for no measurable precipitation for at least a couple of centuries." What had gotten into Noah's head? All logic, reason and common sense told him the whole idea was just plain stupid.

But then, all at once one day it started to rain. Maybe just a little bit at first and no one was concerned. After the years of warm weather it was almost a welcome relief. Then it rained harder, and harder and just did not let up. The ditches filled with water. The fields turned to lakes. Water ran through the streets and starting seeping into people's homes. Now it was becoming a real nuisance. Someone remembered what Noah had been saying all those years while he hammered nail after nail into that ark of his. Even as the water rose to dangerous levels there were those who made their way to Noah's place. But Noah was nowhere to be seen. The door to the ark was shut and no one was able to pry it open. There was no response to their shouts of inquiry or their frantic knocking on the door. Where was Noah? Had he already drowned? The water became death and death seemed to be everywhere and there was no escaping. People raced for higher ground but the water continued to rise. They fled to the hills and the highest points all around but the rain continued to pour down in torrents and the water kept rising.

Water is life. Three-quarters of the planet is water. More than three-quarters of each one of us is water. But this much water became death and desperate men and women could stay afloat only so long after the last bits of dry ground were claimed by the flood.

On a clear and cold night in April 1912, the RMS Titanic went down in the north Atlantic after what seemed like a fairly incidental collision with an ice berg. There were 2300 people on board. Captain Edward J. Smith, with more than a quarter century of experience, made a mistake. We do not know why. When morning came, 1,500 bodies bobbed on the surface of the north Atlantic. Titanic is a well-known story and thanks to the blockbuster, popular multi-Oscar winning, film a new generation knows of the tragedy. Titanic had everything going for it. It was the largest ship of its kind on the seas. It was luxurious and had an impressive passenger list. Some had boasted, apparently, that even God could not sink Titanic. I attended a dinner party in Washington marking the centennial anniversary of the disaster and we reflected on the event.

There were two floods. The one that came in on Titanic and the other that came down upon the old ark. The water rose and Titanic went to the bottom of the north Atlantic. The water rose and the ark floated. E.J. Smith was an expert, but he was never seen again. Noah would not have known the first thing about maritime navigation but he lived another 400 years after that maiden voyage. Titanic was built by experts, the ark was built by an amateur. The ark had nothing to commend it and Noah and his sons must have been kept very busy just shovelling the waste over the sides. Even the steerage passengers on Titanic were not as bad off. The story of Titanic is an abject disaster. The story of the ark ends with a bird bringing Noah a small leaf in its beak. That indicated the waters were receding and hope for deliverance was near.

A number of years ago a television film called *The Day After* got a lot of attention. It depicted the aftermath of a nuclear strike on America. In a moving scene near the end, someone in a makeshift hospital ward makes a poignant statement: "Tell me about hope." There were two floods, but only one hope; hope for deliverance, hope for salvation from the cruel, cold, uncaring sea. Thomas Merton noted that no one was free until they were able to live in pure hope. For Christians, hope is always connected to God. Christ in us is the hope of glory and in hope we are saved.

One of the stories I remember vividly from my childhood were those about Brer Rabbit and his two persistent enemies Brer Bear and Brer Fox. The rabbit always seemed to outwit his foes but on one occasion Brer Fox had him dead to rights and it looked like the end of the trail for poor old Brer Rabbit. In desperation, and in a last ditch attempt to save himself from the evil hatched up by Brer Fox, Brer Rabbit hollered out: "O, do anything you want to me, but please, please whatever you do, don't throw me into that briar patch!" Brer Fox thought this was a capital idea and so he tossed the rabbit into the briar patch. Of course, having grown up in the briar patch, this is exactly where Brer Rabbit wanted to go. In hope, that his enemies would take him literally, Brer Rabbit was saved. Indeed, the briar patch was his only hope.

Tell me about hope. How can we do that when there does not seem to be any hope? The list seems endless when one begins examining the hopelessness in our world: Famine in northeast Africa; war crimes in the Balkans; war in the Ukraine; nuclear build-up in Pakistan and India; slumping economies; crime and violence; war against terrorism; little kids killing other little kids with guns; little boys under the age of ten sexually assaulting little girls; the awful evil of the World Trade Center disaster; the devastation of floods in Central Europe; refugees floating in unseaworthy boats off the coasts of Australia; the Covid-19 global pandemic; and the list goes on and on. Those who hope in Christ can no longer tolerate these realities but must suffer in these situations and live in contradiction to them. I saw a sign once: "God does not take sides." I do not believe that statement to be true. We need theologies, ministries and strategies of hope for our world. God does take sides with the poor, with the exploited, the minorities, the abused, the weak, with the hopeless. God takes sides with those who need God. Some of us behave and live our lives as though we did not need God. We embrace cocksure theologies on practically anything and issue stern warnings to anyone who dares trespass or ask penetrating questions. We close down debate. We seem so certain of everything and have become self-reliant and arrogant in our assumed salvation. To what extent are empty pews and empty sermons witnesses to lost hope?

Hell is hopelessness. Above the entrance to hell in Dante Alighieri's "Divine Comedy" is the vivid sign: "Abandon hope, all of you who enter." The pop song "Vincent" includes the line: "When no hope was left inside of you, you took your life." The absence of hope is the absence of God. Luther encouraged us to wait for God, but waiting is sometimes very difficult. Waiting for God, however, does not mean idleness, or sitting around or just praying around. The old ark that Noah put together was not much at all. As ships go, it must have been pretty pathetic. The ark that may come for us may not be much either but it was enough for Noah and his family and it is enough now for us.

Titanic was quite a bit. It had everything imaginable; everything the passengers could possibly require on their cruise. That is, everything except an adequate means of salvation. There was possible salvation for less than one-half of those on board. When the sea roared in, Titanic was no better off than the old ark. In fact, within a few hours it proved to be a rather distant second to the ark despite its celebrated billing. The majority of those on Titanic died. In the ark, everyone was saved. The ark is where people come together in such a way that all the differences and obvious barriers are obliterated: Theological differences, political differences; church/religious differences; economic differences; social differences; gender differences; cultural differences; ethnic differences; racial differences; intellectual differences and so on. But what of those fences and walls and barriers that we insist on maintaining?

In the film *Titanic* there is a scene during which the great ship is in serious danger and it is evident to all on board that she is lost and there is precious little time to escape the impending watery grave. In this scene a small boy is found in one of the lower deck corridors crying. A few moments later his father reappears. The father had gone back to his room, apparently, to get his suitcase. The time spent retrieving the bag was fateful. The father gathers up his boy in one arm, has his precious suitcase in the other, when the water breaks through. They do not make it. The father dies still clutching his suitcase. What are we going back for? The door of the ark is open. What else do we need except to enter? What are we insisting on clinging to, to our own destruction as well as that of others?

The New Testament encourages us to "lay aside every weight and sin that so easily hinders." What are those unnecessary suitcases, weights and sins? It is not just about sex. Some Christians seem to think that all there is to sin relates to sexual misbehavior and misconduct. Sexual sin is certainly well down the list of God's sins that divide the body of Christ and push hope beyond the reach of those who so desperately need it. These sins include those of intolerance; prejudice; bigotry; back-biting; self-righteousness; criticism; bitterness; anger; fault-finding; attitudes; hatred; dogmatism; theological arrogance and a hundred more. The ark is where these sins have been committed to the cleansing stream of blood that flows from Golgotha. The ark is where there is hope.

Titanic is what we mistake hope and salvation for. What is your Titanic? Can you hear the flood? Can you feel the water billowing all around you? Can you feel its frigid, icy grip? John A.T. Robinson in his last sermon at Cambridge spoke of the Christian taking his or her stand not on optimism but on hope. There is a crucial difference. Hope is not pie in the sky, it is not the best of all possible worlds. Hope ignores pie in the sky and transcends this and all other worlds. Noah was regarded as mentally unstable by his jeering peers; a true knave. But his persistence produced a means of salvation from the onslaught of the flood. Jesus likewise did not seem too bright, nailed to a cross, but his death also brought salvation from a different kind of flood altogether. In Christ, God is our father, mother, sister, brother and friend. We need good fathers and mothers, brothers and sisters, as well as friends along our pilgrimage. For each of us will have floods to endure, caused by the icebergs on the seas of life. There is only one hope. There is Titanic; there are numerous Titanics, but there is also an ark.

In order to find hope in the Christian faith we must be taken back to the scandal, the dying and the awfulness of the cross. For only in the death of the one on the hill can hope be born. We must proclaim his death by our own dying, so that his life can become ours. Union with God in Christ is certainly the key to finding rest for our restless hearts. Two floods, but one hope. The one on the hill is the little piece of olive leaf that a little bird brings to each of us. It is hope.

In the name of the one who saves the world from drowning, we dare to say these things.

Half Moon Bay, Roatán, Honduras

Cathedral Rock, NSW, Australia

Wind Mountain, Washington

DWELLING AMONG THE TOMBS

The synoptic gospels – Matthew, Mark and Luke – all record the story of Jesus encountering the so-called demoniac called Legion. All three gospels note that the person in question was disturbed in some way. Matthew says there were two men while Mark and Luke refer to one individual only. All three accounts note that the place of this encounter was "across the lake" in the region of the Gerasenes or Gadarenes and the man lived among the tombs. All three versions attribute great strength to the man (or men), Mark and Luke say he was in constant torment in solitary places and these two writers give him the name Legion. All three accounts say that he recognized Jesus upon meeting him, that he feared being tortured, that he was exorcised by Jesus and that the demons that lived in him fled into a herd of pigs nearby. Matthew has no unique material. Mark says that Legion was always crying out and cutting himself with stones while Luke adds that the man expressed fear of ending up in the abyss. Mark has the most detailed version of the story (5:1-20) and Matthew (8:28-34) and Luke (8:26-39) can be viewed as parallel texts. The story in its general content is familiar.

There are several details of historic significance within the story that can be briefly enumerated. The precise physical location for this tale is hard to ascertain for the New Testament manuscripts are not consistent. The general region of the Gerasenes is southeast of the Sea of Galilee. The place of the tombs is likewise not a reference to a literal cemetery in the modern sense for these did not exist in the ancient Near East. There were many caves in the general region, however, and these can still be found up to the present day. The presence of pigs in Decapolis is not significant since it is well known that this area was mainly Gentile. Jews, of course, tended to altogether avoid swine as an unclean beast. Owning pigs constituted a breach of Hebrew ceremonial law. However, we must be somewhat indefinite about who actually owned the herd of pigs. The name Legion was a commonplace Latin term for a Roman military unit usually comprising five to six thousand men. The man called Legion has generally been considered to have been demon-possessed. But this conclusion is not necessarily imperative. We now know that there were many diseases, illnesses and disturbances that were put down to this alleged malaise in the ancient Near East during the time of the New Testament. Legion may well have been possessed in the classic, theological sense, but there may be other explanations for his condition. The notion of madness according to the Talmud might be assessed according to four characteristics: Walking abroad at night, spending the night on a grave, tearing one's clothes and destroying what one has been given. The Talmudic definition invites comparison with the story of Legion. If Legion were mad, the porcine stampede might be attributed to the shrieking and flapping about of the madman. According to the Talmud, anyone spending the night among the tombs was a suspicious character. It is also rather perplexing to understand why Jesus allowed the wholesale destruction of someone else's property, that is to say the herd of swine. How might this possibly be justified?

The other matter of interest is the idea of being beyond the lake. How often does Jesus go across the lake in the narratives of the Gospels? How much happens with reference to this or another lake? Confining ourselves to the Gospel of Mark we find the following:

> Walking by the lake 1:16
> Goes out by the lake 2:13
> Withdraws to the lake 3:7
> Teaches by the lake 4:1
> Crosses the lake and calms the storm 4:35
> Crosses the lake and meets Legion 5:1
> Crosses back across the lake 5:18

Goes away in a boat 6:32
Walks on water 6:45
Goes to the sea 7:31
Gets into a boat 8:10
Crosses the lake again 8:13

What does this puzzling story mean to us today? This is a strange story representing a radically different world view than shared in ours. Several questions emerge: What are the tombs? What are the stones used for cutting? What does it mean to cross the lake? Each of these are clues to unlocking contemporary relevance. Dwelling among the tombs does not surely mean living in graveyards. Instead, it is reasonable to think of these tombs as sin, failure, sickness, loneliness, despair, grief, fear, condemnation, hopelessness, addiction, bondage, and these likewise become the stones with which we lacerate ourselves. The evil spirits that filled Legion are not just demons in the classic sense. For us today these evil spirits are the demons of fear, loss, despair and so on. The world, our worlds are filled with tombs and the floors littered with sharp stones and often we cut ourselves on the serrated stones of sorrow and on the ruthless rocks of grief.

One of the tombs amid which many of us dwell is the tomb of lost love. We do not even know how to properly define love, but we know when we are in love and we know when we are without love. One of the classic love stories of all time is *Wuthering Heights* by Emily Brontë. The main characters are Heathcliffe and Catherine Earnshaw. They grow up together, fall in love, have a torrid, if strange romance and just cannot make it work. Catherine marries someone else and dies in childbirth. Heathcliffe becomes a strange and shadowy figure stalking the moors of northern England, haunted by Catherine, dwelling among the tombs of lost love and dies in the end of a broken heart hoping against all hope that his death will allow him to be re-united with Catherine who is his life anyway and life without her is not worth the trouble. Love can do that to you; it can put you high upon the highest pedestal and also send you to the deepest depths of despair. Have you ever loved and lost?

I loved a girl once. Her name was Debbie. She was the prettiest girl one could possibly dream of. We exchanged correspondence, eagerly visited each other, fell in love. She sent me a photograph of herself, my goddess, the meaning of life itself. I was enthralled. I still have that photograph somewhere, I think. One summer evening I was at the annual camp meeting. After the evening service I emerged from the tabernacle (as they called it) into the darkness of the evening. The moon shone brightly upon the calm lapping surface of Harvey Lake. And there before me was my love, Debbie … holding hands with another guy. I was crushed. I knew my life was over. I crept away in the gloom to die. I was eleven years old.

I got over Debbie. I saw her across a room in a restaurant about twenty-five years later, most unexpectedly. She was not nearly as lovely as I had remembered all those years ago. I began to wonder if I had really loved her at age eleven? Anyway, I was not all that sad that things had happened as they did. Still, that incident is not really what I mean about loving and losing. I still recall the email I received at the end of June 2000 while in Prague on a research trip. I was at a social function and decided to slip into the back room and check my email. The message was terse: "Thomas, Phil passed away yesterday. A freak accident while sky-diving. He never regained consciousness and died on the way to the hospital. Remember Laurie and the girls in prayer." Phil and Laurie were friends of mine and former students. Both had been my advisees in college. Laurie had gone on to pastor a church and Phil was a one-of-a-kind youth pastor. We often bantered, Phil and I. His shoulder-length hair flapping in the breeze was frequent occasion for me to say good-naturedly: "Get a haircut" to which he would reply: "Get a real job." I was a mountain climber, he was a sky diver. We often talked of how more likely it would be that we would die in a car accident as opposed to diving or climbing. He had jumped over 1,500 times and was clearly a professional and very good at his sport. On the day he died, it was just another routine jump. But 150 feet from landing Phil was hit with an unexpected wind shear that caused his parachute to collapse. He did not have quite enough time to recover and instead of a soft landing hit the ground at 40 miles an hour. His legs were crushed. Despite the full head helmet one eye was knocked out. One can hardly imagine his last thoughts as he fought for his very life; a battle that lasted only seconds, a fight he did not win. One can only imagine Laurie's reaction when she received the phone call. They had been married twenty years and had two teen-age daughters. Phil was her entire life. I tried to call Laurie immediately but could not get through. A few days later I changed travel plans and went directly to Montana to find my friend dwelling among the tombs.

To love and lose is to be hurled into a dwelling among the tombs of lost loves where one can do little else than cry out and in agony cut oneself with the sharp stones creating another pain that sometimes relieves the other pain, if only temporarily. In the grief and loss of hurt and pain there is a need for a new heart. "A new heart I will give you, and a new spirit I will put within you; and I will take out of your flesh the heart of stone and give you a heart of flesh" (Ezekiel 36:26). The sharp loss of significant love relationships often turns one's heart to stone and drives one into the deepest regions of the tombs.

Another of the places in which many of us dwell is the tomb of shattered dreams. When I was a teenager I became very much involved in church music and I began to dream of a life and career in music. I wrote songs, more than one hundred of them, church choirs performed them. I had a small group, we sang regularly in various places. I went off to college to major in music and realize that dream. I studied piano. I learned to play two or three songs. That was about it. In musicianship classes I was a disaster. I even failed one term. Music theory did not come easily to me; in fact most of the work was a hard slough. My teachers, the late David "Doc" Wasmundt and Dana Rowe, the latter later found fame on

Broadway, must have despaired of my ineptitude. My ability as a singer was average and I was never much of a sight-reader. Try as I might, try as I may, I had slowly to come to the realization that my dream was out of reach. I cried great tears, I rebelled, I moaned, I groaned, I tried harder. The dream got no closer. I felt despair. I retired at length to the tombs.

One cannot change the past, one cannot roll back the clock, one cannot possibly change at all what has already happened. To live in the past is to die a little bit everyday. Still, as we persist in the tombs we flog ourselves for our mistakes, our failings, our sins. But Christ has already forgiven, he has already made atonement, effected reconciliation, bought salvation with his blood, died that life might indeed prevail and that to the full. J.B. Phillips once noted insightfully that most people in his experience were not so much sinful as they were bewildered. In that bewilderment there is a tendency to give up, retreat to the tombs and cut oneself endlessly with the sharp stones that fill the tombs of life. In the novel *The Brothers Karamazov*, Dostoevsky has the monk Zossima approach a woman who has committed an unspeakable crime and is afraid to die and the monk speaks these words: "Man cannot commit a sin so great as to exhaust the infinite love of God. Can there be a sin which could exceed the love of God?"

There are those who think that there are unforgivable sins or that sin sends one to hell eternally and irrevocably. But the existence of an actual hell is beyond reason, impossible to consent to and grossly offensive. It is quite impossible to reconcile the notion that God created the world and humanity with a view towards an eternal hell, or that God somehow determined the existence of hell prior to creation with some role to play in divine justice. It is further problematic to assert that God tolerates such a place or reality to exist alongside the kingdom of God. Should such a proposition be true it would be an admission on the part of God that both creation as well as redemption had failed. That idea is both unthinkable and illogical. Faith in a loving God does not permit such conclusion. For God to deliberately allow the existence of eternal torture means that God is not God in any sense but is rather more like the Devil. The idea of hell is one derived from our daily lives with the human system of rewards and punishments. From God's perspective there cannot be any eternal hell of punishment and torture. To allow for such a theology is so preposterous that it means effectively to deny God, to deny the irresistible love of God and to deny that in the end God will win. It is to conclude that God creates only to annihilate.

Still, like poor old Legion, we sometimes try to curb inner turmoil with the use of outward restraints. So Legion was bound with chains in an effort to control him. But the madman broke the chains and raved again among the tombs. We too wind up crying out, breaking the irrelevant chains forced upon us by those who think they are doing good, we cut ourselves and in the end remain dwelling among the tombs. Of course not all ideas that come to mind are useful or profitable. At age nine Leo Tolstoy believed God would help him fly and thus plunged headlong through a third-story window. He survived the abrupt unexpected crash landing and learned the lesson of his young life.

A third dwelling is among the tombs of aging, decline and death. This is a route we must all follow sooner or later. A few months ago world news carried the story that 15,000 people were dead in India as a result of a massive earthquake. The Lockerbie air disaster trial ended recently bringing a sense of closure for the families and loved ones connected to the bombing more than a dozen years earlier. These tragic events only overshadow the slower trip to death we all participate in. There is no escaping death. I stopped by to visit a former retired colleague in Oregon a few months ago. I had not heard the story and Charles was visibly moved as he related how a few weeks earlier his 41 year old son, elk hunting in Wyoming, father of three, was swept away by a freak avalanche into the arms of death. His hunting companion only a few steps away was spared. Time is the fire in which we burn. One week after the disaster, the man's 38 year old wife learned she was pregnant. There was nothing I could say to my colleague as he threw his arms about my neck and wept. I wanted to cry with him for I could see that he too, at least for the time being, was dwelling among the tombs. There is nothing one can do about lost loves, shattered dreams, age, decline and death. We have simply to accept these things. But we must give up our security blankets for they will only keep us longer among the tombs. Still, that is very hard to do and Linus, from the Peanuts comic strip, comments most shrewdly on the matter of security blankets: "Once there was a time when I thought I could give up thumb-sucking. Now I doubt if I ever could. I'm hooked." But if only we could give up thumb-sucking – theological thumb-sucking too – we might understand what the 101 year old man meant when in Frederick Buechner's novel *Godric* he commented that what's lost when compared to what is gained would scarcely fill a cup.

The only real remedy for those dwelling among the tombs is what Karl Barth called "total help for total need." How long have you been on the other side of the lake? How long have you been dwelling among the tombs? This is not something God has caused, determined, or brought about. Commenting on the epic of the Book of Job, Carl Jung remarked in this question: "Is it worth the lion's while to terrify the mouse?" It is not God's desire that we dwell among the tombs, crying out, alone, cutting ourselves with sharp stones, tormented night and day. It is not God's wish that we remain forever on the other side of the lake. The matter of perception is very important. A light house was moved in North Carolina to protect it from the encroaching sea. It was jacked up, placed on a foundation, and moved so slowly that officials up in the lighthouse could not tell exactly when it started to move. More than 500 observers could not tell either and yet by the time it was done the light house had been moved 1600 feet inland.

On the night of 23 February 1987 an astronomer in Chile observed the explosion of a distant supernova. The blast was so powerful that it released as much energy in a single second as our sun does in about ten billion years. Did this event actually occur on 23 February 1987? On one hand, indeed it did. From the perspective of planet Earth it truly did. On the other hand, the supernova blew up approximately 170,000 years ago but the light generated from that explosion travelling almost six trillion miles a year took all of those 170,000 years just to reach our galaxy.

For those dwelling among the tombs, there is the possibility of hope. That hope is Christ. The cross is lost love, shattered dreams and death but the cross conquers all and the hope lit so long ago might just now be reaching the tombs in which you dwell: "Then I saw a new heaven and a new earth and I heard a loud voice saying now the dwelling of God is with humans and God will live with them. God shall wipe every tear from their eyes. There will be no more death or mourning or crying or pain (or hell!) for the former things are passed away" (Revelation 21:1, 3-4).

When this occurs, every hill shall be exalted and every mountain made low. The crooked places shall be straightened and the rough places made plain. The people who have been walking in great darkness shall see great light. Those who dwell in the land of the shadow of death shall have a great light break forth over them. For unto us a child is born. Unto us a son is given. The government shall be upon his shoulders. His name shall be called Wonderful, Counsellor, Mighty God, Everlasting Father, the Prince of Peace.

He comes to us as one unknown and in our own experiences across the lake, up in the hills and among the tombs, we shall learn who he is. There is no other way. He comes to us there across the lake, up in those same hills and among those old familiar tombs and reveals himself to us and in that revelation we receive the possibility of escape from the tombs and we also come to the place of learning who he is.

In the name of the one who comes to us among the tombs we dare to say these things.

Young thinker, Canterbury, New Zealand

The 'both-and' Theological Working Party

DOING THEOLOGY WITH THE PEN OR THE PENCIL

While a PhD student at Cambridge I happened upon a book written by S.R. Maitland called *The Dark Ages* published at London in 1844. On the frontispiece was this epigram: "I know nothing of those ages which knew nothing." I immediately wondered what was wrong with that arresting statement. Tertullian once queried: "What has Athens to do with Jerusalem?" I wondered what does this mean? If Maitland knew nothing about the Middle Ages how could he be so sure that they knew nothing? If education has no relation to faith, was there any point in thinking theologically? Medieval thinkers used to refer to theology as the queen of the sciences. It is still a business to be taken with utmost seriousness. Theological thinking and "doing theology" should stretch one in every dimension and it is therefore important that one's theology should find expression in writing with the pencil rather than with the pen.

Theology is never finished, never concluded, and it is never ever neatly wrapped in a box. It is rather like a powerful play that goes on and on and each of us can contribute another verse. The study and practice of theology is a thorough and uncompromising examination of life and thought in all of its intricacies, difficulties and contradictions. There is of course a tendency to dogmatize things and to argue to conclusions and unalterable truths in theology. Voices loudly cry out for a dismissal of reason as the "Devil's whore," others forbid investigation and still others enjoin one not to examine but simply believe. I had a student once who blurted out in great agitation to forty or so other students during class that he did not interpret the Bible, he just read it. These approaches demand the pen. I suggest the pencil.

Doing theology with the pencil means that one can change the writing easier than if one uses a pen. Ink is much harder to erase. Pens are permanent markers. Pencils are not. Ink runs deep and dark on the page. Even if one succeeds in erasing ink, it often leaves permanent traces of the effort. On the other hand, doing theology in pencil often means finding the world upside down as often as it is right side up. Pencil-wielding "theologians" are more apt to experience spiritual and inner turmoil. Pencilled theology can be much more isolating than doctrine written in black ink. Pencilled theology often brings with it the charge of ambiguity and uncertainty and an unwillingness to take a stand. Theologians with pencils are often accused of compromise.

The road of those who tell new truths is often a difficult one. Socrates seated on the steps drinking hemlock. Jesus crucified with criminals. Jan Hus burned alive. Galileo badgered into denouncing his own proven theories. Anne Hutchinson banished. Oscar Romero murdered at the altar. The trail of blood can be followed through the corridors of time and human history. There is some resentment to new ideas. Messengers are often killed because of the message they bring. Few of us welcome the discomfort and disturbance of being challenged in fundamental ways. It is difficult to maintain different opinions in a climate where opinions are discouraged. But if we are truly serious about theology and God then we must be brave enough to use the pencil. Even when the multitudes demand the pen we must offer only the pencil. There is no profit in supplying easy answers written in ink. The best response is more hard questions written in pencil.

To look at things in different ways, to find new ground, to strike out on one's own, pencil clutched in hand, in fearless pursuit of knowledge, understanding, truth and God, opens up the possibility for each one to contribute a verse to the powerfully evolving play of the divine drama in the world. Walk in the presence of God, seize the light of knowledge, and lay aside all those things that hinder especially theological pens and ink wells. It is truly meritorious to suppress the urge to write theology in ink with the pen of arrogance. Instead, it is salutary to write the words and ideas lightly in pencil; subject to modification, revision and re-wording. A theologian is one who attempts to understand and practice their own faith. A ThD or PhD degree is not required.

Doing theology with the pencil is rather like grapes. Paracelsus put it this way. "The one who knows nothing, loves nothing. The one who can do nothing, understands nothing. The one who understands nothing is worthless. But the one who understands, also loves, notices, sees. The more knowledge is inherent in something, the greater the love. Anyone who imagines that all fruits ripen at the same time as the strawberries knows nothing about grapes." Doing theology is not just a discussion about strawberries. It must also deal with grapes. In Luther's *Table Talk* a shrewd question is asked: "Just what was God doing before creation?" The answer: "God was making hell for those who ask such questions."

There is the delightful story of St. Augustine, the bishop of Hippo in northern Africa, as he labored on his understanding of God. Walking on the beach at Hippo he saw a little boy (who was really an angel in disguise) digging a hole in the sand and then filling it in with water from a cockle shell. The bishop asked him: "What are you doing?" The little boy said: "I am trying to empty the sea." Augustine replied: "Son, that is quite impossible." To this comment the boy replied: "It is no more impossible Augustine than for your finite mind to comprehend the mystery of God." A matter of grapes. According to Frederick Buechner, theology is a study of God and God's ways. There is some chance that beetles study humankind and our behavior and call it humanology. If that were true, we would probably be more amused than irritated and God probably feels the same way about our numerous theologies. If that be true, there is all the more reason for us to do theology with the pencil and keep in mind the grapes.

Many people of course see no importance in doing theology and find the whole enterprise mainly irrelevant. Others perceive action as more significant than thinking and many Christians in their own curious ways are anti-intellectual, preferring the sensation of warm fuzzies, and the artificial goose-bumps of piety. These enemies of theology must be scorned. One should be liberal in reading, in thinking, in approaching theology, in trying to understand God, in understanding the human condition. The older I get, the more deliberately I attempt to be liberal. There is no other path either safe or sensible which is open to us other than the proven way of the liberal. What exactly do I mean? I mean that theology should be done with the pencil rather than the pen. I am talking about grapes. Theologians change their opinions as they learn and experience more. This should not cause mistrust for complete trust belongs only to God.

Growing up in Canada, I often heard much about the Arctic and the strange frozen world way up there. I remember specifically a statement I heard as a school-boy. After one has spent five years in the Arctic, one is an expert. After one has spent ten years in the Arctic, one is a novice. It is the same way with God and with doing theology. The pencil prevails for it becomes clear that the pen cannot go on. The strawberries have ripened and sometimes rotted, now is the time for the grapes.

Theology can either be a coat of mail that absolutely crushes people and squeezes the life out of them or it can be a means of liberation, freedom and understanding. In other words, theology can either be corpses of lifeless ideas or events of vibrant living reality. Theology can either be all strawberries, or strawberries, apples, oranges, bananas, and grapes. Theology can be written in ink with a pronounced period at the end of the text, or it can be written in pencil with plenty of room for addition, alteration and amendment. God is greater than all theological systems and the revelation of God is unending. Theology must always be ambivalent; never to be taken lightly nor as the be-all and the end-all of religious thinking.

Being a liberal, eating grapes and writing theology in pencil are all related. Doing theology in pencil and eating grapes, however, does not mean that one has all the right answers. Indeed, that is the whole point of using the pencil rather than the pen. Approaching theology from this perspective, undoubtedly means walking along some forbidden and foreboding pathways in our search for the sources of life. There was a fellow named Paul about 2,000 years ago who said: "O, that I might know him. Not just in the power of his resurrection but in the fellowship of his suffering." Participation in this experience is best approached in a liberal fashion, doing theology with the pencil rather than the pen.

Mt Assiniboine and Magog Lake, Canadian Rockies

Eiger Nordwand, Switzerland

A life lived (109) and a life to live (11) – The Quiggs Report

HOLY SPIRIT OR HOLY GHOST?

In the name of God, creator, redeemer, life-giver. Amen. I once heard about an old Pentecostal preacher in the backwoods of Maritime Canada. His name was Ellery Cady and because he used to work in the mines some called him "the man from the bowels of the earth." Preacher Cady used to snort about people who referred to the Holy Spirit. "Holy Spirit," he said dismissively, "Holy Spirit! It's Holy Ghost!" Apparently there was a world of difference. "The spirit of the Lord is upon me" therefore I have some things to say. This coming year my friend Bob Sullivan will be elected the leader of the nation. My other friend April Purtell will enter and win in record time the Portland Marathon, and another friend, Steven Clark, now at age 60 will experience a late growth spurt and add eight inches to his stature by Christmas. "Thus sayeth the Lord!" Amen.

I said just a moment ago that "the Spirit of the Lord is upon me." I was clearly being facetious. My prognostications cannot be taken seriously by any thinking person. Moreover, I would neither stand in this pulpit, nor before any congregation anywhere, and make such a claim. Yet in a synagogue in the town of Nazareth, Jesus did just that.

Now there are those who actively participate in the "yea, thus sayeth the Lord" sort of discourse saying all sorts of things and claiming divine sanction for their pronouncements. More than forty years ago I was in an Evangelical revival church meeting in eastern Canada. The preacher was a man from Florida named Baker. On that occasion, ostensibly under the influence of the Holy Spirit, he told a woman that unless she made a commitment for Christ that night and turned her life around she would be dead within the year. It seemed like a rather astonishing thing to say. Forty years have passed. I looked into the matter in the last year or two. The woman in question never made that commitment. She is still alive and well. The preacher? He has been dead a long time. It appears his counsel to that woman all those years ago was not guided by the Spirit of the Lord. Twenty-eight years ago this month I took a telephone call at my home in Portland. Among other things a woman on the other end of the line said: "God told me to tell you something." I was to call her back and she'd relay the message. I never made that call. We must be very careful what we say God said. We must likewise be cautious in claiming that the Spirit of the Lord is upon us. Equally important, we need to know when not to follow specious claims or make phone calls that open the gate to the broad road.

The reading from the Gospel of Luke leaves me with two questions. The first question is this: Does the Spirit of the Lord come upon men and women, and if so, how can we tell? There are perhaps as many as 140 million Christians in the world today who identify themselves as Pentecostals. By comparison there are probably only about half that number who belong to the Anglican-Episcopal communion. If you ask a real Pentecostal this question they will say that when the Spirit of the Lord comes upon a person that individual will experience glossolalia and speak in tongues. Is it true that only tongue-talkers have the Spirit of the Lord? I think not. Speaking in tongues is not even an exclusive Christian phenomenon. Indeed, it is a pan-religious and a trans-cultural occurrence. It would seem ill-advised to claim that such activity is proof of the Spirit of the Lord. The second question is this: Does one know if, and does one know when, the Spirit of the Lord comes upon them? Does the Spirit make one tingle just so? Is there an outward or visceral manifestation? Does the Spirit enable one to go faster than a speeding bullet, or leap over tall buildings in a single bound, or make one more powerful than a locomotive? Does the Spirit empower one for living as some Christians vigorously claim? Just what is this Spirit of the Lord and what exactly is its function? A paragraph from a classic in American literature provides yet another view of the Spirit.

> I use ta get the people jumpin' an' talkin' in tongues, an' glory-shoutin'
> till they just fell down an' passed out. An' some I'd baptize to bring 'em
> to. An' then you know what I'd do? I'd take one of them girls out in the
> grass, an' I'd lay with her. Done it ever' time. Then I'd feel bad, an' I'd
> pray an' pray, but it didn't do no good. Come the nex' time, them an'
> me was full of the sperit, I'd do it again. I figgered there just wasn't no
> hope for me, an' I was a damned ol' hypocrite. But I didn't mean to
> be... Here's me preachin' grace. An' here's them people getting' grace
> so hard they're jumpin' an' shoutin.' Now they say layin' up with a girl
> comes from the devil. But the more grace a girl got in her, the quicker
> she wants to go out in the grass. An' I got to thinkin' how in hell, s'cuse
> me, how can the devil get in when a girl is so full of the Holy Sperit that
> it's spoutin' out of her nose an' ears. You'd think that'd be one time
> when the devil didn't stand a snowball's chance in hell. But there it was.

That's the Reverend Jim Casy anxiously confessing to Tom Joad in
John Steinbeck's 1939 novel *The Grapes of Wrath*. What is the "spirit of
the Lord?" Was it really the Holy Spirit that came upon Steinbeck's
characters? Ellery Cady might have insisted that was the problem and
they needed the Holy Ghost. Be that as it may, could I suggest that
sometimes it is not easy to distinguish the prompting of the Spirit from
our own inclinations. But now we must return to the synagogue at
Nazareth in the Gospel of Luke.

In Palestinian synagogues during the time of Jesus worship consisted of
several elements. There was a recitation of the Shema: "Hear O Israel
the Lord our God is one Lord." This was followed by readings from the
Law and the Prophets. Then an explanation was given of one or both
passages. We might call this discourse a sermon. The worship ended
with a blessing by a priest or a concluding prayer. Theoretically anyone
might read and preach be they a member of that particular synagogue
or a visitor. Of course they had to be male since women were excluded
from such public offices. It was customary to read standing and to
preach or explain the texts sitting. Jesus stands to read, then sits down,
not because he is done but because he is about to preach. It is most
unfortunate that the editors of the lectionary chose to break the text at

verse 22. This is not a natural break and it disrupts the narrative. We get the reading. We have to wait for next week for the actual sermon.

The writer Luke assumes the Spirit of the Lord rests upon Jesus. He claims Jesus was filled with the power of the Spirit. The Gospel text creates a religious scene at the synagogue in Nazareth paralleling the worship format just noted. Jesus reads principally from Isaiah 61 though there is one clear interpolation in the text. Once the reading is concluded two remarkable things then occur.

First, Luke says everyone was looking at Jesus: "The eyes of all in the synagogue were fixed on him." Not that they were looking at him as he read, but that they continued to stare at him after he took his seat. Their eyes were fixed on him. The mood is one of suspense. Perhaps their attention was riveted to Jesus because of the Spirit of the Lord. Second, Jesus makes a claim that is both extraordinary and provocative. He embraces the declarations of Isaiah and says – what you have just heard, written perhaps 550 years earlier, is coming true in me, right now, in this very moment, before your very eyes. Were I to make such a claim – what I have just read is being brought to fruition in me – I expect an air of silent skepticism would pervade the church. Someone would say (or at least think) who does he think he is? But let us rewind the reel 2,000 years.

The lector for the day comes with a reputation. "A report about him spread throughout the countryside." Luke lapses into clear hyperbole claiming Jesus was praised by everyone. This is most unlikely. He had his detractors everywhere. Jesus was the son of Joseph, a carpenter. One of the local boys. We find out next week the reaction to his sermon. Suffice to say at this place it is sometimes quite difficult to sense the extraordinariness of transformation when it comes to us in the things we have allowed to become all too familiar. So familiar that it is part of our nature. We just can't help it. It is so familiar, so natural. It reminds me of that marvelous fable of the scorpion and the frog. This is a Russian tale possibly built upon a late medieval Persian story.

One day a scorpion came down to the bank of the river. He wanted to cross to the other side but scorpions cannot swim. He waited for a little while and pretty soon a frog hopped down on the bank and prepared to jump in. "Hey, Mr. Frog," the scorpion cried: "I am so glad to see you. I want to get across the river to the other side, but as you know I cannot swim. I wonder if you would be so kind as to let me sit on your back while you swim over?" The frog looked at the scorpion for the longest time with narrowed eyes. Then he croaked: "No way, Mr. Scorpion, I certainly would not." "But why not?" asked the scorpion. "Because," croaked the frog, "I know what you will do. You will sting me." "No," protested the scorpion, "I wouldn't do that. It wouldn't be in my best interests now would it?" The frog thought it over for a few minutes and decided that the scorpion was right. It would just be plain stupid for the scorpion to sting the frog. "Okay," said the frog, "get on my back and I'll take you over to the other side of the river." So the scorpion got on the frog's back and they set off for the other bank. About half way across, the frog felt a searing, stinging sensation in his shoulder. Sure enough, the scorpion had stung him. As they began to sink beneath the surface of the river the frog croaked: "Why did you do it, Mr. Scorpion, for now we shall both die." "I know," said the scorpion, "but I just couldn't help it. It's in my nature."

Not everything that is natural – not everything that is normal and comfortable to us – is good and profitable. That's where the Spirit of the Lord comes in. We may come to church week after week after week and do the same thing over and over without thought, without feeling, oblivious to the latent seeds of transformation that may be all around us. Perhaps the Spirit of the Lord could stimulate our whole being.

The text that Jesus reads in the Nazareth synagogue from Isaiah 61 is generally regarded as a clear messianic pronouncement. The year of the

Lord's favor surely refers to a new era: The kingdom of God. Later in Luke's gospel (7:18-23) we find John Baptist locked up in prison. He sends word to Jesus: "Are you the one?" Jesus replies: "Tell John the blind can see, the lame can walk, the ill are healed, the deaf hear, the dead are coming back to life, and the good news is being proclaimed." These things occurred because of an awareness of the Spirit of the Lord. But there is a salutary lesson to be learned. Sometimes things are not what they seem and one must be aware of the immediate environment. There may be factors that will determine the outcome of any given action. A number of years ago, a farmer in Idaho had to deal with a troublesome rat that took up residence in his barn. There were efforts to evict or trap the rat but each plan failed. After a while the farmer decided to address the problem head on. Armed with a double-barreled shotgun, the intrepid farmer took up a comfortable position in the barn and waited for the pesky rat to appear. He did not have long to wait and pretty soon the unwanted rodent appeared on a rafter overhead in the hayloft and took up a perch atop a box. The farmer took careful aim and pulled both triggers. There was an enormous explosion. The farmer was hurled backwards through the open door and landed flat in the yard while the entire barn was blown to smithereens. In his single-minded attention on eliminating the rat, the old farmer had forgotten that the box in the hayloft was filled with dynamite. As farmhands rushed to the scene the dazed farmer was heard to mutter aloud: "Boys, I believe I got that rat." Sometimes the Spirit is simply not there. If it isn't, it cannot be manufactured. Attempts to do so are often regrettable, if not fatal. One might get the rat alright, but is the price of a barn worth the effort? The Spirit of the Lord is upon me. The discovery of authentic spirituality as well as God may not come easily. There is the possibility we may not discover God as we hope. That is a risk one must be willing to take, but it does seem like a risk worth running.

Earlier I asked two questions. Does the Spirit still come upon men and women, and how can we know? The answer to the first query must be in the affirmative. As for the second question, when the Spirit of the

Lord comes the ethics and mission of Jesus continues. And what is that? Good news for all, freedom for those in bondage, release, recovery, sight to the blind. These are the priority. The Spirit of the Lord never leads anyone to avoid these issues while engaging in activities and behaviors to their detriment. Søren Kierkegaard tells the story of a gang of thieves who broke into a jewelry store in Copenhagen. The robbers did not steal a single thing. Instead, they changed the price tags on all the items. The next day customers were able to buy an expensive antique clock for a few pennies, while a roll of string worth only a few pennies now cost several thousand dollars. Is there some chance we have ignored the Spirit of the Lord and paid too much attention to the lesser things? Because the Spirit of the Lord is present, whether the Holy Spirit or the Holy Ghost, and because this is the year of the Lord's favor, we need pay nothing for the gifts of God.

In the name of the one who comes in the power of the Spirit, we dare to say these things. Amen.

Cochran Lane Cliffs, Welsford, New Brunswick

How Good is Your Eyesight?

In Mark's gospel, Jesus and his followers arrived in Bethsaida and the townspeople there brought a blind man to Jesus and implored him to do something for the poor unfortunate. So, Jesus took the man by the hand and gently led him outside the village. There he did something extraordinary. He spit in the man's unseeing eyes! The onlookers must surely have been disgusted. Then Jesus placed his hands on the man and asked him whether or not he could see anything. After the spitting, the question must have seemed a bit odd. Was this how healers normally went about their business? The blind man, seemed not at all bothered by the fact that a stranger had just spit in his face, presumably not once but twice! He answered: "I see people walking but they look like trees." How did he know what trees looked like? Jesus again laid his hands on the man, this time upon his impaired eyes, and what the spit did not do completely, the hands of Jesus did and the man's eyesight was restored and he saw all things clearly (Mark 8:22-6).

In John's gospel, Jesus appears to take a different approach to blindness. He tells the people that one of the reasons he came into the world was so that those who could not see might have sight, while those who saw perfectly might be made blind. A rather strange statement indeed. Some religious leaders standing nearby asked Jesus if he thought they too were blind. Jesus offers a cryptic answer: "If you were blind you would not be guilty, but since you say we are able to see, your guilt remains" (John 9:39-41).

The number one fear among American adults is, surprisingly, not death. Instead, it is blindness. Being unable to see, whether temporarily or permanently is a very disorienting experience. One becomes uncertain, hesitant, and even paralysed, leading to fear. Blindness is a serious handicap. I took my son Jakoub into Ape Cave beneath Mt. St. Helens in Washington state for the first time when he was seven years old. Ape Cave is about two-and-a-quarter miles in length and is the longest lava tube in the United States. For spelunkers, it is a great adventure. In the upper half of the cave there are numerous rock falls to get over, side tunnels to explore, an eight foot wall to climb, measurable wind currents and absolutely no light. Jakoub did not believe me before we descended into the depths. Once we had moved up the tube a short distance we stood close together and turned both lights off. I instructed him to hold his hand at the end of his nose and tell me what he could see. There was not a sliver of light in that cave and brought home to him the meaning of the saying, "you couldn't see your hand in front of your face." With no source of light, the experience could be absolutely terrifying. There is of course both physical as well as spiritual blindness.

Jesus came to enlighten humankind. According to the fourth gospel: "In him was life and the life was the light of humankind. The light shines in the darkness and the darkness had not overcome it. There was a man sent from God whose name was John. This man came for testimony to bear witness to the light that everyone might believe through him. He was not the light but came to bear witness to the light. The true light that enlightens everyone was soon coming into the world" (John 1:4-9). According to this passage, the advent of Christ had everything to do with blindness. So, how good is your eyesight?

Blindness is a dominant theme in the gospels: In Matthew, Jesus heals two blind men (9:27), instructs the disciples of John Baptist to tell John that the blind see (11:5), he heals a blind demoniac (12:22), declares that if the blind lead the blind everyone falls into the hole (15:14), heals two other blind people (15:30), heals another two blind men (20:30), heals two blind people in the temple (21:14), denounces the Pharisees as "blind guides" (23:16), "blind fools" (23:17), "blind guides," again (23:24) and then declares a series of woes against the "blind Pharisee"

(23:26). Mark records the story of the fellow into whose eyes Jesus spat (8:22), the sad character of Bartimaeus (10:46) who is twice referred to as "the blind man" (10:49, 51). In Luke, Jesus reads that the Spirit of God is upon him for the purpose of recovery of sight to the blind (4:18). Jesus asked: "Can the blind lead the blind?" (6:39). Then he asserts that whenever a feast is held the blind should be invited (14:13), and in terms of the great banquet he instructs the workers to compel the blind to come (14:15ff.). In John, blind people wait at the pool for healing (5:3), another blind man is instructed to go and wash in the Pool of Siloam (9:1), and later Jesus tells the Pharisees they are blind (9:39-41). When questions arise about his ministry Jesus asked, "can a demon open blind eyes?" (10:21) while the mourners at the tomb of Lazarus wonder could Jesus not have saved him since he had opened the eyes of the blind (11:37). Elsewhere in early Christian literature, the motif continues. Paul is struck blind on the road to Damascus (Acts 9:3ff) and the sorcerer Elymas is blinded by Paul for attempting to hinder the gospel (Acts 13:8ff). In the Gospel of Thomas, Jesus says: "Recognize what is in your sight, and that which is hidden from you will become plain in the sight of heaven. For nothing that is hidden will not become manifest, and absolutely nothing covered will remain hidden without being uncovered" (Thomas, 5).

Saul of Tarsus went blind on the Damascus Road but that blindness brought forth light in the Apostle Paul. What did Paul see that made such a change? What do we see beneath the lamp of the gospel? People as trees walking?

Seeing can be deceiving. Things are not always what they seem. In his *Republic*, Plato tells the famous and well-known story of the cave. In the cave, people sit facing the rear wall and can see the shadows cast there from the light outside. They think the shadows on the wall are real, but those outside the cave know it is not so. The frog in the well knows nothing of the great ocean. The greedy dog in Aesop's tales comes bounding across the bridge with a thick piece of juicy meat in his mouth.

All at once he glances down into the water and sees another dog with a thick piece of juicy meat in his mouth. Determining that he ought to have that piece of meat as well, the greedy dog makes a vicious lunge for the second piece of meat but gets nothing but a mouthful of water and loses his own piece of meat in the bargain. The cavemen saw what they believed was reality. The dog saw what he thought looked like a fine addition to his meal. In both cases, we know that the cavemen and the dog were quite incorrect in their assumptions. Seeing and perceiving are related very closely to reality and truth.

Edgar Allan Poe wrote a short story once called "The Spectacles." The story is about a young man who needed to wear glasses but always resisted on the grounds that he thought his eye sight was good enough. The setting is in a theatre and the young man looking around sees a very attractive lady in the far section. Their eyes met. She was truly lovely. Poe tells us that the young man even saw her looking at him through her theatre binoculars and he determined at once that he had to meet this treasure. He was wild with excitement. Never in his twenty-some years had he beheld such a magnificent creation. So through one or two intermediaries a meeting was arranged. The young man entered the room and the pleasant lady he hoped to get to know much better greeted him. But there was something wrong. Her voice sounded very strange. Getting closer, her hair looked considerably lighter than he had remembered from the theatre. Her skin was not nearly as smooth and delicate as he imagined. Fumbling for his glasses he hurriedly put them on only to be shocked into the reality that the beautiful young woman he thought he had seen in the theatre was in fact a slightly withered 92 year old grandmother.

How good is your eyesight? Seeing is believing, they say, or is it? What do you see? There is an old saying: "If I had not seen it, I would never have believed it." On the other hand, there is considerable substance in the observation, if I had not believed it, I would never have seen it. Sometimes we see what we want to see. Sometimes our presuppositions inform our "seeing" to such an extent that we unconsciously create "reality," or is it just another piece of meat in the pond?

There is of course the right kind of glasses needed for different kinds of circumstances. There are times when our eyes need some assistance in order to see clearly and accurately. For reading, some of us need reading glasses but these kinds of glasses are of no help in the bright sun. In the brilliance of the sun, one needs sunglasses, preferably with ultraviolet protection. In order to see something very small in size, one needs a magnifying glass. To see something very far away, a pair of binoculars, or a telescope. While skiing, a magnifying glass is useless, but ski goggles are indispensable. Scuba divers do not require reading glasses, they need diving goggles. If one is working with wood or metal and there is danger from splinters, then safety glasses are essential. It is important to have the right kind of glasses for the right situation.

Having the proper aid for seeing in concert with the situation is not always as easy as it might seem, especially when it comes to the spiritual realm. A scene from Sesame Street makes the point about the proper implements for a given situation: "Is everybody ready to play baseball?" One kid pipes up: "I've got my bat." Very good. Another says: "I've got my catcher's mitt." Very good. Another says: "I've got a baseball." Well done. Then another kid interjects: "I've got my tennis racket." Uh, oh, somebody's not ready to play baseball and so the routine must be repeated. The next time, the kids bring gloves, bats, balls, but one kid shows up with a fishing rod. So it is with seeing. Is everyone ready to see? Sometimes the problem with our inability to see clearly is with our eyes. There is always some chance, though, that our eyes are fine, and the problem lies with what we are trying to see through.

In the story from Mark's gospel noted earlier, we discover that the restoration of sight to the blind was gradual. This is somewhat unusual for miracle narratives wherein normally that which is wrong is put right immediately. But this gradual ability to see is more like our lives. No one sees all of God, or all of truth, in an instant. Most of us will not see all of God or all of truth in a lifetime. Some people think that when they have reached a certain plateau, or experience, they have arrived spiritually. Nothing could be farther from the truth. Partial or incomplete healing, or seeing, or experiences can leave one with blurred vision or a skewed, undeveloped perspective. Like the blind man, we "see people as trees walking." Macbeth paid no heed to the prophecy that he would be in no danger until Birnam Wood came to Dunsinane. How silly to imagine that an entire forest could just walk over to the castle. Macbeth took the prophecy too literally, seeing and understanding it according to his own wisdom. It was too late when he was informed that the enemy was advancing holding in front of themselves tree branches from Birnam Wood to obscure their advance.

To insist on the same glasses, or the same perspective, can result in blindness. Commenting on the Johannine passage when Jesus answers the query of the Pharisees about their blindness, Rudolf Bultmann notes that "blindness is no longer simply a wandering in the dark which can always become aware that it is lost, and so have the possibility of receiving sight; for now it has forfeited this possibility." The kind of enlightenment that Christ brings is a paradoxical one: "The blind see" and "those who see become blind." How can this be? Such blindness can come from a refusal to accept new slants on life, on truth and on God. It can set in from a steadfast refusal to question our faith and our experiences as well as our presuppositions. Blindness may result from a refusal to accept the light of knowledge. If one truly wishes to see one must not refuse the proper glasses. It makes no sense to get suited up in scuba diving gear and jump off the boat holding a magnifying glass. It is equally inane to try and see the jagged contours of a mountain through a drinking glass.

Spiritually, how good is your eyesight? Are you grabbing at reflections in the water? Have you bowed down to shadows on the wall? Have you spent your life on a cheap or clever imitation? It is frightening to think perhaps we have. But to have light shine upon us and refuse to see, we become in that moment ever more profoundly blind and that is far more frightening. We cannot keep looking too far into the past, or into the future. The mists of time dim our eyes, the clouds of life obscure our vision, and the glare of the future can be overwhelming. If the only thing one can see is one's own "experience" of forty years ago, it is probably time to get a new pair of glasses. If all one can see is heaven and the sweet by and by, one likely needs to have their eyes checked. We need to have our blindness healed now. We need spiritual enlightenment. We need to be able to see what God is doing now in the world. God has already come to enlighten all people, to give sight to blind eyes and to those who sit in great darkness God has promised to shine a great light. How good is your eyesight?

Bohemian Forest Trail, Czech Republic

Cascade Mountains forest, Washington

Valley of the Winds, (Olgas), Australian Outback

CHRIST THE CLOWN

Throughout the centuries of time, people have asked this profound question of the man who walked the shores of the Sea of Galilee: Who are you? Each of us, in our own time must ask the same question. One cannot avoid encounter with the person of Jesus Christ because he is alive. With some care one can avoid Martin Luther because he is dead and has been quite deceased since 1546. Yet even to those who walked with Jesus, he remained a mystery. He was always the friend that some just never got acquainted with. He was Jesus alright, but his identity was somewhat more complex than the carpenter, the son of Mary and Joseph from Nazareth. There was indeed a definite mixture of opinion regarding who he really was. Even among those who believed he was someone quite special there was still diverse opinion.

In the New Testament there is something of a clear evolution of the revelation of the person of Christ. He was not known in his truest identity all at once. Through time and relationship, people came to a newer and clearer understanding of who he really was. The disciples of John Baptist who came to him regarded him as a teacher for they addressed him as "rabbi." A demon-possessed man in Luke's narrative called him "messiah." In a moment of personal enlightenment Peter announced that he was "the son of the living God." But when he appeared to Thomas after the events of death, dying and resurrection, Thomas blurted out: "My Lord and my God."

Who is he to you? Each person must answer that query for themselves. The question cannot be answered for anyone else. It is important to understand that Christianity is Christ, not the structure that men and women have built around him. There is a world of difference between Christ being "teacher" and being "lord." To people in the first century he was their rabbi, to others he was messiah or the Christ, some went further and acknowledged him as the son of God or as Lord. Today, he remains for some the moral teacher *par excellence*. To others he is just a fool on the hill. To still others he was clearly a deluded lunatic. To a few he is still Lord.

Søren Kierkegaard tells the story about a small circus that travelled from town to town in Denmark in the nineteenth century. The pattern of the performances in this particular circus seems to have included arriving in the community, circulating announcements of the upcoming events and then putting up the big-top on the outskirts of town where the festivities would be held. One day, after arriving near the site of their next performance the big circus tent somehow caught fire. All of the members of the troupe were in the midst of dressing for the show. The only one who was fully clothed was the clown. So he was dispatched to the town to get help to put out the fire. The clown rushed off into the village and implored everyone he met of the situation and begged them to come at once and help put out the blaze. Everyone thought it was a great ploy and some applauded the ingenuity of the clown in his efforts to drum up business for the circus. "Well done," they cried, "very clever" and some of them threw a few coins to the clown. After all, each one had previous experience with circuses and clowns. They knew full well that one should never truly take a clown seriously and especially literally. Kierkegaard writes that the villagers heard the clown with their eyes only. They assumed that he had come to the village to lure the people out to the great circus tent and what was happening was simply the employment of new tactics. Only when someone looked up and out towards the circus tent and seeing the suspicious red glow on the horizon did they begin to realize that the person before them was not a clown at all. Rather this was a real human being who only looked like a clown who had come not to amuse and entertain at all, but had come with a very urgent message.

It is helpful perhaps to see Jesus as a clown. Think about it. His claims about the kingdom of God in the face of the Roman Empire surely seemed a little absurd. His talk of the power of God, even in his own weakness seemed a bit far-fetched. His assertion that he and the father were one was not even a clever joke, it was just plain silly. Who did he think he was anyway? Everyone knew very well that he was just the illegitimate son of a poor peasant woman. Indeed, this Jesus was quite a clown. To those who only heard with their eyes, to use Kierkegaard's phrase, Jesus was, at best, "rabbi." But to those who listened to him with their hearts, by faith, he was "lord." So, he appears to a nonchalant world as a clown. But this clown, like the other in Denmark, brings to you and to me an utterly urgent and serious message. We must hear him not only with eyes and ears, but also with hearts of faith.

Jesus is the clown urging us to respond to the fire of God that is consuming the world. The world sees him as a real clown because they equate him with religion, which many consider a crutch for the weak. But he is not the structure. He is seen as a real clown because the world tries to believe that it is self-sufficient.

In 1962 Karl Barth made his first and only trip to the United States. He was already 76 years of age and was famous the world over. Following a lecture at a seminary in Virginia, Barth was approached and asked if he could summarize his theology in a single sentence. He paused and took his pipe out of his pocket. He made no reply as he filled it with tobacco, lit it up and took a couple of long puffs. His face seemed to disappear in the billow of smoke. Remember, this is the man who wrote a large work called the *Church Dogmatics* that runs to fourteen volumes and was left unfinished at his death in 1968. This is in addition to the many other works he wrote. The question was still unanswered. The smoke cleared briefly and Barth was heard to say in his heavy German accent: "Jesus loves me this I know for the Bible tells me so." Naturally, this does not work for some people (as a priest in Prague once told me gently) and others find it an unsatisfactory response. Nevertheless, the simplicity of a Sunday School song that kids are taught was the line Barth chose to sum up his life-long theology project.

Jesus appears as a clown, but beneath the façade, the paint, the rubber nose, the baggy clothes, the big shoes, and the funny face, beneath all of that is the power of God for salvation; salvation from everything one needs saving from. Can we hear the message? Can we perceive who he really is? Is he only a clown? Or is he truly the Christ who only looks like a clown? To some he is simply a clown, to others he only looks like a clown who has come bearing a serious message. Is he your teacher, or is he your Lord?

Grand Manan Island, Canada

Touched by the Sun/Son

The church is a community of faith, not a repository of knowledge. The church has neither answers for every problem nor solutions for every dilemma. The church is rather one of God's signposts on the journey through the drama we call life. Life is full of perspectives; many times quite different and contradictory perspectives. I once heard a tale of a fellow being pursued through the jungle by a hungry lion. Knowing that escape was quite hopeless he knelt down and prayed: "O God, make this lion a Christian." What happened next was truly quite startling. The lion paused in its frenzied flight and bowed his head and great mane and said: "For what I am about to receive make my heart truly thankful." This was not what the fellow wanted at all. Different perspectives. The apocryphal *Acts of Paul* tells the story of a "Christian" lion who refused to harm the apostle when he was sent into the arena. Our runner in the jungle was not as fortunate. Obviously his lion was still rather carnal!

Perspectives are sometimes best fleshed out fully after the fact. It is not uncommon for old people, near the end of their careers or lives to sum it all up, setting forth their views, writing their memoirs. This brings me to consider again the book of Ecclesiastes in the Hebrew Bible. The anonymous "preacher" seems to have written his memoirs at the end of the day, at the end of life in old age. Tradition ascribes the composition to Solomon but there is no good reason to accept that theory and indeed a number of scholars are quite certain that Solomon did not write these musings. Koheleth, or "the preacher," as the author calls himself or herself, is in the feminine form in Hebrew and the text was possibly written around the year 200 BCE.

Recently, as I read through the book again I was struck by a number of features in the narrative: Profound pessimism, the repeated notion that "there is nothing new" and that "everything is useless." The meaning of life is set forth no fewer than five times and is summed up in the sentence: "Eat, drink and try to be happy." The other thing that struck me was that the sun is referred to no fewer than 35 times and light is mentioned three further times. The repetition invites scrutiny.

Of course the sun is essential for life. The planet Earth is situated 93 million miles from the sun; close enough to be warmed but not so close as to burn up. Any farther away and the planet would literally freeze to death. Its light is essential. The sun is perhaps the central cosmic symbol of life in our solar system. So much depends upon its light, its warmth, and its life-giving presence. May I suggest that the anonymous preacher of the Book of Ecclesiastes had never been touched by the sun. I base this assumption on his or her very own memoirs.

The larger picture of life is made up of many, many components, experiences and events, the little things. In his 1978 Christmas letter the great Reformation scholar Roland H. Bainton wrote: "Simeon the aged, held the baby Jesus, one would assume, for less than a quarter of an hour. Yet he could say that he had seen a light for revelation. Life is so full of brief encounters." How, in the brief encounters of our lives, can we be touched by the sun/son? Life is indeed so full of brief encounters, some of them are the briefest. For Simeon, one of the last events of his long life span was a brief encounter, but an extraordinary encounter. Simeon's response to this brief encounter is most instructive and is perhaps best understood when it is contrasted with yet another extraordinary brief encounter in the life of Christ. That event was on the mountain of transfiguration. When Simeon held baby Jesus he said: "Now let your servant depart in peace." On the other hand, Peter who was an eyewitness to the transfiguration of Christ said: "Let's stay right here." We have a tendency to want to make certain places holy on account of something that has happened there. Unlike Simeon who departed from one brief encounter to the next, we are more like Peter and we make a valiant effort to nail God down; hoping that God will come again to the same spot ignoring all the while the sage observation that lightning seldom strikes the same spot twice. As Harry Emerson Fosdick once put it: "If you can't find a burning bush, don't worry about it. Any bush will do. God only wants to talk to you."

For the old man or woman writing his or her memoirs as the Book of Ecclesiastes, there is nothing new, everything seems worthless. Did she spend too much of her life looking for burning bushes? Did he look for God too high up and too far away? In 1994 Carly Simon recorded a song that speaks in contrary fashion to the preacher.

> If you want to be brave
> and reach for the top of the sky
> and the farthest point on the horizon
> Do you know who'll you'll meet there?
> Great soldiers and seafarers, artists and dreamers
> Who need to be close, close to the light
> They need to be in danger of burning by fire.
>
> And I, I want to get there
> I, I want to be one
> One who is touched by the sun.
>
> Often I want to walk the safe side of the street
> And lull myself to sleep
> And dull my pain
> But deep down inside I know
> I've got to learn from the greats
> Earn my right to be living
> With every breath that I take
> Every heart beat
> Let my wings of desire soar over the night
> I need to let them say,
> "She must have been mad."

I climbed Mt. Hood, Oregon's 11,240 foot peak for the first time on 6 April 1983 with a college friend. We congratulated ourselves on a job well done as we neared the summit and we sat there on our packs eating our lunch and looking at an awesome panorama in every direction. There was not a cloud in the sky and we were thankful for our sunglasses for the glare of the sun reflecting off the snow and glacial ice was overpowering. I remarked to Eric as we descended: "Hey, we are going to get a great sun tan." I awoke the next morning with second-degree burns on my face. I felt a bit like Icarus who, ignoring the advice of Daedelus, flew too close to the sun and the heat melted the wax holding his wings together and he fell into the Aegean Sea and was lost. Neither Eric nor I bothered, in our ignorance, to put on any sun screen! His ears were swollen up, my lips were two-and-a-half times their normal size. We were incredibly stupid. We were incredibly lucky. Being touched by the sun and being burnt by the sun is not the same thing. For the anonymous preacher in the Book of Ecclesiastes there was evidently little motivation to explore life. Everything was meaningless; there was nothing new at all here or anywhere. The sun/son, however, can make everything new and bring an entirely new perspective into view.

The presence of light can change everything. To those who sat in darkness, a great light has shone. It is unbelievable what difference light makes and how drastically it changes our perception of our situation. We tend to avoid some places for we perceive them as unsafe. So we walk the safe side of the street. We do not want anyone to say: "She/he must have been mad." We hang in the darkness from the trestles of our lives in fear of what we believe, thinking there is a chasm below. The writer of the Book of Ecclesiastes says: "Eat, drink and be content." That's all there is, that is the meaning of life. Some people are content to live their lives; others create theirs. There is little or no sense in the Book of Ecclesiastes of being touched by the sun.

Change is the most difficult thing most of us have to do. We take the view that what has always been is good, right and proper and if anyone needs to change it is surely not us but the next person. A few years ago a story circulated of two naval battleships engaged in manoeuvres for several days off the eastern coast of Canada. It was a foggy night and on deck was the captain and one of his officers. A light was spotted dead ahead. The captain asked the officer: "Is it moving or it is stopped?" The officer replied: "It is stopped sir." The captain signalled this message: "You are on a collision course. Change your course twenty degrees." A response signal answered: "Change your course twenty degrees." The captain fired back: "I am a captain, change your course." The answer came back quickly: "I am a second class seaman. Change your course." In exasperation the irate captain signalled once more: "I am a battleship, change your course right now." The short response was terse: "I am a lighthouse." Sometimes we are just like that captain. We think that everyone and everything else ought to conform when perhaps we need to undergo some reevaluation and make a change in our direction. As in the case of the battleship, it would definitely be for the best. The preacher of Ecclesiastes does not seem to think that a change in outlook might be beneficial.

I think the Book of Ecclesiastes might be too narrow and exclusive to adopt totally and completely as a guide for life, though I must confess that the text has long remained one of my favorites from Hebrew literature. The preacher might well be right in his or her conclusions, but it would be folly to accept them uncritically without first-hand knowledge and experience. The only way to truly live is to be touched by the sun/son.

Being touched by the sun/son means often discovering God where God is least expected. Salvation is sometimes encountered in very unlikely places. On 5 August 1949, a crew of the United States Forest Service's elite airborne firefighters, the Smokejumpers, stepped into the sky above a remote forest fire in the wilderness of Montana. Their story became the drama of the Mann Gulch Fire. They jumped at 4:10 p.m. By 5:00 p.m. they had collected their gear. One hour later it was all over.

No one could possibly have foreseen that between 5:00 and 6:00 o'clock on the afternoon of 5 August 1949 in Mann Gulch, Montana one of the most feared phenomena in the work of fighting forest fires would occur. Firefighters call it a blow-up. This is a towering wall of fire, two to three hundred feet deep. Even before Mann Gulch there were recorded blow-ups that had demolished two square miles in one to two minutes. The men were trapped. Their foreman ordered them to throw down their heavy gear and literally run for their lives. Their charge was a flight of panic. The crew of sixteen men tried to outrun the rapidly advancing inferno to the top of the ridge. The fire notwithstanding, 5 August 1949 was the hottest day ever recorded to that date in nearly Helena, 97 degrees Fahrenheit.

Halfway up the slope the foreman, a chap by the name of R. Wagner Dodge, realized he and his men would never make it to the top in time. He stopped in his flight, took out some matches and in the path of the roaring inferno lit another fire. Then he attempted to persuade his crew to enter that fire with him. They would not listen. Instead, they strained with all speed and might for the top of the ridge. Dodge covered his head and laid face down in the ashes of his own fire. No one at that point could possibly have known it, but the fire Dodge started was the last sure place of salvation. Almost immediately beyond that spot the crosses begin that mark the place where each of the thirteen men who perished fell. Dodge's fire seemed unintelligible. Had he panicked? Was he just plain nuts? Was Dodge a coward? These and other thoughts perhaps went through the minds of his men in the seconds before they made their last unsuccessful bid for life. Dodge laid down in his own fire, the main fire burned over him and he found salvation in a most unlikely place.

In the midst of the fires of life, light another fire, fuelled by the son and be warmed by His glow as the raging fires of life sweep past. That is what faith is all about. God is the Lord of life and life is a gift. Live it to the fullest in the warmth of being touched by the son/sun. Sometimes there is salvation so quickly, so unexpectedly. Sometimes there is the sun/son so quickly, so unexpectedly. It can make all the difference.

Cathedral Rock, NSW, Australia

Tom Dick and Harry Mountain, Cascades, Oregon

Cape Spencer, New Brunswick

Little discoveries, Portland, Oregon

THE MOISTENING OF THE HEART

Come my friends, Tis not too late to seek a better world…
Tho' much is taken, much abides; and tho'
We are not now that strength which in old days
Moved earth and heaven; that which we are, we are;
One equal temper of heroic hearts,
Made weak by time and fate, but strong in will
To strive, to seek, to find, and not to yield.

Thus said Tennyson the famous poet. It is never too late to seek newer or better worlds. There is always plenty to detract one from that quest, however for it is infinitely easier to conform, to accept, than to go against the grain and ask the probing questions. Canada's thirteenth Prime Minister John G. Diefenbaker was widely described as the sort of chap who took the approach: "Show me the grain and I'll go against it." Dead fish flow with the current but it takes a live fish to swim upstream. To strive, to seek, to find is very hard work indeed. There is much that enjoins us to go ahead and yield. But the quest for spirituality urges us to go beyond complacence, comfort and calls for deliberate living; for swimming against the stream and for active, intentional striving and seeking.

One of hardest things for many of us to do, especially those of us who earn our living by talking, is to be silent. I was with a group of students many years ago staying overnight at a Cistercian abbey in Oregon. One of the young men on that trip expressed his view to me that he did not enjoy the monastic setting whatsoever. When I pressed him on why that was so, he replied that it was just too quiet. Solitude is intentional, it is something we choose. It is not loneliness. Loneliness is a feeling that happens to us. Are there passageways to God in the silence?

Native American spirituality contains within it the idea called the "moistening of the heart." I have no idea where I copied this down from, but among my files I found this statement reflecting that perspective: "The stories are friend to us. The silence is friend. The land is friend to us. The dead are friend. The quest is friend to us. It is simple to be a friend, but it is not easy. It must be learned. Take care, friend, and may your heart stay moist." This "moistening of the heart" is the counter condition to hearts of stone or hard hearts. In silence one can explore spirituality. But first the cup of ourselves must be emptied. During the Meiji era the Japanese master Nan-in was visited by a university professor who wished to learn about enlightenment. Nan-in served tea. He poured his visitor's cup full and kept on pouring. The professor watched this until finally he shouted: "Stop, it is full, nothing more can go in!" "Indeed," said Nan-in: "Like this cup you are full of your own ideas. Unless you empty your cup I cannot show you anything." In order for hearts to be moistened one must do as Francis Xavier advised and give up your small ambitions.

Hearts that are moistened cannot be obtained all at once. Time is the great revealer of all things. Time is also the great teacher. Even in spiritual matters there is no substitute for time. A young man once went to a master and told him he wanted to learn everything he could about diamonds. The old man agreed to share his wisdom and knowledge with the eager young man. Each day the apprentice hurried to the workshop for his lesson. Each time the old man handed him a diamond. At first this was exciting but as the days turned to weeks the young man became quite frustrated. The master told him nothing, gave no lessons, provided no instruction. Finally the young man determined that if this happened again he would tell the old man what he thought and just leave. Sure enough, on the next day the old man handed him a stone. The apprentice exploded: "Who do you think I am? I've been coming here for weeks and you have taught me nothing. All you do is give me a diamond to hold and look at and today you even had the nerve to give me a fake."

Through silence and observation the apprentice had learned more than he realized. The famous Spanish painter and sculptor Pablo Picasso was approached by a woman in a restaurant in a small village in southern France. Having recognized the great artist the lady approached him with much hesitation. She handed Picasso a napkin and asked him to scribble a sketch on it, anything. She would be prepared to give him whatever he asked. Picasso looked at the woman for a moment and then took the napkin. For a few seconds he hunched over the table and made several strokes across the napkin. Then he handed it back to the woman and said: "That will be 10,000 francs please." "TEN THOUSAND FRANCS," the woman shrieked: "But that took you only a few seconds to draw!" "No," replied Picasso: "It took me forty years to do that."

Seeking new worlds of spirituality means experiencing the moistening of the heart. This moistening requires courage, takes time, and also mandates careful reflection. Some things are not as they seem. Quick decisions can sometimes be rather fateful. Even doing the right thing for the wrong reason can be somewhat precipitous. Tom Sine tells the wonderful and true story of the wild mushroom harvest and feast. Two people went into the hills one day and spent the entire day gathering mushrooms. Realizing they had too many for their own use they invited a number of friends over for a great feast. Several mushroom based dishes were prepared. Everyone ate until they could eat nothing more. It was a delicious dinner applauded and enjoyed by all. The leftovers were put in the cat's dish.

A few hours later the guests prepared to leave the home when someone discovered the cat laying on the kitchen floor in great agony. The cat was thrashing about, crying, kicking and in much distress. Then they remembered the dinner leftovers. Frantically, the doctor was called and everyone was advised to report to the hospital emergency room. At one o'clock in the morning eight people had their stomachs pumped. What a wretched conclusion to a lovely dinner party. When the ordeal had ended all returned to the house to collect their belongings. Someone remembered the poor cat who in the midst of the confusion and panic to get to the hospital had been forgotten. They tip-toed to the kitchen and peered in. There was the poor old cat laying motionless on the floor surrounded by eight new kittens.

Christianity cannot pass from the incarnation to resurrection without going through the passion. It takes all three – incarnation, passion and resurrection – to moisten the heart. Incarnation is a good thing and resurrection is even better. The passion is something most of us would just as soon avoid. Jesus said whoever put their hand to the plough and then looked back was unfit for the kingdom. Who would not hesitate at the prospect of going through the passion? Still, there is no other way to get from incarnation to resurrection. So he beckons to us just as he did to those men on the lake shore so long ago. "Follow me." He speaks to each of us and calls us his friends. He says: "Come." Do we dare follow? He promises new and better worlds. Our hearts of stone think only of that which will be lost and that which shall be taken. He speaks to us of that which abides and of that which shall be gained. Human reason focuses on the weakness brought about by time and fate. But he speaks of strength – of striving, of seeking, of finding. He promises eternal presence, the comfort of the Holy Spirit and the fullness of a better world – righteousness, peace and joy – the kingdom of God. And as he calls and beckons and urges us away from the security of the lake shore, to those who act in faith they experience the moistening of the heart. For the spirit and the blood are one.

In the name of the one who summons and sustains, we dare to say these things. Amen.

WHERE IN HELL IS GOD?

In 1831 the influential German philosopher Georg Wilhelm Friedrich Hegel died. His last words were reported to be: "Only one man ever understood me and he didn't understand me." These words are an echo from ancient literature.

> My God, my God, why hast thou forsaken me?
> Why art thou so far from helping me,
> from the words of my groaning?
> O my God, I cry by day, but thou dost not answer;
> and by night, but find no rest.
> I am poured out like water,
> and all my bones are out of joint;
> my heart is like wax,
> it is melted within my breast;
> my strength is dried up like potsherd,
> and my tongue cleaves to my jaws;
> thou dost lay me in the dust of death.
> Yea, dogs are round about me;
> a company of evildoers encircle me;
> they have pierced my hands and feet –
> I can count all my bones –
> they stare and gloat over me;
> they divide my garments among them,
> and for my raiment they cast lots.
> But thou, O Lord, be not far off!
> O thou my help, hasten to my aid!
> Deliver my soul from the sword,
> my life from the power of the dog!
> Save me from the mouth of the lion,
> my afflicted soul from the horns of the wild oxen!

(Psalm 22:1-2,14-21)

Can we relate to these words? Can we identify in some way with the absolute despair of the poet? "My God, my God, why have you forsaken me?" Why are you silent? I am being poured out like water. I am being crushed into oblivion and my God, you have forsaken me. Why? I have been plunged into the depths of a personal hell and I have been forsaken by the God I believe in, by the God in whom I trust, by the God in whom I worship. "My God, my God, why have you forsaken me?

I think many of us can relate in one way or another with the poet. We can identify with the cries of anguish. I think it is possible to join our voices with his in this heart-rending and agonizing query. There is no good reason why we should not cry out: "O God, why? Why? Why?" What sort of relationship precludes questions? In my experience is it folly to just accept whatever happens as the will of God, keep a stiff upper lip, never question, just accept and go on.

The question, where, in hell, is God?, that functions as the title for this reflection is a query frequently heard in the world, in one form or another, but rarely in the church and especially across a pulpit. This I think is most unfortunate. For it is a question that needs to be raised and we must not shrink back from the answers that may come. It is fair to say that I have no concern whatever in this context with the historical and theological notions of hell – that proverbial and mythical place – the burning lake of fire and brimstone, where the worm does not die and the fire is not quenched; where poor slobs are tormented night and day by small horned demons equipped with pitch-forks. The likelihood or viability of such religious constructs is a matter for another context. For my purposes here that highly apocalyptic image of hell is not relevant. Hell must be re-considered. But first, it is essential to consider who God is.

I do not think we should envision God as *der übermensch* or Superman (or Wonder Woman), or the old man upstairs who has all the answers, like the God who spoke clearly to Charlton Heston in the movie *The*

Ten Commandments. Only in the movies is God quite like that. It is very important that we should be quite clear about who God is. By the same token, we should make every effort to understand that hell is a matter we must all deal with in the here and now.

Hell is always a rather frightening and fearful experience. If you have not experienced hell, you will. Wait a little longer. Life will take you there. Hell is like dying, it is part of living and can scarcely be avoided forever. The Psalmist described hell in graphic terms: The absence of God, the unresponsiveness of God to all cries, prayers and entreaties, the virtual disintegration of life, the overwhelming despair, alienation, suffering, pain, loss and the list can be extended. Geography is not necessary to hell. The old three-tiered cosmology – earth here, heaven up there and hell down below – is of no value or use whatsoever. Hell is not a place that can be located with maps, compass and stars. Hell is a state. Hell is an experience.

There have been hells – both physical and psychological – throughout recent history, to say nothing of the course of human history from the beginning. The Nazi war camps: Buchenwald, Dachau, Auschwitz, Treblinka. In our own times the terrifying disaster of 9.11.01 when the mightiest buildings in all the world fell before our eyes. The abduction, rape and murder of the little girl in Los Angeles. Two ten year old school girls – Holly Wells and Jessica Chapman – in Soham, England, happy, playing, contented one moment and then gone. Ten days later their decomposing bodies discovered. A young man and a young woman – both in their twenties – arrested and charged. The 118 men abroad the Soviet submarine Kursk who died in the North Sea, trapped in a steel coffin while their air supply slowly ran out. The African refugees, forced from their boats whose bodies have washed up on the ruthless rocks of Gibraltar. The dozens of Russian children who died over southern Germany when two planes collided as a result of an air traffic controller's error. The senseless suicide bombers in Israel wreaking destruction on innocent lives and similar atrocities perpetrated in the

West Bank and Gaza Strip. An 89 year old woman raped and murdered in her garage in suburban Christchurch. All of these, and many more examples besides, are images of hell for these people and for those left behind to grieve, suffer and mourn. Where in hell is God? Some would reply that we should not even ask the question, or ask God why. I do not admit that such response is valid. For a closed mind is like a closed parachute. It's deadly.

Listen to the words of the prophet Habakkuk: "O Lord, how long shall I cry for help, and you will not hear? Or cry to you "Violence!" and you will not save? Why do you make me see wrongs and look upon trouble?" The prophet questioned. He posed the hard questions, he put God on the spot. Habakkuk saw the outlines of hell. He did not understand. He was aghast. He found it unacceptable. He said so. He asked God for an explanation.

Hell is not flames and burning sulphur. Hell is not just physical torment or slow agonizing death. Hell is another enemy in pursuit. Hell is not some future state where the bad guys go, where God finally gets rid of his more questionable creations. Hell is the eternal now (or so it truly seems) that never ends until one finds and experiences deliverance, redemption and reconciliation. Hell is that long and winding road that leads nowhere. Hell is the grief that feels like cold, naked fear that grips one with icy talons and that will not let go no matter how hard we sob, how loud we scream, how mightily we struggle. The experience is hell for as long as it lasts. Hell is the jealousies that can consume, twist and torment. Hell is hot lust, that inordinate desire for people, positions, possessions or all three. Hell is anger and resentment that keeps one awake at night, that causes one to drive for hours through city streets going nowhere. Hell is unfulfilled desires that drive one here, there and everywhere without fulfilment, without hope. Hell is unforgiveness that constantly keeps the past in the present and forces one to live their lives – in whole or in part – in the past. Those who live in the past die a little bit every single day. Hell is self-hate, self-doubt, loathing, depression that pierces through one's very being, that stabs like a million darts until one is dulled by the pain, and misery becomes one's only friend. Hell is addiction to virtually anything negative: Alcohol, drugs, sex, gambling, pornography. Hell is truly being in hot water. As Rita Mae Brown once noted: "people are like tea-bags. You never know how strong they are until they're in hot water." Our tea-bag existence often comes apart in the scalding hot water of our hells. And where in hell is God?

Hell is the experience of the absence of God's presence, or what is even more terrifying, the presence of God's absence. The sheer horror of that experience can never be put adequately into words and no one should try for words only trivialize the inexpressible. Sometimes, along with Moses, we would be contented if only we could just see even part of the back side of God. That would be enough to let us know that we are not completely alone, that God is there, somewhere, not too far away, perhaps about to turn to face us. But when even the hind parts of God cannot be seen it is difficult not to cry out, "my God, my God, why have you forsaken me?" It is not a cry of weakness, of unbelief, or sin. It is natural. The tale in the Hebrew Bible about Jonah in the belly of the great fish is another kind of hell wherein Jonah cried. Commenting on this passage Martin Luther wrote if one can just cry, your agony is over: "Hell is not hell anymore if you can cry to God. But no one can believe just how hard this is. We can understand wailing, trembling, sighing, doubting, but to cry out, this is what we cannot do. Conscience, sin, and the wrath of God are about our necks. Nature cannot cry out. When Jonah reached the point that he could cry, he had won. Cry unto the Lord in your anguish, and it will be better. Just cry and nothing else." "My God, my God, why hast thou forsaken me?" This experience is indeed what some of the medieval mystics sometimes called the "long dark night of the soul."

There may be San Francisco earthquakes and Hurricane Hugo's and these create different hells for many people. But there are also personal earthquakes and hurricanes. Where is God in these disasters? Where is

God in these hells? Again it is Luther who reminds us that there is a difference when God is there and when God is there for you. Where in this hell is God? What about the hurricanes of frustration and rejection? What about the earthquakes of a sexual situation relating perhaps either to gender or orientation? What of the hellish hurricane of Aids, cancer, Covid, or some other dire sickness? What about the earthquake of the abyss of a relational hell, when a marriage or other close relationship goes terribly awry?

Sometimes God is there, or so it seems and there are waves of comfort and closeness. But often God seems distant and absent as the poet wrote in Psalm 22. How can we pray "our father who art in heaven" when we feel with all our hearts and lives that there is no father in heaven? How can we force ourselves to believe when our fervent prayers are only echoes at the top of the stairs and we suffer alone in the hell of the silence of God? I have sometimes described myself as an Evangelical Deist. I long for that personal relationship with God but I cannot shake off the nagging suspicion that God is the cosmic clock-maker. God created the clock (the universe), wound it up carefully and went away, God's work completed. The clock continues to run – tick, tock, tick, tock – through the ages of time.

We are, in these hells, like Goethe's Faust, at a very dangerous and desperate moment in our lives. The poisoned cup already uplifted to our lips. Then we hear the strange words: "He descended into hell." The Apostles' Creed contains an article of the faith often overlooked but it constitutes an essential part of the faith: "He descended into hell." Of course there are several interpretations of the phrase. One of them can be read to include the idea that he partook of the entire experience of humankind, in life and in death too, and that he endured the worst experiences and enjoyed the best. What was his hell? His hell consisted principally in Gethsemane and on Golgotha. At the latter place, the place of the skull, it is said that he too cried out loudly and literally the pained words of the poet: "My God, why have you abandoned me?"

For some people, it can only be concluded, like Jesus on the cross or John Baptist in prison there is no God for them in their hells. All they have is the sense of the presence of God's absence. John Baptist was the man for whom there was no miracle and Jesus truly did die at Golgotha, Godless, alone, in a God-forsaken hell and there was seemingly no deliverance, or redemption or reconciliation, not even for him of all people! Some people will say to those suffering in the same state of hopelessness: "Don't worry, be happy." This is nothing other than a cruel rationalization that denies essentially the realities of life.

This would be the natural point in a discussion on this topic to invoke the well-worn advice of Romans 8:28 which reads that everything that happens, occurs for good, to those who love God and proclaim that on the basis of that text that all things will be well. I cannot turn that corner nor can I draw that conclusion. Romans 8:28 is simply not true in the context in which it is generally used. It is, once again, an example of cruel rationalizing. The New Testament does not support that popular view, and neither does common sense and reality. It is folly to say: "Only believe sister" or "Just have faith brother." It is neither a matter of the faith nor is it of faith to chant the mantra, "all things work together for good." Some things simply create hell and there is no use in denying it. To argue that a woman was brutally raped in order to bring her to God is appallingly bad theology. To tell grieving parents that their child untimely deceased is in a better place and that this was the will of God in order to save Aunt Bessie is madness, offensive and infantile. Some events are without meaning, they have no positive value and deny all goodness. It is nonsense to say that everything contributes to that which is good. According to the New Testament scholar C.H. Dodd, Romans 8:28 means literally: "With those who love God, God cooperates in all respects for good." Paul is not saying that somehow hell is always good, positive or part of the plan and will of God. But Paul does mean to say that God is always there in some form or fashion. No matter what hells we may make for ourselves or the hells we may find ourselves in here on this earth, Jesus will descend into them with us and aid us if we will turn to him. Even if one makes their bed in hell, God is there. Now that is a strange and wonderful thought; even in hell God is there.

Luke 14:27 enjoins us to take up our cross if we truly wish to follow Christ. Those who decline cannot be his disciple. There is no evidence that this phrase was regarded as a metaphor for voluntary martyrdom. It is not simply the historical cross of Christ that we must take up, but our own crosses. Each one of us must assume our own passion. Each one among us must bear up his or her own cross. The cross is our responsibility. Resurrection is God's responsibility. This is the only way to grow, in fact it is the only way to live the life of faith.

Karl Barth claimed that it was quite impossible for humans to grasp the magnitude of their sins unless it was likewise possible to glimpse the magnitude of God's grace. Yet all too often we insist on clinging to something other than the cross even though it leads us downward along that broad road to destruction. The story is told of a man watching eagles in the mountains. One of them seemed intent upon some prey in the valley below. All at once it swooped to the valley floor and moments later rose triumphantly clutching in its talons its prize. Then something inexplicable happened. The eagle began flying very erratically and then crashed headlong into the valley. Puzzled, the eagle watcher climbed down from his perch and at length found the dead body of the eagle. A brief inspection explained the whole tale. The animal grasped in the eagle's talons was a badger, a most ferocious animal when trapped or confronted. It had simply gnawed away the eagle's belly. But having once grasped its prize the eagle was unable to let go even though it meant certain and final destruction. Sometimes we are just like that eagle. What are we clinging to? In the end it may be the things we simply cannot let go of: Theology, comfort, personal gain, power, prestige, wealth or fame, or some skewed idea of freedom that ultimately damns us.

What is my cross? What is your cross? Prison, misunderstanding, exile, death, self-denial, weakness, something that makes us different from everyone else? Accepting our cross and our hell could be the means of finding God. This is, however, not a licence to leave off discipleship. In the Christmas Oratorio, W.H. Auden's Herod says: "I like to sin. God likes to forgive. The world is admirably arranged." That attitude is as perilous as the following jingle is theologically irresponsible: "Free from the law, O blessed condition. I can sin just as I please and still have remission." This is not what I am speaking of in accepting our hells. We are sinners. This is true. So Luther wrote: "We should sin boldly, but believe and rejoice in Christ more boldly still." That is true. There is no point denying the cross and the sin. To spend our lives trying to renounce our crosses is counterproductive. It is these crosses through which God is revealed. Søren Kierkegaard had a girlfriend. Her name was Regina. They were going to get married and then spend their lives together. Kierkegaard called it off. It broke Regina's heart. The Danish thinker explained that he did not believe he could love Regina and serve God at the same time. So he sent Regina away and chose God. Martin Buber roundly criticised Kierkegaard's way of thinking by saying that God comes to us through the Reginas God places in our lives, not in the renunciation of them.

As Paul Tillich so powerfully preached so long ago we must simply accept the fact that we are accepted and we must accept that we are accepted with our crosses. Indeed, there is no place or experience in life in this or in any other world that is beyond the reach of the love of God as we know it in Jesus Christ. Our hope must be in the one who has already descended into hell, who has already experienced the silence of God, who has already been through the valley of the shadow of death, the one who has already experienced being abandoned by God. For this one, ever and again, descends into our hells with us.

How can this be? Where in hell in God? God is there and God descends into our hells with us in the form of the community of believers. That places a great deal of responsibility upon us as believers, as people and pilgrims of faith. We have two options. Either we can simply tell others to trust in God alone in some cold, dark, lonely corner mouthing the words of Romans 8:28 or we can become a Christ to them in their hells. Harold Kushner put it this way: "God is found in the courage of the human soul" particularly in the earthquakes, hurricanes and hells of life. "God is found in the human beings capacity to cherish something as being more valuable than life itself" in those very same earthquakes, hurricanes and hells. "God is found in our willingness to love" in the midst of the utter despair of earthquakes, hurricanes and hells. "God is found in our insistence on finding our way through the valley of the shadow" in these very same earthquakes, hurricanes and hells in what seems to be the complete and irrevocable absence of God.

No one is ever lost...not really...not forever. The winds blow, the sea billows do sweep men and women away. And it is hell. But God's grace retrieves what belongs to God. Safe return is guaranteed. Some of us are lost at sea in gales no one can gauge. But God is there and what seems lost is never beyond the God who has already descended into hell. We must not give up regardless of the depths or horrors of our hells. We must not fail to continue to live deliberately in whatever faith we can muster believing all the while that God will come to us through those who are God's disciples. We must love, and forgive, take up our crosses and be prepared to move fences. We are instruments of grace, it is our duty to allow God's grace to make our lives sacramental. To say to another: "I forgive you all of your sins" is not blasphemous at all. Part of finding God in our hells is through the love and forgiveness of others. That task is not easy, God does not always appear and sometimes God never appears. We hope for epiphany while realizing the darkness may prevail. But even in the darkness of hell, in the dismay of God's silence we would all do well to consider the Quaker phrase "to hold you in the light." The continuing presence of Christ in each of our hearts and in his community assures us that God is always present in Hell and that presence can perhaps sustain one even in Hell.

In the name of the one who never forsakes us, not even in hell, we dare to say these things. Amen.

Crowlink, Seven Sisters Cliffs, East Sussex, England

'Safe Return', (Memorial to fishermen lost at sea)
Squalicum Harbor, Bellingham, WA

St Martins, New Brunswick

Homeless in Gatesville, Texas

Love Lets You Do Whatever You Want

In the year 441, Bishop Cyrus preached a Christmas sermon in the obscure Phrygian town of Cotyaeum. The complete text consisted of this: "Brethren and sisters, let us honor the birth of our God and Savior Jesus Christ in silence because the Word of God was conceived in the Holy Virgin through listening alone. To him be glory forever and ever. Amen." His rambunctious and overexcited parishioners had lynched the previous four incumbents but they loved the brevity of the homilies delivered by Bishop Cyrus and he won their hearts.

"Love and do whatever you please." I could stop right here, say "Amen," and thereby make this the shortest homily ever delivered in the history of St. Anne's Episcopal Church. But I fear that if I stopped at this point, there would be too many questions in the minds of too many so I shall say a bit more on the subject. The words are not original with me. In fact I lifted them directly from a sermon I read while preparing for this homily. That sermon had been preached a long time ago, in faraway North Africa around the year 420 by one of the most important and well-known figures in Christian history. St. Augustine's sermon was based upon the same text that I have chosen to elaborate on this morning. "Love and do whatever you please." That is what he said and I endorse it. Keep that thought in mind for the next few minutes. For in the end I am going to leave it up to you to figure out what it means.

Born 700 years ago in 1304, Francesco Petrarch was the greatest poet of his age. He wrote over 300 love poems to a mysterious and beautiful woman named Laura. These stirring poems have captivated Europe for centuries, inspired other writers like Shakespeare and Chaucer, and continue to influence how we view romantic love today. At the Church of St. Claire in Avignon (in southern France), on April 6, 1327, Petrarch first saw the woman who would be his muse until long after her death in 1348. The identity of Laura (and even the question of her existence) is uncertain, but from the moment Petrarch set eyes on her, the poet was captivated by her. It must have been love!

More than a dozen years ago now in a history course in the Texas prison system, I read a poem about love to a group of women. It was a moving poem about the undying love of a man for a woman. A deep hush settled over the room as I read. The poem reached an emotive and passionate conclusion. I then asked if anyone would like to respond. There was another moment of complete awkward silence. And then one woman, whose name was Sharanna, sitting in the back row spoke. I can still hear Sharanna saying (with a tear in her voice): "I wish someone loved me that much." Indeed. Love is one of the greatest mysteries and wonders of human existence.

In the epistle reading for Easter V the word "love" appears in various forms 27 times! We have heard the text and its summary is significant. Love one another. Love comes from God. Whoever loves is of God. Whoever loves knows God. God is love. Whoever does not love does not know God. God's love is revealed in Jesus. Love is how God dwells in us. God's love is perfected in us through love. There is no fear in love. We are able to love because of God's love. Professions of love for God are only meaningful in love that is expressed for others. Put all together, there is an amazing philosophy of love contained in these short few lines penned 1,900 years ago.

It seems to me that if God is the ground of our being, and I would be prepared to argue that point, then love is the means by which we live in wholeness. No one can live without love. One may exist without love, but no one can truly live in wholeness without love. According to the church calendar, we are still in the season of Easter. Easter is about incarnation and continuing incarnation. I would suggest, based on the text before us, that every act of love is incarnational; that every act of love extends the meaning of incarnation. The God of love creates; the God of love reconciles; the God of love sustains. Therefore, it seems we would do well to follow that path, to love first, and thereafter do as we please!

"I love strawberries." "I love my girlfriend." "I love God." One word, used three times in three separate statements, but each time there is a shade or variation of meaning. One cannot love strawberries, another person, and God equally in the same way or in the same sense. Sanskrit has ninety-six words for "love;" ancient Persian has eighty. We are impoverished inasmuch as the English language has but one word to express such a profound concept. Happily, the first epistle of John was not written in English but in Koine Greek. In the Greek language of the time, there were four main words that were used to express different understandings of "love." The first was *storge* which we may associate in English with the word "affection." This implies a fondness and a familiarity and is often expressed in a familial context. A second word is *philia*. This word expresses our social understanding of "friendship." Here we see a clear bond, a dispassionate virtuous quality. In the New Testament, the word *philia* in verb and adjectival forms appears at least fifty-two times. A third understanding of love comes from the word *eros*. This speaks of "passionate love," implying sensual desire and longing. In English we have the word erotic which is derived directly from this Greek expression. *Eros* is not used in New Testament, though it does appear twice in the Septuagint (the Greek translation of the Hebrew Bible), both times in Proverbs (see 7:18 for example). And just because it is not used in the New Testament does not mean that it has no relevance for authentic meaningful love. Finally, there is *agape*. This is unconditional love, without expectation of return, the kind of emotion or posture that has absolutely no strings attached. In verb and noun forms the word *agape* appears in the New Testament no fewer than 226 times. It is this word – *agape* – that appears so often in I John 4. I think all four of these concepts are important for Christians.

Based on our text then, the conclusion seems unavoidable: Love is the essence of the Christian life. It cannot be equated with the outward signs of Christianity. People may make the sign of the cross, they may be baptized, they may go to church, they may even build churches, some may even be priests or bishops, they may say "Amen" and "Alleluia," and may even come to the Lord's table to receive the body and blood of Christ thus implying solidarity with Jesus. But such people can only truly be called Christian if they live in love. Without love, you may be Anglican/Episcopalian or Baptist, but you cannot be Christian. There is a difference.

The second coming of Christ occurs in the love that Christians live in. According to John, whoever does not live in love denies the incarnation even if they are able to recite the Nicene Creed forwards and backwards in the original Greek. It is such a fundamental element of the faith that without it the faith is vacuous. Think of it this way. Take love away from God and one is left either with a tyrant or nothing at all. Take love out of Jesus and we are left with just another itinerant teacher of the ancient Near East. Remove the idea of love from Christianity and what remains are interesting stories and propositions but no power to transform. Take love and loving out of human relationships and one finds using, misusing, abusing, and confusing! Love really is that essential.

The place of love in the Christian faith and its purpose among the followers of Jesus is underscored by Jesus himself. He said that the criteria for knowing the identity of his disciples was neither doctrine nor religious practice, but love. As Jesus put it: People will know you are my disciples if you have love for one another! That's the crucial issue, not technical points of theology. Thich Nhat Hanh, a Vietnamese Buddhist monk has written a little book called *True Love: A Practice for Awakening the Heart*. In that book he enumerates four aspects of love. First, a willingness to understand another. Second, the ability to ease the pain of another. Third, the ability to bring joy to another. And fourth, true love makes free. Applying Thich Nhat Hanh's ideas is perhaps a greater challenge than appears at first blush.

Bartolomé de Las Casas, a sixteenth-century Dominican who witnessed the Christian missionizing and Spanish colonization of the New World, tells a story about a Cuban tribal chief named Hatuey. Hatuey heard of the atrocities that accompanied the Christian Europeans – missionaries and conquistadors – and he fled. A series of events occurred and the conquistadors tracked him down. Since he did not wish to cooperate he was condemned to die. Before the execution was carried out, a priest shared with Hatuey the gospel and tried to convert him to Christianity. He told Hatuey that if he accepted Jesus as his lord and savior he would go to heaven and live with Jesus. If he refused he would have to go to hell and suffer torture for all eternity. All of this was new to Hatuey so he listened carefully to all of this. Then he asked: "Will there be many Christians in heaven? Will there be people like you there?" "Oh yes," the priest answered: "There will be many of us there." Hatuey thought about this and then replied: "Well, I'd rather go to hell." So the followers of Jesus solemnly burned him alive at the stake on 2 February 1512 in southern Cuba.

The incongruity between the treatment of Hatuey, the teachings and ethics of Jesus, and the statements in our text are striking. No one surely requires further commentary on that point from me. Nothing but good can come from love. Love does not create to annihilate. The rose in our culture symbolizes love. Men of the romantic persuasion sometimes buy a rose, perhaps even twelve long-stemmed red roses, and give them to the woman they consider the center of the universe; the one they feel they simply cannot live without. The red rose is a powerful and positive symbol of love. But the flower for many Christians unfortunately is the daisy. "God loves me," "loves me not," "God loves me," "loves me not!" It's a very poor symbol for true love. The traditional practice of plucking daisies is not God or love. It's just bad theology. Why? Because God is love and there is no fear in love. One must never fear coming to that last pluck and finding out "God loves me not." So far as God is concerned that nightmarish eventuality is quite impossible.

Even with that assurance, there are times in our lives when we overlook the gift of God's love. Sometimes we miss the love in our lives. Love gives meaning when everything else seems lost. God has seen to that. I remember a line from a film, based on a true story, where a condemned man was asked why he had kept a bunch of incriminating letters from his lover. He answered that he had done so in order to always remind himself that once he had been loved! Perhaps the boxes in our lives that we think are empty and worthless are not quite as empty as we assume. That is not only possible but quite certain because God is joined to God's creation inextricably. God does not leave us. God never "breaks up" with the object of God's affection. That is because love does not create to annihilate. And God's love is the most unconditional of all. It can be relied upon as nothing else can in all the universe.

The famous writer Mark Twain stopped going to church many years before he died. In time so did his wife Livy. Twain once asked her why she no longer went: "Well Mark," she said, "If you are lost, I want to be lost with you." The Christian faith is not about being lost. Christianity is about being found and made whole because of love. So St. Augustine once more: "Love and do whatever you please." After all of this, I will resist the urge to explain that statement further. Instead, I hope you will keep some of these things I have shared in mind as I dare you to go out into the world this week to "love and do whatever you please!"

There is a song sung in some Christian communities that is apropos: "In the stars that grace the darkness, in the blazing sun of dawn, in the light of peace and wisdom, we can hear your quiet song. Love that fills our life with wonder, love that warms the weary soul, love that bursts all chains asunder, set us free and make us whole." Pie in the sky, or real hope? "Love and do whatever you please." It's truly that simple. It's that difficult.

In the name of the One who is love, we dare to say these things. Amen.

Hooker Valley Track, Mt Cook, New Zealand

GOD IN THE BOOKS

When I went up to Cambridge as a doctoral student, I became aware of the fierce rivalry in Oxbridge. I heard that Oxford always alleged that learning at Cambridge was like a closed book. To this the Cambridge men and women replied: "The book is open at Oxford, but always to the same page." An old Roman proverb warned: "Beware the man of one book." I have often heard it said that one can tell quite a bit about someone from the books in their library. I have loved books from a very young age. My parents were avid readers. There was no television in our home when I was growing up. Dad was a keen collector of books and it seemed that half of the master bedroom in those years was full of books. Vacations were generally spent in Maine or elsewhere in New England. This was principally on the grounds (at least according to Dad) that there were no decent used book shops anywhere in New Brunswick! Our trips often followed a beaten path from one used book shop to another. As the years passed by, I came to believe I knew every used bookshop in the state of Maine for even when the others had wearied of the incessant treks and remained in the car to rest, I marched right along beside Father into each one of them and then promptly disappeared into my section of interest.

Not only did I know where the shops were, I knew most of the owners by name and was still only 10 years old. We used to go to the University of Maine at Orono's bookshop but it wasn't much good for they didn't have the stuff I was interested in. There was Lippincotts in Bangor and the old book barn in Brewer run by a chap named Rupert Watson whom Dad said had a horn growing out of his head. He did have a bit of a large bump on his beak (as Dad called it) which, once the thought had been put into my young head, did rather resemble the stump of a horn.

Rupert was a real hoot. Whenever I presented Rupert with good old Canadian cash, that horn on the left temple seemed to swell ever so slightly and he would glare at me with disdain. "What am I going to do with that confetti?" he would bark, referring to the colorful Canadian bills. He would feign great exasperation: "Oh, just take the book and be gone." I made off with several volumes from Rupert Watson over the years because he couldn't be bothered dealing with the bank over the exchange rates. Dad began to see an excellent strategy and thus we went frequently to Brewer and never failed to look up Rupert Watson. In Stockton Springs was Aimee McEwen's place and it was quite good. The problem there was that it was always in a bit of a mess. Aimee knew where everything was but she proved sometimes hard to pin down to get directions to exactly where one wanted to get to in the crowded shop in her house. Her husband Maynard was useless. He hadn't a clue, I don't think, between novels and philosophy, science fiction and theology. "O my God," he would say with a worried look on his face when asked a question about a book: "Let me go see if I can find Aimee." They knew Dad so well that even if they were closed, he usually got in to have a quick look and that meant I got to slip in as well.

Farther on down the coast was Camden and the shop owned by a woman Dad called "the old rogue." "The old rogue" was in truth Lillian Berliansky and she was so named on account of the fact that her books always seemed to be much more expensive than Rupert Watson's and the McEwens. Dad would pull the car off the highway into Camden and Mother would say: "Now where are you going father?" To this he would reply: "Oh, let's go see the old rogue. Maybe she's knocked her prices down." She never did but still we went and occasionally I would be able to buy another book. Inland, at Augusta, was a nice fellow by the name of Leon Tibbetts. He had books upstairs and downstairs and was fairly reasonable as I recall. Dad went to visit him a few years ago as he lay dying of cancer. The books were long gone and I can only faintly remember his face. Down outside of Portland was a place on Pope Road though I have no recollection of who the owners were now. Seems like a couple ran the place. It was in a large barn on a farm and I collected quite a few titles from that location. But the best and the biggest of all was in Portland run by a fellow who always asked a hundred questions named O'Brien. Dad facetiously called him, "O-bree-in" or just plain "Obie." His was a large Victorian style house filled with books (or so it seemed) from cellar to attic: "Let's go see Mr. O-bree-in," Dad would announce whenever we neared Portland: "And he'll get a good crack if he's got nothing good." I spent quite a bit of Dad's money in those days paying off "O-bree-in" for the various titles I simply could not live without. And there were more shops, in Bucksport, Ellsworth, Bar Harbor, Belfast, Bath, Auburn, Gorham, Biddeford and so on, here and there, down that lane, over that hill and I suspect we took them all in at one time or another. All in all, books came to play a big role in my life: In those days stories about Gene Autry and Roy Rogers, the adventures of the Hardy Boys and books with interesting titles like *Vanishing Liner*, *The Secret of Tibet*, *Left on the Labrador*, and *We Almost Lost Detroit*. I read about mad scientists, explorers, the wild west of the cowboys and outlaws, and the compelling tales of Albert Johnson the so-called "mad trapper of Rat River." Later I got into Einstein. I still have my copies of *The Special and General Theory of Relativity* and another tome called *Investigations on the Theory of Brownian Movement*.

After I moved to the American west coast I only indulged my passion further. There were shops in Seattle, especially Shorey's, Henderson's in Bellingham, Windows in Eugene, Moe's on Telegraph Avenue in Berkeley, shops in San Francisco and farther south as well. But Portland beats them all. I have read that Portland has more book shops per capita than any other major American city. Cameron's used to be a regular haunt in those early days. The Title Wave sells old library books and occasionally one finds treasures for a dollar or two. I purchased many books from the Paper Moon on Hawthorne, now long gone. The Great Northwest on SW10th Avenue was always fun. It suddenly became less interesting after they relocated only a few blocks away and organized themselves. It was more fun digging through piles of books on the floor and finding something at the bottom one could hardly believe their luck at unearthing. At Holland's on NW12ᵗʰ Avenue, the chap there often rounded things down. If three books totalled $11.50 he might ask, how about $10?" But Powell's is by far the very best. A million titles covering a full city block with branch shops in several other local locations. Who knows how many hundreds of dollars I have left there? Each Christmas, I am certain to get from someone a gift certificate to Powell's. One must spend hours there on each visit.

Skip Paynter and I used to go to the annual Multnomah County Library book sale on N.E. Knott in Portland. It would open at 8:00 a.m. on a Saturday. We arrived at 7:00 just to ensure our place at the head of the line. It would not do to have some knucklehead getting in ahead of us. We always had advance strategy. We brought cardboard boxes and we knew which section to head to, since everything in those days was organized according to the Dewey decimal system. Our plan of attack was simple. Skip started at one end, I at the other. We grabbed anything that looked interesting all along the aisles, threw those titles into our boxes and sorted them out later. It was much easier to put the titles back we didn't want then try to wrestle books from the clutches of others just like us. We were pretty successful, even if we were occasionally ruthless. On one occasion we made off with more than 60 volumes. Nowadays I make annual trips to Portland. When I lived in England I haunted Blackwells in Oxford, Heffer's in Cambridge, Foyle's in London and a dozen other shops. I take an empty suitcase to Prague each time I go and it always comes back filled with finds from the back street used book sellers there. Books remained a big part of my living experience so much so that my son gave me a sweat shirt for Christmas many years ago which had emblazoned across the chest a quotation from Erasmus: "When I get a little money I buy books; and, if any is left I buy food and clothes."

The *Times Literary Supplement* ran an interesting list in its 3 December 1999 issue listing the top books of the past millennium. There had been some type of criteria for inclusion and a sort of voting process by certain people. I copied down the list. Leading the way was the King James Version of the Bible and Shakespeare, both garnering five votes. Next came Dante's *Divine Comedy* with four votes followed by Darwin's *On the Origin of the Species* and the works of Marcel Proust with three votes each. There was a three-way tie in the next position with two votes each and these included Montaigne's *Essays*, Beowulf (which may be older in fact than the past millennium) and the *Adventures of Don Quixote* by Cervantes. The remaining list all had just a single vote: Descartes' *Meditationes*, Giambattista Vice's, *La scienza nuova* from 1785, Emily Brontë's *Wuthering Heights*, James Joyce's, *Ulysses*, Dostoevsky's, *The Brothers Karamazov*, Hildegard of Bingen's, *Scivias* (twelfth century), Edward Gibbon's *The Decline and Fall of the Roman Empire*, Jane Austen's, *Emily*, John Milton's, *Paradise Lost*, Jean Jacques Rousseau's, *Les Confessions* and Spinoza's, *Ethics*. An unusual list. I knew most of them.

For me books mark personal development, the maturation of ideas, turning points in one's life and so on. I have always had a library, even from the time I was a small child. From 1983 onwards, I began to build a personal library to reflect my emerging scholarly interests. In those early days, we always rented two bedroom apartments so that one room could be used as my library. As time went on, I needed the whole room. After becoming a university professor, the institutions I worked for always provided me with an office so my library became my place of work. It became habitual for me to read or look at books while I ate whenever I was alone. I read dozens of books on the light rail in Calgary riding to and from work as well as during lunch breaks. I am probably the only person ever to have read Rudolf Bultmann's *Jesus Christ and Mythology* in the atrium of the Toronto Dominion Center in downtown Calgary. Often through the years I took great comfort in my books and almost thought of them as friends. Many came as gifts over the years; the names of colleagues and friends inscribed therein.

In 1995 I accepted an invitation to join the faculty of the University of Canterbury in Christchurch, New Zealand. I had far too many books to ship. So I gave my Biblical Studies library, on an extended loan basis, to my friend Eric Loy who was pastoring a church in Christmas Valley, Oregon. I sent my Theology library, on the same loan basis, to a former religion student of mine who was then also pastoring a church in Great Falls, Montana. I knew Laurie Moore would make good use of them. My church history books were all boxed up and shipped off to the antipodes. Five and a half years later I was in Montana to preach over two Sundays for Laurie. It was quite wonderful to see my old friends again after the long passage of time. One evening, while everyone was engaged in other activities, I stole over to the church and slipped into the church office where my books were. For some time I wandered about the room looking at them and being amazed at how many I had forgotten I owned. I made a few notes. First, I ticked off the names of authors and titles in my theological library that had contributed to my development: Helmut Thielicke, *Exercise for Young Theologians*, Tillich, Kierkegaard, Thomas Merton, *Lutheran Book of Worship* (a leather copy with my name in gold letters presented to me by the congregation of Epiphany Lutheran Church in Denver, following my stint there as assistant pastor), Schweitzer, Barth (there were no fewer than fifty-five volumes!), Malcolm Muggeridge (whom my old and long deceased mentor Don Fisher introduced me to), Bonhoeffer, Brunner, liberation theology, feminist theology (I was surprised as how many titles I had), Frederick Buechner (whom my close friend and former professor Irv Brendlinger had brought to my attention), Buber, Nikos Kazantzakis (in whom I had found a great deal of useful theology), the Niebuhrs, Schleiermacher, Bultmann, John A.T. Robinson, Clarence Darrow (the agnostic trial attorney whom some said was more Christian than the Christians), and many others besides.

I noted the titles of the books I had used in teaching or had required students to use as texts: *Faith Seeking Understanding, Jesus in Global Contexts, Models of God, Theological Crossfire, A Theology of Love, Man as Male and Female* and a few others. Then I noted a few titles I had used or read as a student: *The Nature of Doctrine, Theology for a Nuclear Age, Plurality and Ambiguity, Religion within the Limits of Reason Alone,* the two-volumes of *Essentials of Evangelical Theology* and a bunch of others.

Looking through these old friends I began to think of some of the writers and how they had specifically influenced me. I did seem always to find some resonance with Karl Barth though I was never sure why but I knew his view of Christ and the Word of God had been highly suggestive to me. Albert Schweitzer's ruminations and life as existential encounter and ethics impacted me. Søren Kierkegaard's "leap of faith" was important and I had no time to waste on Francis Schaeffer and his dismissal of it. Thomas Merton on contemplation, Dietrich Bonhoeffer on the cost of discipleship and his theology of fragments in his prison writings caused me to think in broader terms. Liberation theology, especially in the specific Latin American context, drew me into a fuller consideration of the social implications of the gospel and the idea of applied theology. Buber's *I and Thou* relation is not something to be written about, but an experience one can only know of by entering into it. John A.T. Robinson, the "heretical" Bishop of Woolwich, was just being *Honest to God* as he pushed out the edges of the theological project and he also helped me to transcend my own narrow upbringing. Martin Luther, my own intellectual and spiritual comrade in arms, had perhaps more than anyone else stimulated me with respect to the eucharist, the cross, justification, faith and Christ. I owed all of them, and many more besides, considerably for their infinitely valuable help along the journey.

I thumbed through a large heavy volume called *What Luther Says* nearly 1,700 pages in length. In the front was the date 5 June 1988 and under that the words: "A small token of our appreciation of who you are and an expression of our love for you." Below this were quite a number of signatures: These included Stephen Hannemann, Ginny Heffer, John O'Connor, Lenora Bruce, Dick and Joyce Booth, Gerry Perkins, Betty

Gass, Lynn Hannemann, Lauryn McCroskey, Norma O'Connor, Mitzi, Gary and others. It was a gift from the old Church of our Redeemer parish where I had preached and once tried to minister. Some of those signatories are dead now, others gone I do not know where. Not one of them have I any current contact with. Most of them I never saw again after the summer of 1988. One person had added this comment to their signature: "Thank you for your beautiful and most powerful ministry to us. Love…" I hardly knew the person. What had been so beautiful? What had been so powerful? I didn't know. I still don't. But there it was.

Lastly, as I searched along the eighteen rows of theological books in Laurie's office, I discovered again a number of specific titles that had functioned as key bench marks along the journey. Some of them were heavily underlined, annotated, and even in the margins of a couple I had carried on a dialogue and debate: John Stott, *Your Mind Matters*; Karl Barth, *The Doctrine of the Word of God*; Joseph Fletcher, *Situation Ethics*; Albert Schweitzer, *The Mysticism of Paul the Apostle* (still in my view one of the best books on Paul); Dietrich Bonhoeffer, *The Cost of Discipleship*; Martin Luther, the large *Commentary on Galatians*; and Luther, *The Freedom of a Christian*. There was also a King James Bible given to me as a gift by Mother and Father at Christmas 1971. It had been so used that the entire text was separated from the binding and now it exists in two pieces in the case. My hardcover RSV was annotated throughout. Underlining, highlighting, pencilled comments and other scribbles fill the pages. During my student days I even outlined the documentary hypothesis in four colors – "J" was pink, "E" was green, "D" was purple, and "P" was blue – and inside the back cover I had taped a list of the Old Testament writings in chronological order which I had worked out one summer while living on a farm in Saskatchewan. Later I then read the Old Testament in that fashion and found some of the more obscure writings made far more sense. I had paid 50 cents for that Bible at a small used book shop (the name of which has now slipped my mind) situated on Hawthorne Avenue in Portland; I had gotten about two million miles of use out of it over many years. A colleague in the

Classics Department told me the other night as we rode on the bus together that "J" and "E" of the old documentary hypothesis didn't exist anymore. So much for the pink and green in the old Bible!

The age of books is rapidly slipping into the past, so far as physical tomes are concerned. A few weeks ago two of my colleagues discovered vast numbers of library books being discarded on my own campus, 40,000 at last count, tossed unceremoniously into huge steel bins out the back doors of the library to be carried away by trucks to the dump. I watched with horror as the truck driver confiscated several huge volumes from the bin, arranged these on the ground in a short stack upon which to place one of the legs of the hydraulic lift needed to raise the book-laden bin onto the truck for removal. One conscientious colleague kindly carried several volumes to my office where we later discovered that library staff had neatly written therein: "Not held in another edition, too valuable to discard." I am a curiosity to many of my students. All four walls of my office feature floor to ceiling books, neatly arranged on shelving, displaying all 7,000 volumes. Actually I have six walls. Two of these were created out of book cases, placed back to back, dividing the office into two rooms. These additional walls are likewise entirely filled with books: twelve feet wide, fifteen feet long, and nine feet high. I take great comfort being surrounded by a veritable fortress of learning and important knowledge. I often comment to visitors: This room represents the man I once aspired to be. The journey continues.

The preacher of Ecclesiastes said that of the making of many books there is no end. True enough and so it should be. Many years ago a pastor's wife on the Canadian Plains told a friend of mine: "It's too bad that Thomas has done all that reading and studying for it has only caused him to lose his faith." She was right. I had lost my faith but in losing my faith I had become grounded in *the* faith. Which was more important? In a way, both were vital. Christ said: "People shall not live on food alone but by every word that comes from the mouth of God." In the last year or so I have read things as divergent as Dorothee Soelle's,

Theology for Skeptics, Howard A. Goss's, *The Winds of God*, and John Spong's, *Here I Stand*, which the monk gave me for my birthday and which I had Spong sign after a public talk at Canterbury University in Christchurch. It is wonderful to think that the word of God comes to men and women through many books. While Christ is still my center, Christianity is not my limit.

Family, food, and fellowship

Strangers, Food and an Empty Pail

The aphorism "you are what you eat" is only true in a very qualified sense. But the connection between life and food is obvious. If one does not eat, one cannot live, not at least for very long. Regular physical nourishment is essential to health, wholeness and well-being. In one sense the gospel reading is all about food. It is an invitation to a meal, a meal with a difference. In this wider discourse of Jesus in John chapter six there are at least forty four references to eating or to food. And it is noteworthy that according to New Testament scholars John 6:51-8 is one of the most discussed and disputed passages in the entire fourth gospel.

There are many assumptions or customs associated with food and with eating. When I was a boy, for example, I could not leave the table until I had cleaned off my plate. But in other contemporary cultures and areas of the world it is considered rude if you do clean off your plate. It is an affront to the hostess or the cook. Some people will not eat until grace has been said before a meal. In western civilization it is customary to use utensils like forks, knives and spoons when eating. Elsewhere, one eats with one's bare hand regardless of what might be offered as the meal. Our culture also practices the social convention of eating together. So it is not unusual to say to someone, let's have lunch, or let's get together for dinner sometime soon. Indeed, a great deal of our social rhythms revolve around food and the practice of eating.

Food. Did you know that potatoes were banned in some parts of Europe as late as the eighteenth century because they were thought to cause leprosy and other diseases? A lack of food results in starvation; the fate of all too many in our world. The wrong sorts of food or foods ill-prepared can produce poisoning. As long ago as the ninth century in various parts of Europe there were outbreaks of ergotism – people poisoned by their daily bread. Rye is susceptible to a particularly virulent fungus called ergot that contains twenty poisons including the powerful hallucinogen lysergic acid diethylamide – LSD. In France this malady was called "St. Anthony's Fire." It wreaked absolute havoc upon the communities and persons afflicted by the poisoning. Of course too much food can result in gluttony; one of the medieval seven deadly sins. Physicians in Europe in the Middle Ages and well into the early modern period proscribed diets that were detrimental to many patients based upon what we now know as faulty ideas about different kinds of food. Anthropologists have suggested that the introduction of cooking may have been one of the decisive factors leading our species from a general animal existence into one more fully human. There is no denying the importance of food to life.

When we turn to the subject of religion, we find that the topic of food has always been an important consideration. Religious laws frequently listed banned various foods – sometimes very long lists – making rigid adherence to such curious regulations nearly impossible for the poorest peasants. For example, in Judaism there are numerous dietary laws. There are also strict prohibitions against the mixing of meat and dairy products. Households conducted on ritual principles require two sets of pots, two sets of dishes, and two sets of silverware – one for meat and the other for milk dishes – in order to avoid this form of contamination and the violation of religious regulations on food. In some areas of contemporary Hindu India, hunger remains a real issue while fresh fruit and vegetables are regularly offered to any number of the thirty-three million deities at shrines and the option of eating any of the 283 million cows that roam freely around India is not even considered even for the slightest moment. The Qur'an notes a number of prohibited foods for Muslims. And medieval Christians were not supposed to eat certain foods on certain days at particular times of the year.

Cutting right through all of this, Jesus has something new to say about food. He announces that he is the living bread. He boldly declares that those who eat of this bread will gain eternal life. That is, he claims, because the bread he refers to is his flesh which has evidently been given for the life of the world. Strange words indeed. What can he possibly mean? It is important to note that the food Jesus refers to is not our food. It does not belong to us. Sometimes we think that it is and we try to control who can actually eat. But the food Jesus speaks of is not ours: It is what is given to you and I as gift.

Jesus says: "I am the living bread. My flesh is food indeed." What does he mean? Are we to understand his words in a literal sense? On 13 October 1972 Uruguayan Air Force Flight 571 crashed into the Andes Mountains between Argentina and Chile. The plane was carrying the rugby team of Stella Maris College in Montevideo. They were travelling to play a match in Santiago, Chile. The survivors spent seventy two days at an elevation of more than 11,000 feet high in the Andes before they were rescued. They survived for one reason alone and that was because they ate the flesh of their dead friends. By cannibalizing their colleagues, they lived. The flesh of their friends saved their lives. Early Christian narratives contain various lurid tales of shocking cannibalism wherein communities of Christians were truly suspected of actually devouring human flesh and imbibing human blood. Is this what Jesus had in mind when he uttered those words to the gathered crowds?

In verse 52 John tells us that those who heard him "disputed violently with each other." They were taken aback. They were not amused. The whole thing sounded rather preposterous to them and their reaction was anything but passive. They argued and debated most strenuously. And those who knew him best, the disciples of Jesus, his friends and closest associates, regarded the words of their leader with a mixture of contempt and astonishment. "What a crock. Who can possibly take this seriously?" or as the New English Bible translates the Greek: "This is more than we can stomach! Why listen to such talk?"

I am not one of those who believes that everything in Scripture has to make sense or has some hidden meaning which if we scour about the text long enough and hard enough it will emerge. Nor do I believe that all Scripture is equally important, or even yet that every line in the Bible is important. But this is not one of those narratives that might be dismissed or relegated to the unimportant sayings. I would suggest that what Jesus is communicating to his hearers is a metaphor. In a rather unusual fashion Jesus seems to suggest that entrance to eternal life is available to those who join themselves to Jesus and become one with him. But the question remains: How does that happen? In the fifth century St. Augustine commented tersely: "Believe and you have eaten already." In the twelfth century, Bernard of Clairvaux argued that the one who follows the example of Christ and suffers with Christ will live with Christ. It is entirely possible that verses 53-56 have Eucharistic application. However, it is important to note that nowhere does John record the institution of Holy Communion. This means that from a strictly literary point of view chapter six cannot technically be regarded as a direct commentary on the sacrament. But noting the date for the composition of the fourth gospel, in the last quarter of the first century, it is fair to say that John assumes the Eucharist. And John's disciple Ignatius of Antioch in writing to the community of Christians at Ephesus around the year 115 spoke of "breaking one bread that is a medicine of immortality to live in Jesus Christ evermore." There is a line of common thought between John's representation of Jesus and Ignatius. Eternal life, the medicine of immortality. It is the same thing. In the *Book of Common Prayer* we find these words in the liturgy for the Eucharist: "Take and eat this in remembrance that Christ died for you and feed on him in your heart by faith with thanksgiving." That said, if these words of Jesus relate to Holy Communion I do not believe that these words of Christ about eating and drinking must be limited to the sacrament.

The medieval German mystic Meister Eckhart, who died in 1329 once asked the question: "What does it mean to me that the son of God was born in a manger 1300 years ago if he is not born in my heart each day?" That is the question to which Jesus provides an answer. Preaching on this same Johannine text in 1531 Martin Luther declared the bread of life enabled men and women to become one with Christ. Elsewhere he argued that this union is closer than a husband and wife, closer than any human relationship we can imagine. Throughout his narrative John does not seem to allow for any religious life or meaning outside of Jesus. But what is remarkably characteristic of Jesus is that he is consistently the man for others. And this oneness which the passage alludes to is in the end more than metaphor, especially if we explore the motif in Paul; the whole business is more than the historical Jesus inspiring us. Indeed, in one sense these words of Jesus proclaim the Christian gospel of redemption, they articulate an important aspect of the kingdom of God, and they underscore the meaningful fellowship available in Christ.

Sustenance for life. It's about food and water. John's narrative tells us more. The scenario was a very unlikely one. He was a Jew and beyond that an itinerant teacher. He was one of those many strangers who roamed the wastelands of Judea, up hillsides and down valleys who could be found among the caves, in deep ravines, on steep cliffs, praying, meditating, talking to themselves, contemplating their own navels, muttering odd things about catastrophes and evil, or sleeping under boulders, searching the night skies for answers or direction. He had a motley group of disciples who generally followed him everywhere and these constituted a strange lot in themselves.

She, on the other hand, was not a Jew. She was a Samaritan! Public opinion in that day from a Jewish perspective already had two strikes against her based only on this meagre information. Gender and ethnic heritage were definitely not commendations in this case. A little later we learn that she had a thing for men. This was not a bad thing in itself but there had been five already who had come and gone and she was presently working on number six. It is not entirely clear what all this means, but there is the possibility that this woman could not be viewed as a role model for those concerned with piety and morality. It does mean that a third strike had been called and this person was definitely out. From the perspective of any God-fearing Jew, this lady was bad news, *persona non grata*, a three-time loser. A woman! A Samaritan woman no less! On top of that, a man-chasing Samaritan woman! This was more than enough to prompt a Torah-quoting Pharisee to curse in Hebrew.

The contradictions, incompatibilities and unlikelihood aside, here they were, the Lamb of God, as John the Evangelist called this itinerant teacher, and that woman of questionable reputation chumming up together on a bench near Jacob's old well. The discourse turned out to be about nourishment. Evidently, he had stopped there to rest and had only asked the woman for a drink since he had no bucket himself. She could not believe that he, of all people, would ask her, of all people, to pour him that drink, as it were. After all, everyone knew that Jews and Samaritans hated each other. The animosity was long and deep. They were both quite convinced they could get along very well without the other, thank you very much indeed! She had come to the well with an empty pail to get a bucket of water. After communing with the Jewish stranger she went home from the well with a life overflowing with a different sort of water, a kind of brew he mysteriously called a "spring of water welling up to eternal life."

But now back to the idea of food. A poor family saved up for years in order to purchase tickets to sail from Europe to America. Once they put out to sea they carefully rationed the bread and cheese they had brought with them. After three days, the boy complained about the steady diet of cheese sandwiches. The father gave him a coin and told him to go to the ship's galley and buy an ice-cream cone. The young fellow was gone so long his parents began to worry. Pretty soon he returned. "Where were you?" the father asked. "Oh, I was down in the galley eating a steak dinner, ice cream and dessert." "You got all that for one coin?" "No, no," the boy told his father, "all the food is free. It comes with the ticket."

When it comes to the real meal; when it comes to the question of eternal life; there is very little you or I can bring to the table. In fact, it's included with the ticket and the ticket is the gift of God. The whole unlikely scene is somewhat reminiscent of those old-fashioned Sunday school picnics many churches used to have years ago. Everyone was encouraged to come and bring their own dinner and everyone would eat together. It always sounded like a great idea but you got home late that day and at the last minute realized you had to take your own food. Murphy's law kicks in. You frantically check the cupboards, the fridge and the pantry. Of course! At the top of the "To Do" list, pasted on the wall, is grocery shopping. There is just nothing much to be found. But then, hidden in the back of the fridge under an empty bag you find a piece of old dried-up baloney. There is just enough mustard left in the jar that you get most of it all over your knuckles just trying to get it out. Luckily, there are two pieces of bread left and one is the heel. Unfortunately, both are stale. However, there is not enough time to go to the store and still make it to the picnic. So you slap the baloney onto the thin coat of mustard between the two slices of stale bread, wrap it up in brown paper, because the sandwich bags are all gone, and you hurry off to the picnic. When the time comes to eat lunch, you sit at the end of a table, pull the rather wretched sandwich out of the bag and spread it out on the table and prepare to choke down your own miserable lunch.

You glance over at the people sitting next to you. The lady of that family was obviously a great cook and had spent a lot of time preparing for this occasion. There was fried chicken, potato salad, home-made rolls (fresh from the oven), baked beans and, to top it all off, a banana-cream pie. To make matters worse, they spread the entire scrumptious feast out on the table beside you. There you are with your baloney sandwich laid out for the world to see. It now looks less like a crummy sandwich and more like something the cat dragged in that the dog would not eat (as Parker D. Mitchell would say). Talk about mortification.

But the family with the great feast, looks over at you and at your baloney sandwich and they say: "Hey friend, what do you say we just put it all together?" The best you can do is a murmured comment like: "O, I just couldn't do that. I couldn't even think of it." But they continue to insist, and they truly mean it. "Oh come on," they all say, "we have plenty of everything, we can't possibly eat it all ourselves and besides we just love baloney sandwiches and we haven't got any." So you relent and the next thing you know your creepy baloney sandwich has been incorporated into the great picnic feast. There you sit, eating like a king when you had come just a few moments before as a pauper.

The woman from Samaria had come with her empty pail, hoping to fill it with well water. Instead, she found something much better – she discovered living water. In other words, she put her empty pail on the ground, sat down by the well, spread out her Samaritan baloney sandwich on the bench by Jacob's old well. What happened next was that she found herself partaking of that Jewish stranger's fried chicken and realizing that it really satisfied her in ways she had never dared to dream of. The gourmet meal was free. She did not have to earn it or pay for it. It was all part of the ticket. The stranger at the well really did not need her old baloney sandwich but the truth was, she desperately needed the food that he had to offer.

Two rather odd people sitting together by an old well. What a strange situation. But God was there. It all says something rather wonderful about the surprises of the Spirit, the needs of humanity and the idea that when one least expects it, God is there and salvation, in its many dimensions, breaks through once again. The combination of these three is always an epiphany of light, hope and redemption.

In the name of the one who fills every empty vessel, we dare to say these things. Amen.

THE TARNISHED KNIGHT

It was early spring; the air was cold and crisp and filled with the sounds of the wilds. A trace of late winter snow still clung tenaciously to the vegetation on the floor of the forest cathedral. High above in the soaring spires of the pines the wind rustled gently and mysteriously. I was standing directly above the head waters of the Metolius River in Central Oregon. I watched those life-bearing waters for quite a long time; they seemed to spring up from the depths of primordial existence and their perpetuation seemed eternal. The waters here are crystal clear and pure, and possess almost a divine aura. Yet the course these waters follow in their ever-flowing odyssey is strewn with rocks and sand and gravel. These rocks are cracked and badly broken and some are smashed into fragments of a former existence. Yet this broken and shattered corridor holds the life of the river in its lap and ceaselessly guides the new-born waters along their journey to the sea. As strange as it may seem, the water and the rocks can serve as symbols for the ideas of ministry and ministers.

We sat on the floor together watching Bugs Bunny and Yosemite Sam wage yet another battle in their unending war. She was glad I had come by. The afternoon summer heat accentuated the awkwardness. We did not know each other that well; she had only been coming to the church for a short time. Sitting there on the floor in my tennis shoes, blue jeans and t-shirt that Tuesday afternoon presented a striking contrast to my image on Sunday mornings when I stand in the pulpit wearing liturgical vestments preaching. Yet as the perspiration beaded our brows we shared together, authentically, our lives and experiences at the level of simplicity and basic need. At length, when I rose to leave, she told me how much it meant to her for me to have come by. Then the door closed and I was left alone with my thoughts. There was something she had not told me. She really did not need to for I already knew. She could accept me sitting there on the floor of her home in my blue jeans, but she could not accept me standing in the pulpit wearing a clerical collar.

A dear friend once gave me a card on an occasion of farewell which, among other things, exhorted me: "Live in Christ, you have much to give." Between the lines, illegible to the uninformed eye, was another message: "You have much to give to others, but not to me. For I know you, I know who you are, I know your weaknesses, your struggles, and I know your sin! You do have a lot to give, but only to those who do not know you like I do." But Albert Schweitzer once said: "The beginning of all spiritual life is fearless belief in truth and its open confession." I do have weaknesses, I am a struggler, and I am a sinner. This I openly confess. But I am also a minister called by Christ, sustained by Christ.

There is a myth that is frequently associated with the idea of ministry. That myth upholds the idea that ministry is performed by "perfect" or "near-perfect" individuals in professional capacities. Nothing is further from the truth. Ministry is woundedness. The idea of a pristine, pure, uncontaminated approach to ministry simply does not exist, nor could it function in any realistic sense. The road to authentic ministry is always under construction. The sixteenth-century mystics, Teresa of Avila and John of the Cross, often complained that a clear path through creative and destructive spirits was not always evident. Indeed, ministry lacks magic and supernatural potions.

The essential ingredient in ministry must be the radical interaction of the "minister" with the need and despair of the needy and despairing. There is, of course, a risk that must be reckoned with. Who can chance to rescue someone from a burning building without risking the flames? Likewise, suffering cannot be alleviated without the healer entering into that suffering. The church must exist not as a museum for saints but as a hospital for sinners. The sinners who suffer in this hospital are not simply the poor and the lonely of the world. Lying on cots next to them are priests and priestesses. Without entering into this suffering there can be no true, lasting healing. As Albert Schweitzer put it: "On a stone on the river bank an old woman whose son had been taken sat weeping silently. I took hold of her hand and wanted to comfort her, but she went on crying as if she did not hear me. Suddenly I felt that I was crying with her, silently, towards the setting sun, as she was."

Those who dare to teach must never cease to learn and those who enter into ministry must never cease to recognize their own woundedness. "Having it all together" is an illusion propounded by those who ignore or deny their own humanness. Henri Nouwen sees the Messiah sitting wounded at the city gates with the wounded of the world. He suffers as they suffer, his weakness is as evident as theirs. The "sin" of the single One there is no different than the "sin" of the many. His wounds are open like the wounds of the tormented with whom he associates. Yet his wounds become a source of healing, wholeness and restoration. The robed individual behind the pulpit and the altar can be no different from those who stand before him or her. Only the charter members of the eternal childhood of the believer club imagine otherwise. The minister is a fellow struggler with those around him or her. Like the masses on every hand, those in ministry have not arrived; they are but fellow travellers. They live in the desert with the nomads of humanity, all seek hope, peace and fulfilment. The search for freedom is shared by priest and pauper alike; neither has an advantage, neither really leads the way. Both struggle together and both arrive together – wounded, struggling, halting. In fact, the greatest irony of all is that the one who at last confronts us with ourselves and with our weaknesses, but who provides "total help for total need," as Karl Barth put it, is neither a superman nor a magician but the God who knows what suffering is, who is also on a journey, suffering, but healing the sufferers along the way.

The last temptation of Christ was indeed the temptation to deny his own humanity. His greatest crisis was to accept and come to grips with his essential humanness. In the living out of his weaknesses, he healed the woundedness of the one and the many, and his own woundedness became healing and the power of God.

The church is people, together on a voyage into the Great Unknown. Ministry is the authentic practice of suffering with the sufferer, of dying with the dying, and in the end, achieving mutual hope and freedom. What price can one place on freedom? I saw Terry Waite in Cambridge not long after he was released from his years of captivity in Lebanon. An Anglican church envoy, Waite had been working to secure the release of hostages in Beirut when he was seized in 1987. I remember him vividly riding a bicycle across Jesus Green, breathing heavily, sweating, the wind in his hair, pedalling hard. Free.

I stand in the pulpit, wounded. I sit on the floor with a friend, wounded. In both cases I am the same man. We are all fellow travellers, wounded in one way or another. But the headwaters of God are crystal clear and as they flow among the shattered brokenness of our lives the cleansing stream cools the pulsating heat of common weakness, struggle, sin and woundedness. And here the spirit of Jesus Christ lingers gently and, as Gerard Manley Hopkins once put it so adroitly: "The Holy Ghost over the bent world broods with warm breast and with ah! bright wings," bringing healing, wholeness and forgiveness.

ARE YOU SAVED?

Thirty-five years ago I inherited a car. That car had a bumper-sticker on the back end that read: "Are you lost? Jesus saves." The first thing I did upon acquiring that car was to painstakingly remove that bumper-sticker. Without context, I considered the message incoherent and silly. However, the idea of escape and being saved is an altogether serious one. The language of "being saved" is short-hand for emphases one encounters more often in evangelical churches than in Episcopal churches. I doubt very much there is a literal, eternal hell from which one needs to be saved. But there are plenty of things in life one may need to be saved from. Psalm 97 speaks of the lightning of the Lord and of mountains melting like wax. This sounds all very dramatic. In the Acts of the Apostles we read a startling narrative filled with dramatic phenomena that includes divination, fortune-telling, money-making schemes, exorcism, arrest, false accusations, a public uproar, severe flogging, imprisonment, a midnight earthquake, chains falling off the wrists and ankles of inmates, doors springing open on their own accord, attempted suicide, conversion, baptism, the cessation of a miscarriage of justice, all in a single day! What excitement. Welcome to exciting and high-flying Philippi! The background to these events in the Acts of the Apostles is a sea voyage across the northern Aegean Sea from Troas (in Turkey), a hop, skip and a jump, an island stop-off, before arrival in Philippi. On board that ship is St. Paul and his travelling companions. The story takes place in Philippi, the leading city of the Roman colony of Macedonia. A young slave girl had been following Paul around for several days. We have no indication he minded her presence. She kept shouting: "These men are servants of the most high God who proclaim the way of salvation." This went on hour after hour, day after weary day. Finally Paul told her to "shut up!" She was telling the truth alright, but

Paul was sick of it. In twelfth-century France, Peter Abelard once said that the same thing over and over is the mother of all weariness. The mother of all weariness finally got Paul's goat that day in Philippi. Had Paul known anything about "Miranda v. Arizona (1966) he may have said to the girl somewhat acidly: "Why don't you exercise your right to be silent!"

There is every indication that the slave girl was possessed and Paul performed an exorcism on the spot. He becomes the Exorcist of Philippi and there were immediate implications and consequences. The owners of the girl had been happy up to that point to let Paul and his group do whatever they wanted, right up until it cost them. The power of the purse should never be underestimated. There are people who will not run the risk of standing up for principle out of fear the bishop won't allocate any more money to the local parish. There are people who control churches through their cheque books! This is not anything new. Indeed, the history of this sort of thing is rather long and sometimes quite sordid. "Dearly beloved, we are gathered here together, in the name of the Lord God, to make money!" That cliché often carries more weight in reality than one might suppose at first blush.

Ron Hubbard once quipped: "If you want to make a little money, write a book. If you want to make a lot of money, start a religion." He did both and accomplished both. His quip is likely true, in many cases, but there is a price for that sort of policy. That cost is illustrated by a sobering tale of Thomas Aquinas in the thirteenth century visiting Rome and being shown the treasures of the Church. The guide showing Thomas the wealth and splendor said: "Peter can no longer say, Silver and gold have I none." To this Thomas replied: "And neither can he say, Rise up and walk." Therein comes the rub. So when the owners of the fortune teller saw that Paul had knocked a serious dent in their business, they took immediate steps to see that Paul and Silas were punished. They were detained. They were brought up on charges (as it were) right there and then in the "marketplace." I imagine Luke meant specifically the "court house." That area in ancient Philippi has now been excavated and archaeologists have determined that the court and prison were located there in the "marketplace." After a bit of a kangaroo court session, Paul and Silas were severely flogged – without due process I might add – and thrown into prison. The incumbent warden was given strict orders the two troublemakers were to be watched closely. The authorities were not going to risk any more social disturbances. The stage is now set for some rather dramatic nocturnal events.

The narrative written up by Luke within the pages of the Acts of the Apostles is a story of escape, though one that's a bit unconventional. Escape tales in ancient cultures often featured conventional themes: Prisoners were often to be found singing despite their incarceration, the intervention of angels or supernatural beings frequently occurred, and doors sometime did mysteriously swing open, and so on. At midnight there was an extraordinary event inside the prison. First, an earthquake struck without warning. The geological history of this region reveals that earthquakes were rather common. This seismic activity at midnight created a crisis situation. The crisis was both immediately good in the sense that the inmates were free to escape. We know that at least some of them had been unjustly treated. The crisis was bad inasmuch as the security of Philippi was threatened and the warden was so fearful of the developing situation that he took steps to kill himself. This seems rather drastic. We must pause to ask why the warden would think to take such immediate and extreme measures. Apparently in that culture, prison administration were held liable if inmates escaped. We need look no farther than Acts 12:19 for evidence of sentries being killed following St. Peter's miraculous prison break escape. Presumably, the head of the Philippian prison considered it more honorable to kill himself than to await the inevitable humiliation of being found derelict in duty and sentenced to an ignominious execution.

But before the panicked-stricken warden could plunge the sword into himself, two surprising outcomes must be noted. First, none of the prisoners attempted to make a getaway. Frankly, this seems rather improbable, but then secondly, the warden up and abruptly converts to Christianity. He rushed to Paul the prisoner with the urgent query: "What must I do to be saved?" One must ponder precisely what the warden meant by his question. I do not think for a moment that the warden's query was a religious or theological question. Paul (and/or Luke) provide an immediate theological answer thereby turning this story into a religious event. It seems more natural to see the warden's anguished query as a sort of "my God, what are we going to do?" type of expression. This is often a normal and natural reaction to a crisis situation. These are cries of desperation, when one has come to the end of their tether, can see no escape, and imagine only the gloom and darkness of pain, suffering and loss. Surely each of us has been there. "What must I do to be saved?" For some reason, the warden of the Philippian prison turned to Paul and Silas (the newest inmates) at his moment of crisis. This is possibly on account of the fact that Paul had just prevented him from committing suicide. What sort of prisoner would intervene in such a manner? Being assured by Paul that things were not quite as dire as he initially assumed, the warden laid down his sword, called for light, and was saved.

Following Paul and Luke's lead this query – about salvation – becomes a religious question. And the answer depends upon one's persuasion. "What must I do to be saved?" Salvation is a religious category and different traditions provide different answers to what salvation consists of. In Islam, it means to gain paradise. In Judaism, salvation consists in fulfilling the law of God. For Hinduism, it implies release from worldly existence and union with Brahman (the supreme being or source of eternal life). Buddhism conceives of salvation as enlightenment (or nirvana). In Christianity, salvation historically has been thought to be eternal life in Christ (heaven). Within the Christian religion, there are various answers to the query "What must I do to be saved?" Possibly the Calvinist will say: Do nothing; it's already been determined whether one will be saved or lost. The Catholic will put stress on good works.

The Universalist is convinced that everyone will be saved, so there is really nothing to be done. The story in the Acts of the Apostles conveys an important truth. Rather than engaging in an academic discourse or discussing abstract theology to make my point, I am going to follow the example of Luke in the *Acts* and share several stories that will shed light on this business of being saved.

In 1862 Henry David Thoreau lay dying. A visitor came to see him and asked: "Henry David, have you made your peace with God?" Thoreau replied: "I didn't know we'd had a quarrel." Jesus prayed in the Gospel lesson for today that they all might be made one in love, and through love. Does this include Judas, and all those, all of us, cowards and betrayers too, mired in misery in all of the deep dark places in our world? What shall be our escape? How shall we be saved?

There may be many answers to the question of what prevents one from being saved from whatever it is one needs to be saved from. The famous scholar of world religions and mythology Joseph Campbell once told of an exercise he underwent in Kentucky years ago. A group formed and decided upon a ritual. They spent a day thinking about seven things they would not want to live without. "What are the seven things for which you feel your life is worth living?" Then they gathered seven small objects to represent the seven cherished things and each one had to remember which represented which. In the evening they went down a wooded road in the dark to a cave. A wooden door covered the mouth of the cave. A man stood there wearing the mask of a dog, representing Cerberus at the mouth of hell. He put out his hand and asked for one of the seven objects that represented the thing you least cherished of the seven. Then they went into the cave itself. On five further occasions thereafter they were asked to surrender that which they least cherished until each of the participants were left with the object they treasured most. And in the process each of them discovered what they valued most. The precise order in which one surrendered each object also was important in helping each person know the order of their priorities and

values. Then the people came to an exit where there were two people
between whom one had to pass. And before each could exit they had to
surrender what they cherished most! Most who did this spoke of an
experience of "release" when they gave up everything. Much of what we
hold onto may be some form of bondage; commitments, expectations,
limitations, the feelings of "ought" and "should," obligations, rules to
keep, restrictions, fears and so on. Campbell said that watching those
earlier bondages go changed one's feeling for the treasures one had
given up. It increased one's love for one's treasures without the tenacity.

But let us return briefly to Philippi. "What must I do to be saved?" The
prison warden provides us with a template. First, one must lay down
one's sword, whatever that sword might be. To be saved means to
surrender. Salvation is not something that can be obtained by wielding
our own swords of self-sufficiency. It might mean laying down in a fire
in the path of an oncoming big fire. Second, one must step into the light
like the warden in the Philippian prison did. In the Christian context
this light is the light of Christ. Third, one must let go of those things we
all hold onto which are perhaps more bondage than liberation. Money
and possessions have nothing at all to do with being saved. Perhaps one
needs to escape from all those bondages too. Fourth, one must simply
accept the gift. Believe on Jesus and be saved.

In John 17 Jesus speaks of love and unity. In Revelation 22 the thirsty
are invited to drink the water of life as a gift: "The Spirit and the Bride
say: "Come." Let everyone who hears say, "Come." Let everyone who
is thirsty "Come." Everyone who wants to drink the water of life as a gift,
"Come." The water of life, the gift of love and the promise of unity. This
is what it means to be saved. Will we accept this gift?

In the name of the one who searches for the lost and never gives up on
those in despair, we dare to say these things. Amen.

How far is it to Bethlehem?

The disturbing truth is that there was no room for Jesus in the overcrowded inn. Theologians and preachers have made much of this as though the inn keeper was a vile knave, a nasty fellow, a contemptible scoundrel, who maliciously put the young couple out into the winter night. That, however, is just rhetoric. That there was no room was perhaps was no one's fault. Had Joseph made reservations? Had Mary given any thought to the fact that the hotels and inns in Bethlehem might all be filled when they arrived? We can never be sure of the historical circumstances but the fact is that when they arrived in Bethlehem there was no vacancy. Tradition tells us they spent the night either in a barn or more likely a cave. Bethlehem was the end of their journey. For Christian pilgrims travelling through the season of Advent, the many roads lead to another kind of Bethlehem.

The journey through Advent brings us to confrontation with the good news of Christ's coming. It forces us to look backwards to the historic birth of Christ but also calls us to look forward to his coming again in the hearts and lives of people everywhere. In this active looking, we are compelled to pause amid all of our words and singing and keep silence. It is impossible, however, not to ask the query: Just how far is it to Bethlehem? The mood is one of expectation, anticipation, longing, excitement, and appearance. Two millennia ago the announcement of the way to Bethlehem was made in a most curious fashion illustrated by a half-naked, loud-mouthed, apparent lunatic stalking the deserts of the ancient Near East. This was a strange figure indeed aimlessly roaming the Judean wilderness, wild, uncouth, and somewhat scary. "There was a man sent from God: His name was John. He came for the purpose of giving witness." What better introduction could a person have than the recommendation that they had been sent from God. What was John's message? Listen to his sermons: "I am the voice of one crying in the wilderness, make straight the way for the Lord." "Repent, for the kingdom of heaven is at hand." "There is one who is coming after me." "Behold the Lamb of God who takes away the sin of the world."

Such preaching invites reflection and even anticipation. This is perhaps illustrated best by a young girl, probably all of 12 or 13 years old, who discovered herself in a rather uncomfortable, painfully awkward, even embarrassing situation. She was pregnant outside of legal wedlock in a culture that tended to not look favorably upon "loose women" and the shenanigans that evidently caused her condition in the first place. Still, there was something extraordinary about this girl and this situation for the Lord was with her and her story is one of trial and triumph.

> Mary was the first one to carry the gospel
> Chosen by the Father and favored by his grace
> Delivered to a sinful world through a precious little virgin girl
> The first to hold him to her breast, and the first to look upon his face.
>
> See her in the evening time
> Struggling up a hillside
> Months were swiftly passing by, her time was close at hand
> Turning with a painful eye, from those so quick to criticise
> That tiny beating heart within, was more than she could understand.

How far is it to Bethlehem? For Mary it must have seemed an eternity since the angel had appeared to her with those momentous words that even she could scarcely understand at the time: "You have found favor with God. You will give birth to a son. He will be great and will be called the Son of the Most High. His kingdom will have no end." It is recorded that Mary's reply was one of wonderment: "My soul magnifies the Lord and my spirit rejoices in God my Savior. From now on all generations will call me blessed, for the Mighty One has done great things for me and holy is his name." But as the days and weeks and months dragged on, the question became increasingly more urgent: Just how far is it to Bethlehem?

After the traditional four week long journey through Advent, Christians reach Bethlehem. There should be a star to mark the spot, but if our sources are right it won't be much. Just a small cave, perhaps a barn. A few animals will be there too (well, after all that is where they lived), a bewildered carpenter named Joseph who was not quite sure whether he ought to be proud or embarrassed, a young mother named Mary and a manger. Lying amid a farm-like scent in that manger will be a child. According to the Christian faith, the child lying there is much more than a new-born baby. The Nicene Creed sums it up this way: "God of God, Light of Light, very God of very God, who for us and for our salvation came down from heaven." So this is Bethlehem. The word became flesh, wrote John the Evangelist, and lived among us. This is exactly what Incarnation means. In Bethlehem, it is rather untheological. It is also surprisingly unsophisticated. With the smell of animal dung and farm odour, it is truly undignified. Wait! Could this be the right Bethlehem? According to Christianity this is the place and this is the way things are. That was then, 2,000 years ago, this is now. Will it be any different in contemporary, post-modern Bethlehem?

How far is it to Bethlehem? After the lonely vigil, the hoping, personal preparations, anticipation and joy, and after the long journey we arrive at long last at our contemporary Bethlehem. The lights are just up ahead. The star does seem to have finally stopped in its weary westward journey. There are "wise men" and fools, saints and shepherds, kings and crooks, all making their way to Bethlehem just like you and I. We pause. We pray. We hear the strains of the medieval verse: "O come, O come, Emmanuel and ransom captive Israel. Who mourns in lowly exile here, until the Son of God appear."

In our own time, just as it was in that first Advent season, there are two discrete searches underway for Christ. In some ways, while the details have changed, the two searches now mirror the two searches then. Two thousand years ago the Magi travelled all the way from the east (wherever that is). They were sincere in their search for Christ. When they arrived in Jerusalem, another search for Christ began. King Herod summoned the Magi to a secret meeting and found out from them the exact time the star had appeared. He urged them on to Bethlehem saying: "Go and make a careful search for the child. As soon as you have found him, report to me, so that I too may go and worship him." Herod might well have said "worship" to the Magi, but he was clearly thinking murder. Herod's inquiry amounted to an insincere search for Christ.

How far is it to Bethlehem? What are our motives for making the journey? Is it to worship the Christ, or is it just idle curiosity? Do we make the trip out of fear, or does love draw us there? It seems as though everyone is heading that way, today, just as they were then. Joseph said to Mary: "Let's go to Bethlehem." King Herod instructed the Magi: "Go to Bethlehem." Angels appeared to shepherds in the hills singing: "Glory to God in the highest and peace, good will to all people." The shepherds said to each other: "Let's go to Bethlehem." So they came, from here and there, far and near to the city of David, to Bethlehem. For us, the many hopes and fears of all the years come together tonight in Bethlehem, just as they did so long ago and so far away.

How far is it to Bethlehem? He is as close as the mention of his name. Bethlehem is wherever men and women, in faith, reach out and receive him. Bethlehem is the end of every sincere search for Christ. Bethlehem is everywhere and nowhere. Bethlehem is God with us, revealed in us. When one reaches that ancient town one can sing again, for the first time, the words of the old medieval hymn: "Rejoice, rejoice, Emmanuel shall come to you, O Israel."

WHAT PHILIP WYATT AND
JOHN JACOB ASTOR HAVE IN COMMON

In the fall of 1991 Philip Wyatt, 57 years of age, was discovered in his bed in the Crumlin area of the city of Dublin. No one had seen or spoken to Wyatt in over three years. Actually, the council worker who broke into Mr. Wyatt's home found only his skeleton. Philip Wyatt had gone to bed in 1988 and died in his sleep. No one had missed him. In October 1993 Adele Gaboury, aged 73, was found beneath six feet of trash in the filthy kitchen of her dilapidated home in Worcester, Massachusetts. She had lain there four years. No one was concerned. In November 1998 Wolfgang Dircks, a 43 year old German man was found dead sitting in front of his television set with his Christmas tree lights flashing beside him in his Hamburg flat. He had been sitting there for five years. No one was alarmed by his absence. In March 2000 a chain of misfortunes led to three deaths in a small Munich, Germany apartment. An elderly woman evidently died of a heart attack. Her wheelchair-bound aged husband, coming to her aid, fell and broke his neck. Their little Yorkshire terrier starved to death. The three decaying bodies were found weeks later. Autopsies told the tale. Marinella Beretta lived alone in a house near Lake Como in northern Italy. Neighbours had not seen her in two-and-a-half years. Apparently, the 70 year old had sat down for a meal sometime in 2019. Her mummified body was discovered in 2022 still seated at the table of her last supper.

All of these people died alone. None of them were missed by anyone for weeks. Several were not missed for years. Their living and their dying had no impact or effect whatsoever. Holy Scripture says that no one lives to themselves and no one truly dies to themselves. Tell that to Mr.

Wyatt, Mrs. Gaboury, Mr. Dircks and the old couple in Munich. Death is a predator that stalks us all, but most of us have the hope that someone might be there when our time comes; that perhaps our lives might have made a difference to someone and that our presence might be missed. One of my New Zealand colleagues spent most of the night in her office marking end of term essays and completing other student assessments. At about 6:00 a.m. on a June morning in 1998 she went up onto the roof of a seven-storey building immediately adjacent to the building where my office was located and threw herself to the concrete below. A graduate student discovered her a short time thereafter. She was still alive but well beyond the hope of living. She was 35 years old.

Sarah Krauss was born on September 24, 1880 and died quietly in her favorite chair in Allentown, Pennsylvania on December 30, 1999 at the ripe old age of 119. Had she lived another 33 hours she would have lived in three centuries. Lucid to the end she could talk of her own memories of the Titanic tragedy, the opening of the Brooklyn Bridge, the Eiffel Tower, seven U.S. wars, the erection of the Statue of Liberty, Charles Lindbergh's solo flight across the Atlantic, Henry Ford's introduction of the Model T and Neil Armstrong's walk on the moon. I once saw a photograph of the former Sarah Clark taken in 1897 when she was 17. I thought she was lovely and I am sure that when the photo was taken she had no idea she had more than one hundred years left to live.

Death is an odd thing and one of the "four last things" according to medieval thinking: Death, judgment, heaven, hell. The tales about it are legion. Friedrich Nietzsche threw his arms around the neck of a horse in the Via Po in Turin and collapsed into a dementia from which he never recovered. Robert F. Scott wrote to his wife Kathleen from the Antarctic ice when all hope was lost and said: "I wasn't a very good husband. But I hope I shall be a good memory." In 1906 a nurse popped in to check on the Norwegian poet Henrik Ibsen and remarked that he seemed better today. His last words were: "On the contrary" and he promptly died. Cardiologists would do well to remember the famous last words spoken by Joseph Henry Green, a surgeon of the eighteenth century, as he was taking his own pulse: "Stopped." The parish register of Malpas, Cheshire in England tells us that while dying of the plague in 1625 Richard Dawson dug his own grave and then laid down to die in it. He was a large man, and, as he explained, he did not wish for his relatives to have to carry him to the cemetery once he expired. Dr. Samuel F. Upham, of Drew Theological Seminary, lay dying. Friends and relatives gathered. At length the question arose of whether or not the great man was still alive. Someone whispered: "Feel his feet. No one ever died with warm feet." At that precise moment Dr. Upham opened one eye and said: "Jan Hus did." Those were his last words.

Two weeks after a local man died a letter from the Greenville County Department of Social Services in South Carolina was dispatched to his home address: "Your food stamps will be stopped effective March 1992 because we received notice that you passed away. May God bless you. You may re-apply if there is a change in your circumstances." Death is that slow winding down of the experience we call life. Death, not sex, is the last taboo. Death is an essential part of life. One can avoid marriage, child birth and child rearing. One can avoid swimming, climbing, tennis and even driving an automobile. One can skip university and going to church. If one is really clever even paying taxes might be avoided. Death, on the other hand, will come for each of us and no amount of money, intelligence, cleverness or planning on our part can make it otherwise. Death is the price we pay for having life.

Life is a gift. What we do with that gift is up to us. It is silly to think that all people are created equal for nothing could be farther from the truth. Still, each of us have choices; some of us have more choices than others. Our lives can be sacred journeys or unholy catastrophes. We even have some control over death, at least its manner and timing, but not over its inevitability. In Christchurch an elderly lady died in June 2001. Among her personal effects was a note with very specific instructions that no man was to carry her coffin. As she put it: "The buggers wouldn't take me out in real life, and no men are taking me out now that I'm dead."

Most of us do not know the hour of our death. On the Titanic many did and it is remarkable the tales that have come down to us of those last minutes. John Jacob Astor, worth at that time 87 million dollars, helped load women and children into life boats. He waved good-bye to his pregnant wife Madeleine, lit a cigarette and waited to die. His last act was to rush below deck and free several dogs from their pens. Chief Steward Andrew Latimer gave his life jacket to a woman who had none and then went down with the ship. The thirty-four engineering officers stayed at their posts and kept the ship's lights going until two minutes before Titanic sank. They all were lost. Five postal clerks guarded the mail room with their lives and went to the bottom of the Atlantic with 3,364 bags of mail and more than 800 parcels. The chief baker Charles Joughin went below for a drink of whiskey and met one of the ship's doctors on a similar mission. Archie Butt, Arthur Ryerson, Frank Millet and Clarence Moore continued with their card game in the first-class smoking room until about twenty minutes before the ship went down. Benjamin Guggenheim and his valet Victor Giglo went to their state room, dressed in their formal evening wear and then appeared on deck. Guggenheim was quoted as saying: "We have dressed in our best and are prepared to go down like gentlemen." The managing director of Harland and Wolff, Thomas Andrews, sat stunned staring at a wall, his life jacket on the floor in front of him. Colonel Gracie bumped into the squash professional Frederick Wright and told Wright he thought he just might cancel his scheduled Monday morning slot. At the time the courts were already under water. Wallace Hartley's band played on until 2:10 a.m. until he dismissed them. None elected to leave and they stood and played another tune: "Nearer my God to thee." Captain E.J. Smith stayed on the bridge and went down with the ship. In third-class rooms Irish-Catholic immigrants recited the rosary while on the after deck Father Thomas R. Byles heard confessions. Jack Phillips, the wireless operator, stayed at his post and kept sending out distress calls until 2:17 a.m.

Philip Wyatt had nothing when they found him. John Jacob Astor had a gold watch, gold cuff links with diamonds, a diamond ring with three stones, £225 in British bank notes, $2,440 in American cash, £5 in gold, 50 francs and a gold pencil. Benjamin Guggenheim was dressed in his best and went down. Adele Gaboury went down in nothing special under six feet of trash. In one sense, they were equally alone. My 83 year old neighbor who lives alone told me she doesn't fear death but does not like the idea of lying there for days on end. As it turned out, Nina lived to be 100 and did not die alone. The last thing Jesus said was: "It is finished." That about sums it up. Whether in squalid inner city houses and tenement buildings or on luxurious ocean liners, the end is the same; the end is death.

The funny thing about all this is that the historic Christian faith speaks of the resurrection of the body. The body dies: Philip Wyatt expired in his bed and decayed there. John Jacob Astor died in the waters of the north Atlantic. Death was their common link. They might also have something else in common. The Bible calls it resurrection and life.

In the name of the one who infuses resurrection into every living thing, we dare to say these things. Amen.

New Jerusalem, New Brunswick

Westmorland Heights, Saint John, New Brunswick

Who is Christ for us Today?

The question, "who is Christ for us today?" is one that must be asked and answered by each generation. It is a serious query. Scholars devote books to the subject, ministers preach sermons and laypeople ponder. There are several reasons to support the idea that Jesus was in fact Mexican. His first name was Jesus, he was bilingual and he was frequently harassed by the authorities. But there are also good reasons for believing that Jesus was black. He called everyone "brother," he liked Gospel and he could not get a fair trial. There are compelling reasons why he might have been Jewish. He went into his father's business, he lived at home until he was in his thirties, he thought his mother was a virgin and she thought he was God. However, there are equally good reasons for assuming that he was Italian. He talked with his hands, he had wine with every meal and he used olive oil. That aside, there are several even better reasons to assume that Jesus was a Californian. He never cut his hair, he walked around barefoot and he started a new religion. None of this can be denied. Still, he might have been Irish. He never got married, he was always telling stories and he loved green pastures. But perhaps the most compelling evidence of all points to the fact that Jesus was a woman. He had to feed a crowd at a moment's notice when there was no food. He kept trying to get the message across to a bunch of men who just did not get it. Even when he was dead, he had to get up because there was more work for him to do. The humor only underlines the diverse opinions. But the question is indeed entirely valid.

From behind the gray walls of the Tegel Prison in Berlin in April 1944, the now-famous theologian Dietrich Bonhoeffer, waiting to die, wrote these stirring words to his friend Eberhard Bethge: "What is bothering me incessantly is the question what Christianity really is, or indeed who Christ really is for us today."

The Gospel of Luke tells the story of a man who went on a trip from Jerusalem to Jericho and was attacked by robbers who beat him up, stole his belongings and left him injured on the side of the road more dead than alive. A priest passed by, but seeing the carnage and perhaps fearing that the criminal gang was still lurking in the vicinity hurried on without offering any assistance. Another religious personality passing along had the same response. A Samaritan man, however, stopped, had compassion, offered first-aid, took the man on to the next village, arranged accommodation, and paid the charges. Who is Christ in this story? Surely not the priest or the Levite. Definitely not one of the robbers. The Samaritan? Well, that makes for good preaching. I suggest however that Christ is more likely the poor fellow lying there beaten, dying, neglected and ignored by the passers-by.

Who is Christ for us today? In Matthew's gospel Jesus describes the Last Judgment as a separation of the sheep from the goats. And the criteria for entrance into the kingdom is predicated upon a most unusual condition. Those on the right hand of the King are granted entrance for as Jesus says when "I was hungry you gave me food, when I was thirsty you gave me drink, when I was a stranger you welcomed me, when I was naked you clothed me, when I was sick you visited me, when I was in prison you came to me." When the righteous ones query this in great surprise, Jesus answers saying: "As you did it to the least of these my brothers and sisters, you did it to me." Those on the left hand are excluded on the same ground with the rejoinder that as they had failed to minister to others so likewise they had ignored Christ. As Martin Luther put it: "So it is that the world is full of God. You can find Christ in every street, outside your door; don't stare up into heaven." But where exactly is the dwelling place of God? In London, on City Road, is John Wesley's church. In front of the church a statue of Wesley can be seen with the words: "The world is my parish." Christ also seems to be saying that the world is his home.

The scene presented in Matthew 25 is truly a radical scene. The world has been gathered for judgment. Not only is the scene radical, the criteria for judgment is all the more so. From the vast sea of human faces each one in turn is singled out. No one is asked about creed. No one is examined on worship style. Not one is investigated about theological preference. It seems not to matter whether one was Catholic or Calvinist, Pentecostal or Arminian. There are no questions pertaining to doctrine. Instead, the entire process is concerned with social issues. Examining the text we find allusions to hungry and thirsty people, strangers, those destitute, sick and afflicted and people locked up in jails. These issues – hunger, thirst, sickness, destitution – are usually related to the underside of life. Those incarcerated constitute the socially disinherited and the stranger is symbolic of all those regarded as outsiders, aliens, those who are somehow different than the rest of us, those who do not fit in. Some of those judged are called blessed and righteous because they ministered to the outcasts. The rest are called cursed and sent off to punishment. What has all of this to do with the presence of God?

Again Luther reminds us that there is a difference between when God is there and when God is there for you. Perhaps not exclusively but God is there for humankind in the person of Christ. But where is Christ and who is Christ for us today? These people are Christ. Look into the eyes of the socially disinherited and the least of humankind and you will find the eyes of Christ looking back at you. Mother Teresa used to say of the poor in Calcutta that they were Christ. Perhaps this helps to explain why she devoted her life to them. Hers was an applied faith; a social gospel.

A minister and a soap maker were walking along a street in a rundown industrial area of a large city: "Well, as far as I can see," said the soap maker: "The gospel and the church have done nothing to improve the world." The minister was silent for a moment. Just then the two came upon a group of children playing in a ditch. They were covered with dirt and grime from head to toe. "Well, it seems to me," said the minister: "That your product has done nothing to clean up these kids." "Wait a minute," protested the soap maker: "Soap must be applied to be of any use." "Exactly," said the minister: "And so it is with the gospel."

The gospel must be applied and lived out in the world. It cannot be reduced to mere proposition or intellectual dogma. If it is reduced to that it has little to no effect. It would be like meeting a homeless person on the street who is very hungry and saying: "I have just what you need. It's an excellent recipe for chicken soup. All you need to do is put the ingredients in a pot, add water and stir while it heats up. It is very tasty and I am sure you will enjoy it." It is no good telling someone in need that you will pray for them and leaving them alone in their need.

The cross must again be raised at the center of the world; at the cross-roads, in the market-places of life. Jesus was not crucified in a cathedral between two candles. He died on a cross between two crooks on the garbage dump of the city. There were so many different types of people about that his offense had to be written in three different languages and pinned over his head as he died just so most people would know what sort of a fellow he was. He died at the place where evil-doers use filthy language, where thieves curse and swear and where godless soldiers gamble. He is no glistening figure in a religious house but rather the dishevelled, smelly wretch on a bench between two whores. It is time to stop romanticizing Jesus. It is time to leave our insulated houses of idolatry and imitate the incarnation.

Who is Christ for us today? He is perhaps the bum in the slums reeking of alcohol and urine. He is the disadvantaged child roaming aimlessly in the urban jungles of our cities. He is the migrant worker in the fields desperately trying to earn a living, clinging to a thread of hope. Who is

Christ for us today? He is also the hated, despised and discriminated homosexual. He belongs to the so-called ethnic minority, the one who is different because of religion, custom, color or language. Christ is the disease-ridden untouchable of a society steeped in individualism which has become too holy, too separate, to even touch the least of these. But this is where he died and this is what he died for.

Perhaps it is high time to take the gospel out into the world and make a difference. Give them not hell but hope and show them the kindness and everlasting love of God. The gospel should be lived in order to give the least of these courage, hope and empowerment. The least of these should be told in word and deed that they have not suffered alone for they are indeed part of the church. They are the people of God; they are Jesus in the here and now. Christ is crucified in these men and women just as he surely was crucified on a Roman cross two thousand years ago on a hill outside Jerusalem. The pain and suffering of the least of these, like his, will yield forth liberation and redemption.

Who is Christ for us today? Malcolm Muggeridge, the late iconoclast of British journalism put it this way: "And you Jesus? I never caught a glimpse of you in any holy shrine of Christendom, or in any paradise – unless you were that old black man smiling from ear to ear shining shoes on that cold windy Chicago street corner. Or that little woman with the lame leg in the Immigration Department in New York – that might have been you." Who is Christ for us today? The Spanish missionary to Latin America in the early sixteenth century, Bartolomé de Las Casas brought forward the passion of Christ to his own time: "Jesus Christ, our God, scourged, afflicted and crucified, not once but millions of times." The suffering of Christ is the suffering of God and this suffering cannot be limited to the historical Golgotha. The Christ present for us today is present in the world as the humiliated Christ; he is the beggar among the suffering and oppressed peoples of the world.

Those willing to take Christianity seriously must stand with God in God's hour of suffering and watch with Christ in Gethsemane. In our contemporary Gethsemanes we must not slumber and sleep as did the disciples of long ago. Two thousand years ago Gethsemane overlooked Jerusalem. Modern Gethsemanes tend to overlook other cities and communities. As Jesus wept over Jerusalem, so now he weeps over racial injustices, exploitation of the poor and other evils of our day. Who is Christ for us today? During my years in Portland I could tell of the man in a wheel chair who takes a knife when he goes to get his disability cheque for he is scared for his life. I could tell about the woman with two kids caught up in prostitution who says: "I just want someone to love me. I want to belong." Or the alcoholic man who says: "How can you challenge me to go on living? I am trying hard to drown out the memories." He had been attacked, raped, and set on fire. What of the pan handler who says: "Yes, I ask for money, but I just want someone to look in my eyes and recognize me as a person?" If we hurry past like the priest and the Levite, what kind of God do we communicate to the least of these?

Too often we look for God in all the wrong places or we restrict God, perhaps inadvertently, to the churches. Maybe we need to expand our conception of where God is and who Christ is for us today. In 1965 the United Church of Christ convened in Chicago. Among its proceedings was this "Litany from the Ghetto."

> O God, who lives in tenements, who goes to segregated
> schools, who is beaten in precincts, who is
> unemployed...help us to know you.
>
> O God, who is cold in the slums of winter, whose
> playmates are rats – four-legged ones who live
> with you and two-legged ones who imprison you
> Help us to touch you.

Who is Christ for us today? Christ is the poor, the marginalised, the exploited, those left out, those referred to in Matthew's gospel. God has always been concerned with social issues and has always challenged the people of God to practice all the social implications of their faith. The prophetic literature of the Hebrew Bible, especially books like Amos, exemplify this in their calls to maintain justice, share food with the hungry, bring the homeless into one's own home, to cease trampling the heads of the poor, to stop selling the needy for a pair of shoes and to do something about the human propensity for ignoring the afflicted.

John A.T. Robinson summed it up this way when he wrote that for all men and women there remains forever two paths. One road is crowded and it is still the one that inevitably leads to destruction. Many people find themselves travelling it. Even on that road each one reaches a point, near or far, where they encounter a figure stooped beneath the weight of a cross. Every person asks where he is going and the answer comes: "I am going to New York, to Kabul, to Portland, to Santiago, to be crucified again in your place. No one surely can bear that encounter forever. For at the intersection of time and eternity – nailed there with the nails of injustice and indifference – he confronts us as a perpetual reminder that in living we die but that in dying we live. This is the incarnation that is marvellous to contemplate and is indeed the light of the world and is the answer to the query: Who is Christ for us today?

Bayham Abbey ruins, Kent, England

Rattlesnake Mountains, Montana

MARY MAGDALENE'S STORY
...IN HER OWN WORDS

"Now on the first day of the week Mary Magdalene came to the tomb early, and while it was still quite dark [she] stood weeping outside the tomb...She turned around and saw Jesus standing...Jesus said to her, "'Mary.'"

John 20:1-18.

Almost 2,000 years have passed. I was one of the original disciples of Jesus. I loved him more than you will ever know. I loved him with my whole heart. I loved him with my whole life. Ever since the time he touched me and healed me I tried to love him by living with him and living for him. I travelled with Jesus along with two of my girlfriends – Joanna and Susanna – and to the best of my ability I supported Jesus financially and participated in his ministry. Unlike most of his other disciples I did not desert him but stayed with him right up to the end. I came from the city of Magdala – that's why they call me Mary the Magdalene – Magdala was a wealthy city in Galilee that had a pretty bad reputation. In fact the rabbis here in Jerusalem later said the city fell because of its overt licentiousness. So I am a Galilean. I came here to Jerusalem with Jesus several years ago along with Joanna and Susanna and some others. It is not often I get to tell my story but I think you should hear it...from me.

Most of you know something about me – since all four of the evangelists (Matthew, Mark, Luke and John) refer to me – but there has been a lot of things said about me that are not true. For centuries the church has told the story that I – Mary Magdalene – was a prostitute when I met Jesus. I was a sinner alright but I assure you there is no good reason to think I was sexually immoral. I never knew Luke but in his account of the life of Jesus he wrote that I had seven demons that Jesus delivered me from. That is true though you mustn't think that I was some raving lunatic, frothing at the mouth. Remember that all those years ago in first century Palestine we often called physical or spiritual illness demon possession. The fact that I was personally afflicted with seven demons does indicate the seriousness of my condition. I truly was in a sad state of affairs until Jesus called me.

Matthew and Mark – I knew both of them – tell a story in their gospels about a woman who brought an alabaster jar of ointment and anointed Jesus. That wasn't me. Luke wrote about a sinner woman who came and wept on Jesus' feet and kissed him and dried his feet with her hair and then anointed his feet with ointment. That wasn't me either. My good friend John also wrote the story of the gospel and he told a story about a woman who had been taken in adultery and the Pharisees brought her to Jesus ready to stone her to death. But Jesus refused to go along with them. He even told the woman he did not accuse her. What a wonderful story. It says so much about him. Lots of people have assumed that was me too but it wasn't. But I really was there with the Lord. I looked on. I followed. I served. I went with him to the end … and beyond.

There are many things I could tell you this morning about Jesus and my experiences with him but I think the most important thing I can share with you is an experience that not only changed me but changed the world. It's what happened after he died and the way John tells it is quite accurate – of course John and I talked about it many times – and it is, if I may be allowed to say so, the most humanly moving of all the stories about Jesus after his death. But let me tell it again in my own words as I remember it.

It was Sunday morning. He was dead! There could be no doubt about that. A couple of days earlier they had nailed him up there on that Roman cross between those two crooks. I saw it happen. I watched him be crucified. I stood there overcome with grief before his naked, blood-drenched body and I watched his life ebb out like grains of sand through a child's fingers: "It is finished." I heard him utter those last words through clenched teeth while quite literally dangling at the end of his rope. I stood there on the edge of the abyss, lost in the shame and agony of it all, and the storm seemed to recede about me.

It was dark then, as the sun hid its face, and it is dark now, as I stand before his tomb. What tortures I have gone through these last days since coming down from the place of The Skull. It is so quiet. It is silent. My heart beats wildly within my breast. I sense only the presence of his absence. I am so terrified that my whole body will not stop shaking. The emptiness, the stark horror of my own guilt press against me like thorns. The moon seems caught in the naked branches of the trees standing erect and motionless against the night now almost completely spent. "Why am I here?" The words come spilling out of my mouth before I can suppress them. Once spoken, I just let my feelings take on a life of their own in words. "The marrow of life has already been sucked out of my bones and I have come here to die with him, as it were, and yet, yet I have not lived. Surely I am raving mad to come to this awful place." My conscience screams out as if to mock me: "IT IS FINISHED!"

There is nothing to do now but run away and hide. But as I turn to make haste from this terrible place, someone stands there in the way. I did not recognize the face at first, but then my eyes flew open wide and I knew suddenly, somehow, he had returned. I wanted to doubt it but found myself strangely compelled to believe. I could not explain it and with great relief I felt no need to try. All at once, I was besieged with fear and I thought to leave, but then fear gave way to an urge to stay. I wanted to hide but found my arms wrapped around him before I could even think. Suddenly I found the oneness of sensing my own being intertwined with his in an embrace of life and in that moment the emptiness of my heart was filled with a fullness I had never known. Then he called me by my name: "Mary," and the sound of his voice caused something to explode within my breast. My tears of sorrow, grief and shame, became tears of joy and the aching of my heart became in an instant the warmth of a presence like none I had ever before imagined. The dim moon-light seemed to give way to radiant sunshine and the darkness had long since fled. The stark branches of the trees against the sky were now filled with the abundance of the fruits of spring and the whole world seemed strangely alive and well. That tomb of death on the side of the hill now burst upward and outward like a virtual fountain of refreshing, life-giving water.

In the moment that he touched me and called my name, thank God, I recognized him and I – Mary Magdalene – was freed – absolutely freed from the power of sin and released into resurrection and life. Oh! He breathed on me the breath of life and I received his holy spirit and he was no longer just my teacher but now he was my Lord.

Luke recorded the story of Cleopas (I knew Cleopas too) and his friend going to Emmaus and while they were with Jesus how their hearts literally burned within them. That's exactly what happened to me in the cemetery. My heart burned like hot fire within my breast when Jesus appeared; burned with an everlasting flame.

I do not know how it happened, but in the midst of this ecstasy, and beyond all my wildest hopes and dreams, I suddenly found myself no longer standing on the edge of the abyss, but on the threshold of new life; and that life was no longer mine, but his. A moment can indeed be everything and this was the moment. I had come exploring and found myself back at the very place where I had begun. But now I knew the place for the very first time and in that place I was reborn.

Oh, I can't tell you how much I wanted to hold him forever in my arms and never let him go but he told me I could not keep him all to myself. He let me know that he had lots to do and miles to go that day. He made it clear that now he was no longer just a hand to hold or a shoulder to lean on. His life was not just a life one could know by touching but he explained that his life can only be known by living his life inside of me and inside all those who seek God. I just knew that Christ in me was hope and pure love, resurrection and abundant life; the means of rising above everything that is wrecked, broken and dead.

I never understood why he appeared to me first. Why did Jesus choose me? What does it mean to be chosen? One would think he might have first gone to Mary his mother. But he did not. Nor did he go to the eleven disciples. Why not to Peter? Or John, the beloved? Or to any of them: Andrew, James, Philip, Thomas (who really needed to see Jesus), Matthew, James, the son of Alphaeus, Thaddeus, Simon the Zealot, or even Bartholomew? Astonishingly he appeared first to me – a woman, a sinner – and by appearing to me made me one of his apostles. Think of it! Me, Mary Magdalene, a healed woman, an eager disciple, now an apostolic witness! I had been with him from the beginning and now I was with him in resurrection and life. I think because he chose me – a woman of no reputation, or no goodness of my own – means that he has chosen you too.

He told me to go and tell the other disciples what had happened. There were many people then who wanted to discredit me. They saw me as a second-class citizen; a woman who should be silent. But Jesus told me not to be silent but rather to speak and in speaking to teach my brothers by telling what I have seen and heard. So I rushed immediately to their hiding place – where the eleven disciples were and told them: "I have seen the Lord!" They were incredulous. But I think they could tell from my face that it was true. Then I urged them: "Don't cry anymore, do not be filled with sorrow. His grace will be with you all and he will protect you. Let us praise his greatness." I also testified: "I have seen with my eyes that you might be able to believe." My witness, through his power, turned the hearts of the disciples towards resurrection and life.

There is so much to say but my life can be summed up in three words: I was there! Because I – Mary Magdalene – was there I have never been the same. I was there with him in Galilee. I was also there with him in Jerusalem. I was there in ministry with Jesus. I was there at Golgotha even though the only comfort I could give him was to stand there while he suffered and died. I was there and I did not leave. I was there when they took his body down from the cross. I was there when they put him in the tomb. I was there on the morning of resurrection. I was there to welcome him back from the grave. I was there to put my arms around him and confess my faith. I was there when he revealed himself. I was there to receive the message and take it to the other disciples who were hiding in fear. I was there and I have always been so grateful to God that I was.

Let us go back to the tomb for one more moment. I remember it vividly. As he took his leave of me that day in the cemetery as the sun came up and started down the path, I thought it strange and wonderful that even though he was walking away he seemed to linger still; ever within my heart. And I have never, never, to this day, ever, been the same again.

In the name of the one who appeared to me – Mary Magdalene – I dare to say these things. Amen.

Gospel of Mark: The Movie

None of the four gospels are signed. Tradition assigns them to writers named Matthew, Mark, Luke and John. The *Gospel of Mark* is thought to be the earliest of the extant gospels and of the four canonical gospels it is the shortest. As a script it really ought to interest Hollywood film makers. It has all of the elements needed to make an interesting movie. The entire gospel is a narrative filled with intrigue and secrecy, miracle stories, compelling controversies, hot sensual dancing and nudity, exorcism, assassination plots, betrayal, violence, disappearing bodies, severed body parts, murder, nocturnal boating, storms, ghosts. It's all there. All the elements for a fascinating film, in the right hands. And at the center of all of this…Jesus!

The narrative moves along quite briskly. If one reads the entire text one will find the word "immediately" used almost 40 times. The gospel narrative opens with a dramatic announcement. John the Baptist has been arrested! The next time we hear about John (chapter 6) he has appeared at King Herod's birthday party in the royal palace. An impressive guest list for the event included the courtiers, the military commanders, and many of the leading citizens of Galilee. I say John appeared…well sort of. His head turned up on a platter! The rest of him was nowhere to be found.

Being arrested means coming to a halt. Something interferes, the arrest alters progression. Mark seems to link the arrest of John with the end of one thing and the beginning of something else. And that "something else," the text tells us, is the appearance of yet another itinerant teacher of the ancient Near East. Nothing unusual about that: At times the Judean desert seemed to be literally crawling with rabbis and eccentric sorts of teachers. Look at John himself: A half-naked baptizer, wearing camel's hair, eating fists full of locust and honey! I gave a thought earlier in the week to coming today as John but I thought the congregation might have drawn the line at having a half-naked preacher eating locusts and getting sticky fingers on the pulpit while he delivered the homily!

Our text addresses the question of origins. This is always important to an historian such as myself. The question of how the "Christian" faith began is not avoided in our text. All too often there are gaps in our knowledge of the past. The Czech historian František Palacký noted: "In vain may a historian send thousands and thousands of questions into the dark and deaf night of the past ages; even if he or she may catch a gleam is it doubtful whether it is light or will-o-the-wisp." And the text that has just been read, seems to present a drama in four parts: Jesus comes, he speaks, he sees, he calls. I would like to draw our attention to these four movements. Think of it as a stage play, if you will.

Act I: "Jesus came." This is an historical, rather than a theological statement. According to early Christian sources, Jesus was a real person who lived at a real point and a real place in time. His coming changed the world. Even if one is looking for something specific, it is sometimes easy to miss one's objective. In the 1960s a young American theological student was visiting the Swiss city of Basel and got on a tram and without realizing it sat down beside the great theologian Karl Barth. They engaged in conversation: "So, what is the one thing you would most like to do while here in Basel?" Barth asked the young student. The student answered: "Well, I would really like to meet Karl Barth. I have read many of his works and would like to meet him." Barth nodded silently, eyeing the student. A moment or two passed and the student continued: "Do you happen to know Dr. Barth?" "Oh yes," said Barth: "I know him very well, I shave him every morning." At the next stop the student got off the tram firmly convinced that he had just met Karl Barth's barber. Sometimes life is like that!

Act II: "He speaks." Jesus announces the "gospel of God" which Mark reveals consists of four aspects: The fulfillment of time, the approach of the kingdom of God, repentance, and acceptance. This "fulfilling of time" – means it is in process, the kingdom of God is arriving. Before the invention of terrorism, one was able to meet friends and loved ones at the specific gate in an airport. One might hear an announcement on the intercom: "Flight 67 from London now arriving at gate 24." The announcement does not mean the aircraft is actually there, but that it is about to be there. It is likely still on a runway, but the message is intended to alert those awaiting its arrival that the time is at hand and they'd best begin to make their way in that direction.

The kingdom of God is the central theme of the message or teaching of Jesus. There is, annoyingly, no explicit definition of the kingdom in the *Gospel of Mark* or anywhere else in the known Jesus narratives. This is not the place to attempt a comprehensive definition of the kingdom but one or two basic observations might then be made. It has apocalyptic, eschatological significance (meaning it has some future aspect and that it has to do with a summing up, a consummation of history), but it also has clear ethical and social connotations. It has something to do with the overwhelming, pervasive, permeating presence of God. It is the future, realized in the present. The kingdom is not of human origin but somehow you and I are caught up in the drama of the kingdom, rather like being taken by the swift current of a river. Whatever the kingdom of God is, it is inextricably linked to the coming of Christ – perhaps one may say the kingdom of God is Christ himself. The Coptic Gospel of Thomas, 82 has Jesus say: "The one who is near me is close to the fire; the one who is far from me is far from the kingdom."

More than one hundred years ago a French Catholic priest by the name of Alfred Loisy said: Jesus came preaching the kingdom of God. We wound up with the church! It is an important question to consider the relation between the kingdom Jesus announced and the church we are familiar with. But that also is a consideration for another venue.

Mark places a clear emphasis upon repentance. The idea comes from the Greek term *metanoia* – that literally means "to turn around." So Jesus would have us turn around, and go in a different direction, but that is not all. He says: "Believe the good news." Good news? What is that? Why should we trust it? We live in a world filled with bad news. Good news rarely makes the news. We thrive on bad news and there is plenty of it whether we speak of first-century Palestine or twenty-first century America. Now John was rather controversial and came to a bad end. Remember Herod's birthday party? Jesus was also controversial, and we are surely not unaware of the direction his path took. Still, I will be controversial too, if just for a moment. The kingdom of God has failed when the reign of Christ and the ethics of Jesus are ignored. The kingdom has failed when racism persists, when sexism is ignored, when young boys are made to kill other young boys in distant countries all in the name of self-defense. The kingdom is marginalized in our lives when materialism becomes a way of life, when poverty is ignored in a land of plenty, when the justice system becomes "JUST US" and the powerless can be locked up for 50 years for little more than recreational drug use. The kingdom has not come when society tolerates violence in our prisons (and it does), condones injustice and inequality in its myriad of manifestations. The kingdom is ineffective in our lives when we are more concerned about socially invented taboos than we are with what God is all about. But the good news, and thank God there is good news, is that Jesus came and challenges all of this.

So as John Murray put it 200 years ago: "Go out into the highways and byways of America. Give the people blanketed with a decaying and crumbling [religion], something of your vision. You may possess only a small light, but uncover it, let it shine, use it in order to bring more light and understanding to the hearts and minds of men and women. Give them, not hell, but hope and courage. Do not push them deeper into their theological despair, but preach the kindness and everlasting love of God." Now that seems like a worthy challenge.

Talking about the kingdom of God is not the same thing as the kingdom of God. It is rather like the difference between merely reading a menu and eating the meal. The poet, Alfred Lord Tennyson once wrote: "Our little systems have their day, they have their day and cease to be. They are but broken lights of thee, and thou O lord, art more than these." Applied to the church this means, we must never mistake "theology" for God; all theology is human attempts to understand the divine.

Act III: "Jesus sees" – He sees Simon and Andrew and he goes on a bit farther and he sees James and John down by the Sea of Galilee (really a lake and other ancient authorities refer to it as such). The body of water is 6-7 miles wide and 12 miles long. There is no mention that Jesus sees Zebedee or the hired help. The pessimistic German philosopher Arthur Schopenhauer out walking on a dark gloomy night was asked: "Who are you?" He replied: "I was hoping you could tell me." One of the great yearnings of the human soul in the pilgrimage we call life is to know and be known. To be known as the individual for who we really are. It is why we seek partners and form close relationships. In order to know one must see (and I do not mean just with the natural eye), and in order to be known one must be seen. "Jesus sees."

Act IV: "He calls" The plot thickens! Follow me – discipleship. Who me? Are you talking to me? Why I thought this was just another Sunday matinee at the "Galilean theater." I came to see, to hear and to be entertained! "Follow me?" Surely you must be kidding! The German Lutheran pastor Dietrich Bonhoeffer during World War II famously wrote: "When Christ calls a man or woman, he bids that individual come and die!" That is hard stuff. It does not sound like good news to me. Death? What about life? It sounds like a set-up, Jesus I thought you said: "Believe in the good news!" There is a cost. It cost John. It cost Jesus. I have no authority to tell you that your cost will be any different. This is where things get a wee bit uncomfortable. Are we followers of Jesus or secular people who just happen to go to church on Sundays?

Tomorrow morning try walking down Main Street and saying two words only to someone you don't know: "Follow me." Keep walking. After three or four paces, look over your shoulder and see if they are following. What was it about Jesus that people found attractive; that caused them to want to follow him? I would be rather unlikely to follow an invitation like that from a stranger. If a particularly attractive woman said: "Follow me," I might be tempted, but I would be wondering all the while: "What is she up to, where is she taking me?" Our text does not make any suggestion or provide even a hint but I think the Galilean brothers must have known Jesus. Perhaps he'd bought fish from them, or they'd all been at a pub the previous weekend. They were just plain, average people, going about their lives, at their jobs. That's good news for us. But how extraordinary. Commercial fishermen just walking away from their business, leaving their boats, and nets, and gear. What in the world did Zebedee think? There is a cost to the call. The illustration on the cover of the bulletin today shows a fishing net draped over a cross. I imagine that later that day Mr. Zebedee went home and told Mrs. Zebedee that some fellow named Jesus happened by. That he called the boys to follow. And they did. And they left him with all the work, and he hasn't seen them since. Just what did Mr. Zebedee think about all of that? And what about Mrs. Zebedee?

The Christian takes his or her stand not on optimism, but on hope. And what is that hope in this season of Epiphany? That he will come to you and to me, that he will speak to us, that he will see each of us, and that he will call us to himself. It happens on the journey; not in some special place. It need not happen here, or there, or in any designated place, though it could. It happens wherever we are and does not, cannot, depend on who we are. That's the compelling part of the movie that the Gospel of Mark can be.

In the name of the one who always "comes," who "speaks," who "sees," and who "calls," we dare to say these things. Amen.

PRESENT IMAGES OF THE PAST

Have you ever stood in a strange place in the silence of the twilight hours and thought you had been there before? Have the blurred faces of a bustling crowd suddenly focused into the form of a familiar face, only to fade away in oblivion? How often have the shadows of history come around full circle to suddenly bring forth again, that which has gone on before? The situation is not unique. Such was the case in the district of Caesarea Philippi about 2,000 years ago. What is it that draws the past from its place in history into the activities of the present? What purpose do things of the past have in the here and now?

While the writers of the Synoptic Tradition of the gospels – Matthew, Mark and Luke – did not attempt to biographically sketch out the life of Christ, they did focus upon his work and mission. The life setting of Christ cannot be regarded as a detached moment of history. He was of his own, he had a heritage. He occupied a place in his time and culture. Jesus was a man of the world even though he had come from elsewhere. His personality, by the testimony of the gospel writers, was colored by the full spectrum of life. In essence, he was not just a divine blob who had rocketed into Bethlehem from the twilight zone. He had come from God for a specific task and this assumption was held by more than a few. But even in Christ, the God-Man, images of the past were perceived, recognized and identified. Was this simply another would-be deliverer of Israel, or the appearance of another "Teacher of Righteousness?"

He was many things to many people, and more frequently than not, the victim of mistaken identity. In the district of Caesarea Philippi he was identified by people there as a specific historical personality. They knew who he was all right, that was common knowledge. He was Jesus an apprentice carpenter in the Nazareth Construction Company. His dad, Joseph, was the president. Yet strangely enough folks felt compelled to identify him as someone long gone, dead and past.

A brief examination of the Christian faith itself and the documents comprising the New Testament make clear the significance of this man Jesus. He is not only the "founder of Christianity" but seems also to be the central object of its faith. More than that, those called by his name seek to become his voice today. That being the case, it seems that what he was then, those called Christians must now be. His person must be mirrored in the present age. The image of the historical figure must be perceived in his followers. But what was the image that people saw? What did they see when they looked at Jesus?

As Jesus and his disciples entered into the district of Caesarea Philippi, he asked the first of his two famous questions: "Who do people say the Son of Man is?" Why would he care? Was he concerned with reputation, or was he just curious? And what a place to ask the question. Caesarea Philippi was a long ways off from the usual stomping grounds of Jesus and his friends. Caesarea Philippi was a type of resort for Roman soldiers, heathens and others quite unsympathetic to Jesus-types. Jews stayed away from Caesarea Philippi. Centurions and Roman police went to Caesarea Philippi for rest and relaxation when they were not throttling Jewish insurrectionists or chasing armed hoodlums around the countryside. The city was a green, lush, place by the sea. Pagan gods of the Romans stood in carved niches; niches that can be seen to this day. Perhaps in view of these gods and idols Jesus just called for a break. Perhaps within earshot of sabre-rattling soldiers he asked the people travelling with him that interesting and riveting question. Instead of being identified as Messiah or liar, he was identified with a voice from the past. Not simply was Jesus connected to this voice from the past, he was somehow, rather mysteriously, that image of the past.

"Some say you are John the Baptist!" To be sure, Jesus was related to the Baptist by birth. But being related would never constitute such identification. "Jesus, they are not saying that you remind them of John, they are saying that you *are* John!" John was a prophet, the voice of one crying in the wilderness. He was a Baptist and a herald of the coming Kingdom of God. But his notable characteristic was his preaching. "In those days, John Baptist came preaching repent because the kingdom of heaven is near." Close affinities can be drawn between the preaching of John and the proclamations of Jesus. So close in fact were these similarities that Jesus was identified with the Baptist, and the Baptist was now already dead. His head had appeared at a party on a platter and had been shown around. I think we can safely say he was deceased.

This image of Christ, though rooted in the past, is a present critical concern. Are we known for our message and for our witness? The Baptist suddenly appeared in the wilderness one day. He came to bear witness to a light; the light that brings light to all people. His message contained an eventful witness: "Behold the Lamb of God." Jesus became an image of the Baptist for he too bore a message of eventful and decisive witness. He came not to testify about himself, but rather to speak on behalf of God. He witnessed in dynamic act and being God's message to the nations. Christians should be known as ambassadors. The message should be heard, not just in words but in the manner of life and the love that is given.

The past image of the Baptist has faded now. His witness has been silenced. His finger no longer points. His body had already been tossed away. After the party was over someone must have noticed the head on the platter. One of the maids probably was called to clean the bloody head off the platter and get rid of it. But his image that mirrored itself in the life of Christ lives on in the present, somewhere...

"And some people say that you are Elijah!" To be identified with the Baptist was one thing, but to be called Elijah was an entirely different matter. This image of the past, this illustrious figure of the ninth century B.C.E., represented a truly unique traditional institution of the Israelite prophets. He is one of the weirdest figures among the Hebrew prophets. "Jesus, they are saying that you are Elijah."

What was so outstandingly significant about this Tishbite? He was the prophet whose "word burned like a torch" (Sirach 48:1). Rabbinical legends grew up in his name and among the prophets of antiquity he is without peer. Elijah's life has historical significance in several areas. Tradition linked him to the eschatological forerunner of the Day of the Lord. The person of John Baptist was, according to some, Elijah revived. Elijah is best associated with miracles and miraculous elements. He is perhaps best related to the concept of power. "Jesus, these people are saying you are Elijah."

Jesus was noted for power too. Not the circus entertainment, attention-getting feats of power, but the strong and creative power of God. To use Paul anachronistically, Jesus did not come with wisdom or with the skills of humankind but in a demonstration of the Spirit and with power. If an image of the past became creative and present in Christ, perhaps it likewise should become a present image of the past in those who are called by his name. Christians possess power, not of themselves, but of God. That power can affect the lives of those among whom Christians dwell.

The past image of Elijah is gone. His miracles have ended. His voice has been stilled. No longer does he stride across the hills and fields. What happened to his power? Did he take it with him or put it somewhere for safekeeping?

"And some say you are Jeremiah!" Jeremiah? Not him! To be identified with the Baptist is one thing. To be identified with Elijah perhaps even prestigious. But Jeremiah? What redeeming quality does this ancient personality possess? He was a man of gloom and sorrow; the author of

"The Lamentations," the figure who bore the epithet, "the weeping prophet." "Jesus, the people here are saying that you are Jeremiah. They say that you are this man." In those days now long gone, people would see old Jeremiah coming and they would say: "There he is, weeping all the time, crying, there he goes again." Was he just a morose figure? Could he have been emotionally disturbed? Do these suggestions truly describe Jeremiah? He may well have been the "weeping prophet" but his tears surely were not indication of emotional instability. His peers undoubtedly wondered about him: "There goes that old man Jeremiah, there he goes once again, crying, weeping." What possible common denominator links this prophet with Jesus?

Christ came to serve, he did not come to be served. His life was lived out in the context of the needs of others. Love motivated his life; compassion ruled his actions, and he poured out his life for the many. Even at the doors of death in terrible agony, he had compassion on a convicted thief and pronounced justification. He loved so much that he gave. Where else is compassion so ably personified but in the life of the Son of Man?

It is not insignificant that Christ was identified with these three images of the past. He did not simply resemble them, he became all that they were; all that they had been, and more. He is the Word, he is the power of God, he is grace. Are we Christian, or are we just religious? Do these images of the past find present expression in Christians? His message must be ever proclaimed, his power must be demonstrated and both expressions must be made within the context of his compassion.

The voice of the Baptist is silent. His finger ceases to point. The power of Elijah has faded into the dimness of the historical night. The tears of Jeremiah have dried where they fell. The footsteps of Christ have ceased to echo, and the images of the past are now only a memory. And who do people say that we are?

Castaway Island, Fiji

Black Mountain, NSW, Australia

Hear This, you Christian Dimwits, Halfwits and Nitwits!

No one appreciates being called a dimwit, nitwit or a halfwit, even when it's true. To call someone a quarterwit is truly insulting, implying that they are not even up to being just plain stupid. I have learned the names of other members of the Wit Family during my time in Australia that cannot be included here. It is also offensive to begin an essay or address by calling one's audience derogatory names. However, it is often the obtrusively off-the-wall that catches our attention. The Hebrew Bible is filled with a variety of characters called "prophets." In this context these "prophets" were spokesmen, not fortune tellers though they sometimes uttered threats about what awful things might yet befall the sons and daughters of earth. Each of these prophets were sufficiently audacious to make the claim that they spoke on behalf of the Lord and Creator of the universe. There is no evidence to suggest that anyone ever asked a prophet home for a meal … at least more than once.

"Fools! Lunatics! Knaves!" That's what they were often called. It did not matter to them. They just went on, as always, sometimes muttering, sometimes actually screeching: "Thus sayeth Yahweh!" We just call them prophets. They were a motley crew to be sure and definitely weird. Calling them weird is putting it mildly. Wherever these clowns went they always raised a ruckus. Take Ezekiel for example. Here was a real basket-case. He was always hearing strange voices. "Son of man, take a brick." So he played with bricks in the backyard. He cooked his food on excrement and laid on the ground for thirteen months. That was the first time. He seemed to enjoy this adventure so much that he tried it again but on the second occasion he did not hold out quite so long, apparently wearied of the strange business after forty days. Later he shaved his head as well as his beard because some voice identifying itself as "the Lord" told him to. This all happened after he ate the book. That's right, this fellow Ezekiel actually ate a book. Chewed it up and swallowed the whole thing. He was not always this nutty. It seems it all began when he began raving about seeing flying wheels careening about in the sky. If his wife had not died when she did there is some chance that this old boy might have driven her straight to the mental hospital. After she died, he took to talking to old dried bones out in the middle of nowhere. Somehow, by hook or by crook, he wrote up an entire book, of considerable size, detailing his eccentric existence and somewhat amazingly it later came to be regarded by posterity as sacred literature and the complete unedited text wound up in the Christian Bible, simply called *The Book of Ezekiel*. Now that is truly a strange one. Have a read!

Or how about that fellow they called Elisha? I have my doubts about him as well in terms of mental stability. Ever since his buddy Elijah, the one they say whose word burned like a torch, took off for a ride in a flying chariot, old Elisha went pretty much off the deep end. He claimed to have picked up a mantle that fell from the sky as Elijah was whisked off. He was also pretty sensitive about his advanced receding hairline. One day on the Bethel Boulevard a couple of pranksters, just kids really, called him "old chrome dome." He became so irate he cussed them out good, in the name of the Lord of course, and then promptly turned a couple of hungry bears on them and their playmates. As a matter of fact he wiped out the entire playground. Forty two children were mauled to death. Now that's seems pretty excessive just because someone made a joke about his bald head. There is a good chance that Elisha might have benefited from an anger management course or gone off to counselling to work through some of his personal issues.

Then there was a tale about a seer who could not see. Now that one is certainly deeply ironic! His claim to fame, however, was not so much his prophesying as his famous talking ass. Not only could the ass talk, it could see, which was a very good thing for poor old Balaam. After giving Balaam an unwanted scenic tour of a nearby field, including smashing his foot against a wall that must have prompted the prophet to howl in pain, and then finally flopping to the ground as mules and their ilk are prone to do, the old jackass saved Balaam's hide from a sword-wielding angel who was holding up trail traffic. Of course these old characters could certainly put on a show too. Isaiah got tired of hanging around the temple so he went down to the city square and promptly removed all of his clothes. He walked around town like that, not just for the afternoon, but for three whole years! He claimed he did this as a sign to the people. One can well imagine that the sign was well read. One cannot help wondering what the city-folks thought of this. It must have been quite a sight; the streaking prophet. Presumably, proper parents advised their kids, especially their teenage daughters, to stay inside and keep the blinds pulled. "Let's just stay inside today dear, Isaiah is still parading around the neighborhood!"

Strange stories about the prophets are a dime a dozen in the Hebrew Bible. Hosea married a whore and Habakkuk talked back to God in a very irreverent and sassy way. Jeremiah showed the people a clay jar and told them that it represented them. Whereupon he then smashed it to smithereens and informed his startled hearers in no uncertain terms that this was what God was about to do to them. On another occasion he went straight up to the temple and bellowed: "Do not trust in these deceptive words, this is the temple of the Lord, the temple of the Lord, the temple of the Lord." Just like a prophet to say it three times when once would have been enough. He wanted everyone to get the message. When he was not up to his armpits in a cistern, or in jail, he was crying all the time so people stopped calling him Jeremiah and began referring to him as "the weeping prophet." On the other hand, Zechariah spent his time watching flying scrolls that he reported were about the size of a small airplane today. If the thing had ever landed it would have taken Zechariah quite a long time to read it. There are no reliable reports that these flying scrolls – ancient UFOs – ever touched down.

The stories of strange behavior could be multiplied to fill a number of pages, but the stories are not the real point. The crucial issue is what does all of this mean? What was a prophet anyway, and what was the purpose of all these strange goings-on? In the Hebrew Bible there is no one word that means "prophet." Indeed, there are at least four: *nabi'*, which generally is translated prophet though the etymology is disputed; *ro'eh*, generally translated "seer"; *hozeh*, which also means "seer"; and *"elohim,"* which means "man of God." One might wonder whether or not the ancient Israelites even truly understood was a prophet was. In I Samuel 7:7-9 we find three of the aforementioned terms used in reference to the prophet. One thing is certain however, prophets played pivotal roles in Israel during the monarchy and throughout ancient Israelite history up until at least the neo-Babylonian exile in 587 BCE. Their messages and actions worked as vehicles of transformation. Contrary to some popular understandings, these prophets did not function as heralds of the far distant future. They were not concerned with providing road maps for the coming end of the world complete with apocalyptic illustrations. Confusion between "foretelling" and "forth-telling" must be carefully avoided. The prophets presented a radical option, a challenge to their own particular setting in life. The prophetic voice spoke out of a particular historical milieu to that same milieu. For example, Habakkuk spoke openly concerning the political circumstances of his own nation faced with the impending invasion of foreign powers. Amos prophesied against his neighboring nations as well as against both Judah and Israel. In our own times, prophecy would follow this same exact paradigm: Social issues, the poor, the socially disinherited, egregious injustice, ecology, politics, racism, sexism, (all the isms!), liberation theology and many other related issues.

It is arguable that the church today does not have a prophetic voice. To be sure, one does hear a lot of "thus sayeth the Lord" but one must wonder whether or not that is merely a cheap imitation of the authentic and radical prophetic voice now long submerged in the dimness of the historical night. No longer does a Malachi stand up in the midst of the people and boldly declare that the Lord is about to spread poop on people's faces. Would anyone believe it? Would the so-called prophet be laughed to scorn, ignored, or escorted out? What would happen today if someone stood up in the cathedral and asserted this was about to happen? While there may be many causes for the apparent decline of the church in this so-called post-modern, post-Christian age, it must be stated that the loss of the prophetic voice may be a contributing factor. "Hear this, you fat cows of Bashan." Truly! That is how Amos addressed his hearers. Crude? Harsh? Insensitive? Politically incorrect? Still, none can disclaim or subvert the prophetic word that he uttered against the social injustices in Israel.

Is it possible that the contemporary church has far too long ignored the radical option of the prophetic word? A visitor to the papal court in the thirteenth century was shown the treasures of the papacy. The pope remarked: "See my good friend, Peter can no longer say: 'Silver and gold have I none,' to which the visitor replied: 'True, and nor can he now say, rise up and walk.'" During the time of Amos, the people looked forward expecting deliverance. Amos told them they had better start looking for something else. God was going to settle their hash in a way they had not counted on. In contemporary language Amos, quoting God, asserted that their church services bored him to tears. Encounter groups, spiritual retreats, and sterile Bible studies made him sick in his stomach no less than their pious prayers and inglorious platitudes. Justice is what God wants, not late-model BMWs, designer clothes and $30,000,000 churches, God wants righteousness like an ever-flowing stream. There is of course a price to be paid for all this. When Jeremiah's "prophecy" was read before the king, the king cut it up, page after page, and tossed the fragments into the fireplace. Amos was exiled and told to go somewhere else and prophesy but never again show his face in that place again.

They are all dead now, all of them. Elijah's chariot ride was a one way ticket. Jeremiah went to Egypt and retired there. Legend has it that folks got so fed up with Isaiah's exhibitionism that they took a saw and cut him in two. None of them lasted long. They were either all banned, jailed, exiled, persecuted or killed. Who among us today has the courage to stand and prophesy as those eccentric lads of old? Micaiah ben Imlah was hated by the king and even got his mouth slapped, literally. Do we try to make sense out of these strange fellows or should we simply read them as curiosities of Near Eastern antiquity? Perhaps the strangest thing about these prophets is that they were not necessarily instruments of redemption. While there may be correlation, the symbolic acts of Ezekiel are not the same thing as the social change agendas of a Martin Luther King or the theologies of Latin American liberation movements.

Does the church today support or tolerate the prophetic word? We must not be too hasty to say "yes" for the preacher might take off his or her clothes and walk around the chapel naked for three years, in a manner of speaking. What a fright that might be! One must not be too quick to answer in the affirmative for one might change their tune when reports begin coming in of flying scrolls and spinning wheels. The prophetic voice may come forth out of a theophanic spectacle like that on Mt. Carmel with Elijah, or it may be spoken quietly in the chamber as Jeremiah did to Baruch. The prophets of ancient Israel are gone and the prophets of the historical church – Hus, Luther, Bonhoeffer, Barth, Schweitzer – are also silenced. And where is that mantle, that rough unattractive hairy old thing? The status quo of ten years ago in the church is probably impotent now. The status quo of today is dangerous. Is the church on the verge of succumbing to the demons of irrelevancy? Perhaps the church needs to find a prophetic word in a hurry to avoid the possibility of becoming inept. Is there a danger of drowning in our pool of mediocrity with our feet almost on the shores of truth? Perhaps there is a pressing need to shake off the paralysis that prevents us from implementing the radical option of the prophetic message.

Like Robert Frost's, a prophet's quarrel with the world is really a lover's quarrel. If the prophets truly did not love the world they would not be bothered telling it that it was going to hell. They would just let it go. But their quarrel with the world is God's quarrel. So where is that unsightly mantle? Has it been destroyed at long last, or just tucked away in the museum for safe keeping? Is Jeremiah now only the bull frog? Why is that fellow over there eating a book? Hear this, you sons and daughters of God. Maybe someone should holler out from the back pew: "Go up thou bald head, go up thou bald head." Maybe the bears will come out of the forest yet again. On the other hand, there is the distinct possibility that a prophetic voice might shatter the sounds of silence.

In the name of the one who acts with prophetic power in our lives, we dare to say these things. Amen.

Cooper Spur, Mt Hood, Oregon

Klausenpass, Uri canton, Swiss Alps

Telegraph Station, Northern Territory, Australia

THE KING AND THE CRIMINALS

"And when they came to the place which is called The Skull, there they crucified him, and the criminals, one on the right and one on the left" (Luke 23:33). This was a rather ignominious end to what some thought would be a brilliant career. Over his head was a sign that read: "The king of the Jews." The king and the criminals. Who is this man on the cross, the one there in the middle? They had called him master, lord, rabbi, Christ, now he hangs there naked, dying, a clear spectacle of obscenity. Forsaken by nearly all his friends there are only a few women who loved him who lingered near the cross. And of course the two crooks. They would certainly not forsake him for they were nailed just as solidly by his side as he was to his own cross, one on the right and another on the left. In this single sentence, Luke the Evangelist presents us with an interesting scenario; a most unusual scene. It is striking to find a king in such a place for it is hardly the place where one expects to find royalty.

The narrative is at once shocking and a study in contrasts. People watch the scene unfold, the authorities scoff at the condemned. Soldiers mock the dying men. The two crooks are slowly dying. They have opposite responses to their plight. One criminal rails on Jesus while the other prays to him. Christ the king is dying in a most unusual way for royalty and certainly in the strangest of company. There must surely be some terrible mistake.

It is of note to observe that his kingship is declared in his identification with the criminals. The criminal element of society – practically any society – denotes those left out, the socially disinherited, those who for various and sundry reasons fail to make the cut into the higher echelons of society. Criminals are those we despise, loath and fear. Yet with this kind of riffraff the king is found and more than this, in this place and with these degenerates the kingdom is declared. The king seems to say at the climax of his life that the entire world in all its dimensions is his kingdom. It is not restricted only to the church or religious circles but fills the whole world.

At practically the last place we might expect to find the anointed one, the very son of God, he appears, not on the sidelines but center stage. Perhaps it is more fitting that he be crowned with a crown of thorns rather than with a golden royal diadem, duly encrusted with jewels and gleaming in splendor. In a sense, his end at Golgotha, the place of The Skull, is fitting when compared to his beginnings and lifestyle. His resume is hardly a recommendation for any king. Born in a cave to an unwed mother, a runaway from his parents, disrespectful to religious authority, violated the law on numerous occasions, took sides with sinners, hung out with whores and crooks more times than anyone could truly remember, taught his followers a subversive radical agenda, refused to conform to acceptable social mores, and died violently under accusation of leading a revolutionary movement. The sign over his head was as much an indictment as it was identification.

It is entirely superfluous for us to proclaim Christ as the king if we are unwilling to implement the radical nature of his rule in our world. He did not come as King to a church, nor did he found a church. Instead, he came proclaiming the kingdom of God in and to the world. So it is somewhat fitting that there was no palace, no gold, no ivory, no marble, but only a rough wooden cross. Indeed, his kingly rule is a paradox. We might say with considerable justification that Christ missed all the usual elements of kingly glory by a rather wide margin. In our story from Luke's gospel, Christ is the humiliated king, the crucified God. The king of kings, as Christian theology lauds him, is here the king of crooks. The Lord of lords is the lord of the losers. The incarnate God has become the incarnate fool. Or so it seems. But the one who seemed so foolish and mistaken on the hillside is Christ the King, the power of God whom one must see with more than just human eyes.

There is one query that each one of us must seriously consider and that question is this: What is Christ the king of? Is Christ the focus of one Sunday in the church year, the last Sunday in the liturgical calendar? Is Christ the king merely the object of a religious ritual? Is he the hero of a Christian epic, or the center of a religious fantasy? We must do all we can to prevent our preconceived notions from concealing his presence from us. Too often Christ was overlooked by the throngs who had an idea of who God was, or who the Messiah might be or who the Savior of the world would probably look like. Jesus always seems to have represented something else. Will we allow our conceptions of Christ to conceal his kingly reign in our world? Is he Lord and King of our lives, of our world?

One might be inclined to wonder if the cross does not nullify his kingship. But Luke seems to be telling us that there is no king without the criminals and there is no kingdom without the cross. Which is more amazing, to find Jesus the king in such bad company, or to find the criminals in such good company? As a matter of fact, both are amazing. The king and the criminals. Both preach the gospel and together both symbolize the kingdom of God.

In the name of the one who extends, and does not conceal, his kingship from criminals, we dare to say these things. Amen.

Harvey Camp, New Brunswick

Round Lake, Camas, WA

Harvey Camp

I grew up in a religious context where conferences and conventions were commonplace. In the summer we all looked forward to the annual camp meeting. I have been to many camp meetings in Oregon, Idaho, British Columbia, Miller Lake in Nova Scotia, Pea Cove in Maine and others, but the best one of all was Harvey Camp. Harvey Camp ground was located on the eastern shore of Harvey Lake just a few miles north of the small township of Harvey Station in New Brunswick, one of the Maritime Provinces of Canada. In 1970 Dad bought a cabin from a guy named Bryce Hargraves that was located on the last road of the camp ground as one went north from the tabernacle. The cabin was a two-bedroom setup with a large front room divided into a kitchen area and living room. My sister slept in the living room. My brother and I got one bedroom and Dad and Mother the other. We had running water but no bathroom. There was an outhouse behind the cabin. Dad paid $1000 for it and we often stayed there during camp meetings and also at other times. On the grounds were several dozen cabins. I can't remember how many but perhaps fifty. Just across from our cabin on the last road was the men's dormitory. A couple of cabins west towards the lake was the two story chapel. At the other end of the camp ground was the girl's dormitory which I am certain was deliberately situated to be as far away from the men as possible. Right beside it was the cook house and the dining hall. Across the yard from these buildings to the east in the direction of the main road, Route 636, was the essential canteen and the bookstore. There was a public phone booth situated there outside the bookstore. South, across a ditch was an open field which, during camp time, was filled with tents and travel trailers. The main structure was the tabernacle centrally located and large enough to seat over 2,000. During evening services it was consistently filled with perhaps two or three hundred more milling about out-of-doors. Off the north side of the tabernacle were the public rest rooms and the water tower. To the west of the camp ground itself lay the body of water from which the camp derived its name: Harvey Lake. Down at Harvey Station at the corner of Route 636 and Highway 3 was a store: "W.W.E. Smith Food Market" founded by the Englishman William Walter Embleton Smith in 1869. We always stopped. The owner loved the summer for as he put it, where would his business be if it were not for the camp meeting. He figured he made enough income off the eager campers to sustain him through the leaner business months of winter.

I do not remember my first visit to Harvey Camp. I remember clearly my last visit and several in between. It was an annual event and everyone who was anyone was there. Going to Harvey was as much a social event as a spiritual gathering. I looked forward to seeing friends I had not seen all year. Keith Phillips, Lloyd Bustard, Stuart Ward, David and Danny Bustard, Daniel Briggs, a bunch of others and of course the girls. What was a camp meeting anyways without the girls? In my view the girls from Perth and Fredericton were well worth waiting for. Between the canteen and the tabernacle was a veritable stage. Girls in their summer dresses. Girls with interesting hair styles. Girls looking around. Girls looking to be seen. Tall girls. Short girls. Blonde girls. Brunettes. Red heads. Skinny girls. Fat girls. Single girls. Beautiful girls. I liked the girls. I spent as much time as I could between the tabernacle and the canteen. I was pretty certain that if God was around, God would be found right there in that area so I decided I'd better hang around too. And I did.

I attended youth camp on those same grounds. The classes were often fun even if I cannot recall a single point of doctrine or theology from them. The girls were too distracting and it was great being away from home for a whole week. That's a big deal when you are fourteen. We played baseball, went swimming (the boys at 1:00 o'clock, the girls at 3:00 o'clock), had Bible Studies and ate lots of ice-cream. We caught bull frogs and put them in people's cabins and listened to the roars when someone discovered an enormous bull frog sitting on top of a fridge. We broke into the cook house and helped ourselves to goodies and then congratulated ourselves on a well-executed plan and on then escaping without being detected. Occasionally there was some trouble. Russell Morehouse, the youth camp director, lost his cool on more than one night when the noise level in the boy's dorm failed to get below 80 decibels or when the front end of his Volkswagen "Bug" ended up on top of a garbage can. Lloyd Bustard laughed himself silly when he was booted out but Blair Crawford cried like a baby when the supervisors informed him that for his shenanigans he had to go home next morning. I chimed right along with the rest of the ringleaders but always pulled in my horns just before trouble loomed. I was better than anyone around at feigning sleep and acting completely innocent. I could ill afford to get sent home. My father believed literally in the "spare the rod and spoil the child" idea. In all the hilarity, notwithstanding, we were encouraged to get in touch with God, with faith and spirituality.

One evening, under the direction of the brazen Lloyd Bustard, several of us escaped from the dorm and crept along the trails between the cabins. All at once Albert Galbraith, one of the pastors, stood before us, blocking progress. He had just appeared out of nowhere. He wanted to know where we were going. Lloyd piped up that we had to use the toilets. Yes, that was it, we all chimed in, we had to use the toilets. "Yes," Albert said in deep voice. We confirmed it was true. Our objective? The toilets. "Yes," he boomed again. We insisted we had to go badly; all six of us at once. "Yes," he said again: "No you're not." Albert Galbraith had bought none of our story. Our plan really had been to make it to the girl's dorm. Doubtless, Albert Galbraith knew that. He was nobody's fool. Thwarted, we were escorted back to where we had come from. Albert was a tough customer but we all knew he had come to Harvey Lake to help us get in touch with God.

At the main camp the grounds were swelled to capacity. Before 1973 E.P. Wickens was the district superintendent. He would lean on the pulpit at the close of the afternoon service and call for volunteers among the men to help peel potatoes in the cook house and also for those to help wash pots and pans. Most people were asleep by then for Wynn Stairs, the foreign missions director, had just spent hours droning on about Africa, South America and other unknown reaches of the globe. The unspiritual were already lining up outside the cookhouse more eager to feed their stomachs than their souls. The radicals never came to the afternoon sessions for by their own testimony they would rather go into Fredericton shopping than sit and listen to Ed Wickens go on since everyone knew he was "weak on the message."

There were truly memorable moments in some of the services in the big tabernacle. One afternoon, Rev. C.B. Dudley preached on the story of Balaam. He told the story in his own inimitable way noting that it was indeed strange that the Lord had to use a jackass to talk to the prophet. "Well," Dudley roared: "I'm the jackass from the Lord here today to talk to you." And he went on like that for about 90 minutes. When they sang the song: "I'm gonna walk all around in that city," Milford Stairs, another elderly minister, would literally walk all around the platform. Raymond Beesley was as big around as he was tall. His hair was as white as the driven snow. He would stalk to the pulpit and say: "Praise the Lord." He would get a murmur in reply. So he raised his voice: "I said, praise the Lord." The color would rise in his face and there would be a pretty good reply. Then a third time: "PRAISE THE LORD!!!" His face would be as red as a ripe beet. Mother always said she was sure he would have a fatal stroke. The tabernacle however erupted in loud Pentecostal praise. At that point one could consider the service good and truly underway. Alison W. "Buddy" Post, who hated his Christian name on the grounds that it was a girl's name, was, when he came to the pulpit, as calm in his dry "glory to God" as Beesley was loud.

Sometimes there were 70 or 80 preachers on the platform and I knew every one of them by name. I watched them come in the rear door and take a seat. They all sat together on several benches on the left side of the platform. They were gods. They were icons. They were heroes all. They were the men of God. Well, at least I believed that then. Buddy Post, Raymond Priest, Paul MacDonald, Dudley, Wickens, Beesley, Stairs, and the rest. Charles Glass was preaching one night on the theme "everything that can be shaken will be shaken." To make the point he pounded the pulpit and a large wooden sign hanging on the front came loose, plunged several feet to the concrete floor with a loud crash and then bounced, just as loudly, several times before coming to a halt. Nathan Urshan had several times to tell C.B. Dudley to be quiet and let him preach. Dudley had the habit of preaching right along with the preacher. Don Carmont stood on a chair directing the choir wearing white shoes. Many people paid more attention to the shoes than the songs. Dad admired him and to the end of his life called him "Pastor Carmont." Freddy Clarke sang "let the church roll on" but Simon Cameron and the singing "Camerons" from Peterhead, Scotland were banned from the platform. Something about Simon's wife cutting her hair.

Before a concrete floor was put in, the floor used to be sawdust. Each year, one could always count on at least one evening featuring a terrific downpour. More than once I was obliged (usually by Mother in a fairly direct way) to lift my feet up and let the water run past. One night the lights flickered and faded and threatened to go out. Keith Phillips and I were sitting with Jack Hatt from Orono, Maine. Jack was middle-aged back then. Jack said to us: "I wish the lights would just go out so I could shout hallelujah." A moment later the lights went out and Jack Hatt was heard to shout out: "HALLELUJAH." Keith Phillips and I were heard snickering. There was a retarded fellow who used to sit there and during the worship would raise his right arm with three fingers only extended. Then very deliberately he would reach up with his left hand, grasp his right arm around the wrist and pull it down. This would be repeated several times to my amusement. Sitting round the cabin later we would mimic the action until Mother said that was enough and we shouldn't be mocking the afflicted.

The tabernacle had a bell located on the southwest side just outside the prayer room that was attached directly to the tabernacle itself behind the platform. The prayer room was used for overflow seating. The bell was rung to announce each service and its sonorous tone could be heard from one end of the camp ground to the other. The other bell in use was a small cow bell in the hand of C.B. Dudley. Campbell Boyd Dudley – the "jackass from the Lord" – was among the ugliest men one might ever meet. He was rather uncouth, uneducated, rough, hulking and utterly committed to his God. At seven or seven thirty in the morning Dudley would stalk around the camp ground, cow bell in hand, ringing it vigorously, waking all: "C'mon," he would roar, "get up and pray. You sit up half the night talking, get up and pray!" His deep bellowing could be heard a hundred yards away. "C'mon you lazy fellows in there, get your pants on, get up to the prayer room and pray." So it went morning after morning throughout the whole camp meeting. Dad called him "Dude" after a fictional character in a Gene Autry book named Dude Dudley. When "Dude" came past our cabin Dad said he would like to get a big stick and go out there and give Dudley a good crack. In 1971 Dudley went through the windshield of a car in Newfoundland with his colleague Don Carmont during a winter blizzard. He was 66 years old at the time but far too tough to kill. Nonetheless, they put a steel rod in his leg from hip to ankle and he walked with a stiff leg the last 25 years of his life. He had to give up his cow bell morning pray meeting walks. But that did not stop him. Now he drove around in his car, blowing the horn, leaning out the window, rain or shine, telling people to get up and pray. Dad said the car horn was even worse than the cow bell. Dudley claimed everyone knew him and invited people to send mail to him with envelopes simply addressed: "Father Dudley, Miramichi River."

I had my favorite spots. Down by the lake between two large rocks just off the corner of Milford Stairs' cabin. I used to go there with my girlfriend Kris and watch the sun set and see the dark shadows claiming the surface of Harvey Lake. I used to dream about spending the rest of my life with her. It never happened. The circle around the tabernacle I used to pace with friends remains a good memory. Down at the far end of the camp grounds by the last cabin was a spot where I had my first real talk with my father. There is another place under the trees in the open circle between the tabernacle and the cabins where one night I sat in a car with Jack Long and he gave me good counsel for the road ahead. I only saw him once thereafter and at the age of 48 he dropped dead of a heart attack. We swam in the lake every year. I was really grossed out once when a huge blood sucker was found on my back and had to be yanked off by a friend of mine before it got a good hold.

In 1981 I was working in Nova Scotia managing a shoe store. I took my annual vacation in order to go to Harvey Camp. I remember quite a few details of that camp mainly because it was the last one I would ever attend. As a matter of fact no camp meeting would ever again be held at Harvey Lake. Two months after the camp ended I left Maritime Canada for the last time and went to Oregon. The next winter, in February 1982, a massive snow fall caused the roof of the venerable old tabernacle to cave in. The venue for 1982 had to be shifted to a convention center in Fredericton. A decision later was made to sell the old grounds – lock, stock and barrel – and keep the camp meeting in the city. It was never the same. Dad sold our cabin. The district superintendent R.A. Beesley later regretted the sale of the old campground and told me so twenty years later. Almost forty years after the last camp meeting at Harvey Lake I had the chance to visit the district archives in Marysville and pore over pictures that provided snapshots of the way things were all those years ago. Dude Dudley, R.A. Beesley and caved-in tabernacle roof.

Nineteen years after I was last at Harvey Lake, quite unplanned, I found myself at Harvey Station. I went in to W.W. E. Smith's, just as I used to as a kid. He was long dead. Someone else had the business. We bought ice-cream just like in the old days. Then we drove up Route 636. I saw the lake. But when I got near to where the old camp ground used to be I was dismayed. The whole area was gone. One could no longer even see the old lake. The space between the road and the lake was totally overgrown. There was no trace anything had ever happened there. It was like a dream that disappears the moment one awakens.

Somewhat saddened, I continued to drive on up Route 636 but as I did I began to think about the old camp. I remembered the faces, some of the names. I could still see C.B. Dudley baptizing people in the lake. I could see Raymond Beesley at the pulpit. I could see the throngs in the prayer room. For a moment I thought I heard a cow bell. The scent of hot dogs and French fries from the canteen, the preachers on the platform, Milford Stairs walking all around loosening up for his junket around the new Jerusalem. I remembered, again, hearing him once say: "I'm a fool for Christ, whose fool are you?" I could see it all just like those days so long ago. I remembered some of the stories Dad used to tell us kids in the old cabin on the last road. Of Ellery Cady boasting of how good a preacher he was. Of Charlie Curtis complaining of how he was never asked to preach at Harvey. I remembered Art McElroy telling Dad to come on up and visit him and joking: "I'll straighten you out on your doctrine." Of H.D. McNair leading the congregation in singing: "How great thou art." I could still hear the strains of the camp meeting music. "Pastor Carmont" directing the choir. I heard again the laughter in the dorms, I could see in my mind's eye pretty girls in lovely summer dresses, hearty handshakes, happy greetings, peeling potatoes at the cook house, the sawdust floor, Jack Hatt hollering in the dark, the bell calling everyone to the service, sights, sounds and memories that had lasted all these years. But everything that could be shaken had been shaken. Harvey Camp was gone. As far as I know there is not a single remnant on the shores of Harvey Lake to even suggest that any of us had ever been there. Harvey Camp lives only in the minds and lives of those who found a sign post there for the journey to faith, to spirituality, to God. And as I rounded the bend I realized that the God I had met there, and the spirit I had felt there, lives on and through the years I have warmed my hands before the fires that once upon a time burned brightly on the lakeshore of Harvey Camp.

A Season's Paradox

Christmas, once again. What is the true reason for the season? Behind the trees, the gifts, the tinsel and the carols, there is a truer and more accurate reason for this occasion: "Unto you is born this day a Savior." But during all the hustle and bustle of this busy holiday season where exactly is this Savior? He does not seem to be found beneath the tree. He is difficult to spot in the glitter and glamor and tinsel. Nor can he be found, at least primarily, in the plush Christmas parties. Moreover, he seems to have abandoned the manger. This Savior is no longer a baby, and no longer a child.

Christmas is a paradox. Frequently, the refrain of "joyous Noel" could be changed to "Season's grief." For every gift that is gaily wrapped and given, there seems to be a corresponding grief. For every song sung of joy and happiness, there are as many sorrows and lamentations. Friends gathering and families uniting sometimes conceal the frustrations and fears which seem, more than any other time of the year, to creep forth. Celebration and suicide seem to go hand in hand. While some people enjoy the fullness of love, laughter and life, others experience only the utter despair of emptiness.

Christmas does seem intended to express the fullness and blessings of life. That said, consider this paradox. Joy came to Mary and Joseph but they had to flee into exile in order to save it. Their Christmas joy wound up in a foreign country, Egypt. The child in the manger in a cave lived, but all the other boys were murdered; butchered by King Herod's hired thugs. Mary's soul may have rejoiced with exceeding great joy at what happened to her, but what about the dozens, or hundreds, of grief-stricken mothers whose children were brutally killed? How could they be consoled? In the face of all this, how can we say: "Peace on earth and good will towards all?" The mothers and fathers of the butchered babies had absolutely no peace that Christmas and as for good will … well, their experience was anything but that. Mayhem and murder displaced any chance for good will.

What should be the proper and appropriate response to the fact that while the Savior came bringing peace and good will, and escaped the butchers of Bethlehem, the rest died? Does it even matter? Is it even an issue that the Lord of life came in the midst of carnage, destruction and death? In fact, it was his very appearance that caused the disaster. Had he not come, the butchers would have stayed in Jerusalem. What can our response be to the fact that while we proclaim the child in the manger at Christmas, many children and adults alike are dying from the increasing cruelty of war, famine and oppression? In some way, it is life itself in all of its sometime ugliness and meaningless chaos. These are the results of choices, of circumstances and tragedies. Does the coming of the Christ, then and now, somehow address the awful waste of human life, both then and now?

In the words of the prophet, he has come to bring good news to the poor. He has come to comfort the broken-hearted. He has come to proclaim freedom to the captives. He has come to procure release for the prisoners. He has come to announce the inauguration of the year of God's favor. We could truly celebrate it, but often we find it somewhat disconcerting. So we have just given lip-service to it, especially around Christmas, but we have not allowed it to come to pass in our midst. We sometimes feel our own agenda is better. We have too often said "no" to taking up the social applications of the gospel. We have oppressed women in our churches and in some quarters openly praise this as salutary. We engage sometimes in racial and religious prejudice. That goes both ways. It is not just whites discriminating against blacks or Christians opposing Muslims. We have refused to speak out on social and political issues, sensing in them a risk not worth running. We have at times turned our backs on the sad drunks, the whores and the more despicable sinners in our midst. And this is supposed to be Christmas.

Where is he? The Magi asked the same question as they searched for the object of the star seen first in the east. We must ask the same query. Where is he this Christmas, if not at the parties, in the gifts, among the tinsel, beneath the lights or behind the trees? He is with the poor, the oppressed, the downtrodden, the sinner. He is with those who have not, for it was to these that he came in the first place. Paul Tillich once commented adroitly that salvation is a child but when it grows up it gets crucified. Only the person who can see strength in weakness, the big picture in the broken pieces, triumph in losing, glory in suffering, innocence in guilt, righteousness in sin, and life in death can truly say: "I have seen his salvation."

He came once to the world as a baby. He comes again to the same world as men and women. The divine imperative is for us to live the gospel, to be a Christ to our neighbors, to give, to love, to serve, and to be an agent of reconciliation. This is how God is best served. Holy Hallelujahs and pious Amens are not the point of service. Luther said there was no point looking up into heaven for him. The tasks which he came to do must be actualized in those who call themselves by his name. The world will know the tomb is empty when they see that our hearts are full. They will know that he is alive when he is seen living in us. The world will know who holds tomorrow when they see his followers holding to him today.

Unto you is born this day a Savior. Unto the derelict on inner city streets is born this day a Savior. Unto the most unlovable old cuss is born this day a Savior. Unto the vilest sinner is born this day a Savior. Let us give that Savior to them, to our world ever and again.

And an angel of the Lord appeared to them, and the glory of the Lord shone around them. The angel said to them: "Do not be afraid. Behold, I bring you good news of great joy which will come to all people. For unto you is born this day in the city of David a Savior, who is Christ the Lord. Glory to God in the highest, and on earth peace, good will, to all" (Luke 2:9-11, 14).

Bay of Fundy, Canada

Rowing on the Bodensee, Germany

VIOLENCE AND THE PRINCE OF PEACE

The gospel reading for today is a disturbing narrative. I intend to give it a bit of a disturbing interpretation. This means some of you may find it disturbing too, especially in my application of it. But before that, it is noteworthy that the Old Testament lesson has a lot of "thou shalt nots" included in it, including the firm admonition: "Don't make idols." The allusion to idols is relevant to the gospel reading. It also reminds me of an anecdotal story about the great nineteenth-century British preacher Charles H. Spurgeon who was famous both for his sermons as well as smoking cigars. One day as he was working on a sermon in his office someone popped in, saw him puffing away, and sarcastically remarked: "At your idol again I see!" To this Spurgeon cheerfully replied: "Yes, but as you can see I'm burning it!" Keep that little story in mind as we turn to the gospel.

When something unusual happens, it makes an impact and sticks in one's memory. On 2 February 1976 one of the greatest storms to slam the rugged coasts of the Bay of Fundy in eastern Canada struck. It is remembered as the "Groundhog Day Gale." Winds of 118 miles an hour were recorded. There were thirty-nine foot waves in the bay. Salt spray from the sea was later found on buildings twenty miles inland. The storm hit around 11:00 a.m. and continued on for eight hours wreaking destruction and devastation. Power poles snapped like matchsticks, the power was knocked out and parts of the city were in darkness for two weeks. Roofs came off buildings, cars were flipped over, oil barges torn from their moorings struck the Courtney Bay causeway. There was over twenty-two million dollars of damage in the city of Saint John. And I was right there in the middle of it. School was dismissed early. We had to walk home. Behind Bayside Junior High School we had to cross the soccer field which was covered with ice. When my friends and I stepped onto the ice, the gale force winds blew us across the field. It was great fun. That night by candle light, we huddled round a battery-operated radio listening to storm reports and the efforts of EMO (emergency measures organization). It was all very exciting. It was forty-six years ago and I remember it vividly as though it were last night.

More than 1900 years before the great "Groundhog Day Gale" another unusual event occurred which people remembered too. The story, or allusions to it, appears in six early Christian sources. These include the gospels of Matthew, Mark, Luke, John and Thomas, along with the Acts of the Apostles. The event also figures into the trial of Jesus where it becomes a formal accusation, an indictable offense, blasphemy. The setting is Passover, one of the great religious events of Judaism and we find Jesus strongly objecting. Jesus goes to Jerusalem but not to engage in the ritual, he does not participate in the festival. He is no longer concerned with the feasts. So why did he go to Jerusalem? Mark tells us that Jesus went to the temple a day early, went in, and looked around. In modern parlance, he cased the joint and then left. The next day he returned and took action. This suggests premeditation.

The following day Jesus returns and drives them out. The incident has been inappropriately called the "cleansing of the temple." Only John tells us how he did that. Jesus was armed. Jesus takes the time to fashion a rudimentary weapon – i.e. a whip. He could have been arrested and charged with being a public nuisance, with destruction of public and private property, with multiple counts of assault, causing mayhem, disorderly conduct, and so on. The district attorney's office there in Jerusalem could have had a field day with this fellow Jesus. Picture the scene. A crazy man lunging into a crowd, likely shouting, swinging a lash, people dashing for shelter, trying to get out of the way. Merchants anxiously trying to preserve their goods, tables turned over, money spilling, coins bouncing across the floors, rolling here and there and everywhere while desperate men try to collect it all the while feeling the burn of the lash striking them over and over. Imagine the oxen, the sheep and the doves panicked. It is silly to assume he was "driving the oxen out" only. The sources explicitly say he drove them out who were doing business. The Greek literally means: "He threw them out." This is an act of violence. Plain and simple. And him the Prince of Peace, the meek and mild and positively gentle Jesus! Understandably, people are uncomfortable with this passage. There have been desperate attempts to tone it down, make it say something else, or when all else fails, simply ignore it. The exegetical gymnastics of some scholars and preachers in handling this narrative are nothing short of astounding.

"Stop all of this," Jesus says loudly: "Stop making the house of God a marketplace." What does this mean? It is an error to read this text as an anti-money narrative, or as an open attack upon religious business, or a protest against the improper use of sacred space. The moneychangers often, and unfairly, get the brunt of the blame. The temple tax could not be paid with the Greek drachma or the Roman denari because these currencies featured a human image – imperial or pagan portraits – so this had to be converted into Tyrian money which bore only the value of the shekel designation but was also prized for its higher purity of silver (90%). There is evidence indicating Tyrian currency did display the image of Melkart, a pagan deity. But that aside. The merchants and moneychangers were properly licensed by Temple authorities, they were legitimate, they possessed official authorization, and they had no reason to feel bad about what they were doing. After all, the temple tax and the temple cult required their services. There is no evidence from the sources that there was anything amiss in what was happening in the Temple. It is specious to argue that the high priests were engaged in extortion, money making, and that Annas (the high-priest) was running a $170 million dollar annual business.

It is necessary to sidebar here just for a moment. Did this event really happen? The Synoptics (Matthew, Mark and Luke) place the story late in the career of Jesus while John places it at the beginning as among the first public acts of Jesus. It is doubtful there were two similar episodes. So how did Jesus manage to do it alone? The temple precincts were perhaps two to three football fields in size. Why is there no opposition? Are we to believe that not one merchant or moneychanger tried to defend himself? Why do the temple police not intervene? Where are the Roman soldiers garrisoned in the Antonia Tower fortress? The fortress overlooked the Temple on the northwest and was connected to the outer court by means of two flights of stairs. Be all of this as it may, the narratives claim that Jesus created havoc that day in the Temple. The religious authorities were upset (to put it mildly). After all, the Temple, forty six years in the making, and still not finished, was the heart and most prominent symbol of their religion, and here's this rabid armed hooligan saying it's all for naught.

Sometimes in our lives we insist on clinging to the sources of our own destruction. Other times we misread the script and prepare badly with acute disastrous consequences. The Revd Mr Bruce was an ambitious preacher in the court of King James VI in the early seventeenth century. The day came when he was granted opportunity to preach before the entire royal court with the distinct chance of promotion. So he prepared diligently as one would. The appointed day came and the Revd Mr Bruce mounted the pulpit. He made one mistake. He selected as his explicit sermon topic to expound upon the doctrine of election and predestination. No mean task. King James considered himself as astute theologically as any layman in the kingdom. After the sermon had dragged on for an hour, yea two hours, in extreme exasperation King James leaned forward in his chair and shouted: "Talk sense man, or come down from the pulpit." Realizing that his chances for promotion had now gone by the board but determined to save face, at least for the sake of his cloth, the Revd Mr Bruce leaned back across the pulpit and said: "I'll do neither." What a desperate moment for the poor soul. What a serious miscalculation. The Revd Mr Bruce vanishes from the stage of history and we hear nothing further of him.

How are we to best understand these puzzling actions of Jesus in the Temple? It is worth considering that the greatest sin of the church is silliness. Jesus was not simply moving furniture about, he was throwing it out...the baby with the bath water. He was tearing the house down, because it was silly. What is it, exactly, that we as Christians are making such a fuss over? I think Jesus is saying, rather forcefully, that there is something more important than temple religion. His detractors tried to kill him, and he was later arrested, tried, convicted, and executed. That is the way of the prophet.

In order to properly understand this story we must see it in its context. The larger narrative involves the *Gospel of John*. One of the main themes in the fourth gospel is Jesus as the replacement of Temple religion. Jesus undercuts Temple religion. He perceived the Temple as a place of corruption, legalism, oppression, practically idolatrous, stifling access to God. There was a fair amount of resentment against the temple. The community of the ascetic Essenes had rejected it. Temple religion was oppressive to poor people. It is significant that the first thing the rebels did in the Jewish revolt in the year 66 was to burn all the temple records of indebtedness. Jesus attacks the idea that people can buy God's favor. It is a rejection of this form of worship. It's not about the temple as sacred space, for Jesus in John does not recognize sacred space. Is the story about cleansing or destruction? Of course the author has the advantage of hindsight. He knows what happened to the cult of the Jews. The Temple lay in ruins for about twenty years before John put pen to parchment. The word "cleansing" is something of a misleading euphemism. The action against the temple underscores the difference between the new religion and the old. The famous twentieth-century theologian Karl Barth said the message of the Bible is that God hates religion. Really? Where does that leave us? The gospel of Jesus Christ is meant to comfort the afflicted. The gospel of Jesus is also intended to afflict the comfortable. That's what this sermon is about. "Everything you know is wrong." Someone wrote those words on the wall in the university library tower stairwell at the University of Canterbury in New

Zealand during final examinations one year. "Everything you know is wrong." Might this apply also to theology and our own doctrines? Do we find that frightening? Sometimes things are not what they seem.

Many of us have difficulty imagining that something in place for so long should be changed, altered or done away with. Is it possible that what has been established and so well entrenched is past its "use by" date? If we truly want to take Jesus seriously, we should allow for the possibility. Reform is never achieved without opposition. In the pew racks in front of you is a red book. The *Book of Common Prayer* is the basis for faith practice in the Anglican communion. But when Thomas Cranmer introduced the BCP in 1549, there were riots in England and 4,000 people died opposing it in Devon and Cornwall alone! Perhaps it is time to riot once again!

Prudence might suggest the sermon should stop here, but I think that might be remiss in my responsibility as the preacher. So let me be as disturbing as Jesus for a few moments. Is the Temple a signpost or the reality? The Temple was supposed to point to God. It became an end unto itself. What needs cleansing or abolishing today? Jesus may be the most admired man in history and the one least imitated. "What would Jesus do?" We see these words on office walls and desk plaques. It is cliché! Empty, trivializing rhetoric. The question may be legitimate but few are truly interested in the replies. The answers are often altogether too frightening.

The United States is a country frequently called "Christian," called by his name, with the best sports stadiums and the worse schools in the developed world. We have increasing stockpiles of guns and bombs but no solutions to health care and poverty. We build luxurious churches, but fail to use them to attack systemic injustice and all too often these structures are characterized by an evident reluctance to publicly condemn political corruption and anti-Christ foreign policy. The IRS investigated All Saints' Episcopal Church in Pasadena and threatened to remove its tax exempt status because the-then rector George Regas preached a blistering antiwar sermon concerning the policies of the Bush administration in 2004, especially the war in Iraq. The incident was an exception. Christianity used to give the Roman Empire fits. Now it has blended in so well with the dominant culture that it is part of the Empire. I think it might be quite interesting and quite wonderful if federal agents entered churches and arrested ministers and other people. On what grounds? Enemies of the state! Think of it! Threats to national security! Subverters of dominant cultural paradigms! Imagine federal agents hauling these dangerous people away in manacles. This is how the first Christians were perceived. This is how the early Church interfaced with culture. But not anymore. We're just too busy trying to figure out ways to be accepted by culture.

Following Jesus is a dangerous path. Dietrich Bonhoeffer who ended his life of costly discipleship dangling at the end of a length of piano wire in 1945 suggested what we needed was "religionless Christianity." What would that look like, I wonder? I think it means burning the idols, driving out the idolaters, it would mean "don't pick up badgers," I think it might mean cleaning the "blue ice" out of our spiritual refrigerators, and above all, it means following Jesus. Jesus made a radical statement in the Temple. What would be an approximate parallel today? If we want to follow Jesus, then it's time to skewer the sacred cows. Such as? Expel all the bishops and pastors right up through the archbishop of Canterbury, the pope, and all the general superintendents. Get rid of all of them. Collect every copy of the *Book of Common Prayer* and the manuals of every denomination and have a great bonfire. Bring in the demolition crews and tear all the churches down. Raze them to the ground! And most importantly, stop this silly practice of worshiping Christ! We have had quite enough of that. And one public word of advice to the search committee: For the love of God and for the sake of humanity, don't hire someone who emphasizes the worship of Christ. Appoint a man or woman who follows Jesus. There is a serious world of difference.

In the name of the one who destroys the temples of idolatry, and who releases us to the energizing power of God, we dare to say these things. Amen.

Konstanz, Germany

Reichenau Island, Germany

THE JOKE OF THE SECOND COMING

I once heard the story of two old men who lived in a nursing home who had the very naughty habit of putting their hats on and then going off whenever it pleased them. Sometimes they would be gone for hours and no one knew where they were or just what they were up to. Try as they might, the staff could never catch those two old crafty codgers. They would grab their hats and off they'd go. One day someone got the idea that if they hid their hats maybe they would not go out. So the hats were taken down from the pegs and hidden. Sure enough, the two old fellows never left the nursing home again except when they were supposed to. Hiding their hats should have done nothing to prevent the two men from going out. But going out and coming in with their hats on was their routine. That's just the way it was. Some of us accept uncritically ideas just because that is the way it's always been. I wonder what might happen if someone hid our customary hats?

In recent years the church has literally suffered an all-out blitz in the media, in literature, in religious institutions and in the pulpit with attention paid to that cataclysmic event known in Christian theology as the second coming of Christ. We have heard the cry: "The time is at hand." We have seen terror and signs in the heavens. There have been wars and rumors of wars. We have heard the galloping hoof-beats of the four horsemen of the Apocalypse. We have anticipated the imminent darkening of the sun, the moon being turned to blood and the fall of the stars. We have expected, in great fear and trembling, the coming of the Antichrist, the revealing of that awful symbol 666 and the outbreak of Armageddon. All around we have witnessed the solemn countdown to the rapture. Hal Lindsay was only a bit off in his chronology for we must surely now be living on that late great planet earth. We have heard the call of the archangel and the last trumpet of God has sounded. Or has it?...so caught up have some of us been in the imagery, the apocalyptic drama, the fantasy of it all. Tyndale House Publishers have been making a fantastic killing with the phenomenally successful *Left Behind* series of novels. But all of this, in terms of the second coming, is a joke. For the second coming has already occurred and continues to occur.

I remember as a small boy hearing preaching about gloom and doom and the end of the world which I became convinced would happen before I got out of high school. I did not like the idea. Heaven did not sound like that good of a deal to me. I privately lamented the loss of life's opportunities and I hoped that God might hold off long enough to let me get to age 21 at least or thereabouts. I recall more than one preacher laboring over arguments to demonstrate that this was indeed the last generation. Somehow, I knew they were probably right. After all, one did not question the man of God. At least that's what they told us: "Touch not my anointed." That was an oft-repeated line. Besides when you are 13 years old, loudly proclaimed arguments can truly make an indelible impression. Forty years is a generation they said. The modern nation-state of Israel – always the center piece of this sort of preaching – had been established in 1948. Forty years implied that 1988 had to be the absolute end of human history. Other preachers got on about the Balfour Declaration of 1918 and something about 70 years but that still worked out to being 1988. Of course one had to keep in mind the "great tribulation." That was to last seven whole years. The question, then, for figuring out the second coming, depended on one's special view of the tribulation. Most of the preaching I heard took the pre-tribulation perspective. That is, the Lord will come before the onslaught of serious oppression. That meant 1981! I remember seeing tracts on the table at the back of the church explaining the "fact" that in 1982 all the planets would be in perfect alignment and this event would have catastrophic consequences for earth. I was afraid that life would be yanked out from underneath me. I was also afraid that I might not be ready for this second coming and would have to face Antichrist and the horrors of the "great tribulation." I certainly believed all of this. In my high school annual all of the graduating seniors had the opportunity to put in a quote by our pictures. Mine reflected this ethos: "It won't be long, then we'll be leaving here. It won't be long, we'll be going home." The words were from a Black Gospel song. As time went on and 1981 passed uneventfully and 1982 did not seem to bring any great terrors I began to shake off the notion that the world was about to go to hell in a handbasket. I came to accept the view that Christ had not come to raise hell at all, but to proclaim the good news of the gospel of God. In 1988 a friend wrote to me and said: "Well, this is the year, isn't it?" I wrote her back and by then was feeling quite cheeky so I said: "Well, Lynn, this time next year, I'll write and tell you what I think."

The more recent lead-up to the millennium introduced another barrage of bizarre theology. The end of the world was upon us and the second coming would occur any moment. In the last night of the year 999, multitudes of people singing and praying, waving torches and palm branches filled the streets and squares of Rome. When the fatal hour struck, the crowds remained transfixed barely able to breathe. It sounds all very dramatic and makes for a great and compelling story, but it never happened. The French monastic historian Raoul Glaber – who was alive in 999 – tells us that many unusual events occurred in the years leading up to and following the turn of the first Christian millennium. But if Glaber knew it was December 31, 999 he was among the very few who did. Most Christians in the tenth century lacked a precise calendar and could not possibly have known what year it was. An exact sense of chronology would have to wait another two centuries. There was in the main no panic about Y1K. But if 999 makes for rather dull reading the same cannot be said for the end of the second Christian millennium. Doomsday ideas have persisted throughout Christian history and under certain cultural conditions a dormant doomsday virus breaks out. Millions of Christians, from St. Paul down to the present, have expected the end of the world and the second coming in their lifetimes. "This generation shall not pass away." Yet generations come and go, even as prognosticators persist in predictions, prophesies and prognoses. Why then, was 2000 any different? It was in fact really nothing more than an arbitrary date on a calendar which any informed person knows was constructed on assumption and calculation now known to be clearly erroneous. No one knows exactly when Christ was born, certainly not the precise year. And what about the year zero? Yet for some reason 2000 was a big deal, even in the Church.

Arithmetically, the twenty-first century began on 1 January 2001 but that date had no appeal. The year 2000 seemed magically attractive. Unlike 1000 years ago our world has a common calendar, in most cases, so the precise end of the second millennium was celebrated globally and simultaneously. In a sense, the whole Y2K mania was a Christian invention. If the world did not largely observe the Christian calendar and went, say by Buddhist reckoning, the New Year would have rolled around in April and would have been the year 2543. That aside, the third Christian millennium began some time ago somewhere between 1994 and 1997. That did not seem to pacify anyone and millennial madness, doomsday fascination and preoccupation with "endings" continued to characterize a lot of Christians. Since at least the 1970s, Christian groups have utilised the Apocalypse of St. John literally, creating a theological discourse of fear and finality. In late 1999 so-called prophets converged on Rome and Jerusalem, fear-mongering increased. Our technological captivity gave rise to many fears that our computers would literally crash, banks would lose their money, nuclear weapons would be accidentally launched, aircraft would fly off course, food would run short and all of this would be the beginning of sorrows. Churches in many areas began to participate in strategies aimed at surviving this event just in case the second coming did not occur simultaneously. Of course none of these predictions came to pass and those obsessed with the end of the world and the second coming were left to revise their charts and graphs. The joke in all of this, of course, is that even Jesus said no one could possibly know the day or the hour. He then went on to confess that not even he knew the date. Only God knows it. Still, that advice has not deterred us from making our own predictions. The joke has been told of a fellow trying to figure out God and thus put several questions to God in hopes of sorting it all out. "God, how long is a million years?" God answered: "Oh, a million years is just like minute." So the fellow asked: "Well, how much is a million dollars to you?" God replied: "A million dollars is like a penny." The man thought this over for a moment and then said: "God, would you give me a penny?" And God said: "In a minute." The whole point about this joke of the second coming is that, as St. Augustine reminds us: "If you understand it, it is not God. If it is God, you do not understand it."

Is it accurate to say that men and women can find God in Christ? The answer must be in the negative. Who are we to think we accept or reject God? We should cry out in praise that we have been found by God. For it is God who finds us in Christ. The moment is everything; that moment when he comes again, for the second time. An old man when asked if he would like to arrange something for the following summer replied: "Son, at my age, I don't even buy green bananas." The second coming is a joke because exactly the opposite of what is expected occurs. Jesus was always found with strange people: The woman at the well, Legion, the adulterous woman. Yet God included them all in a mighty, miraculous and marvellous way. All who labor and are heavy laden are promised peace and rest in Christ as he comes to them. That must include controversial figures such as Donald Trump, head cases like Charles Manson, bad guys like Osama bin Ladin, and the alluring girls who make up the centerfolds in *Playboy* magazine. Or does it?

If we wait for the God of the galloping apocalyptic riders, God might be, in the words of J.B. Phillips, too small. If God is the child of Bethlehem alone, perhaps God is too small. If God is merely a once-for-all-time historical man, there is a good chance that God is too small to make a difference. If the second coming of Christ is just a literal eschatological event, it is not enough. Some things have second comings that are quite different from what one originally envisioned. On 11 March 1995 the

Oregonian newspaper in Portland published a small photograph of a fellow named Dick Fitzgerald in Shreveport, Louisiana holding up a small rather battered looking postcard. It had just been delivered to his home, on 9 March 1995, where his parents used to live. He had mailed it to them from a post office in Italy in 1945.

I recall a theological joke from seminary days about an Arminian who was walking down a flight of stairs. All at once, he tripped, went head over heels down the steps to the bottom. He got up, dusted himself off and said: "I'd better be more careful next time." A short time thereafter a Calvinist came down the same flight of stairs and also tripped and did exactly what the Arminian did. As he dusted himself off at the bottom he was heard to say: "Well, I am glad that's over with." The flower of the Calvinist is a tulip; an acronym for the five points of Calvinism. On the other hand, one might well say that the flower of the Arminian is a daisy: "Loves me, loves me not, loves me, loves me not." I am not promoting Calvinism, but where is our assurance? What is the foundation of our faith? Is it God or our response to God? Do our theologies sometimes play jokes on us?

Christ has come once as a child. He comes again. Not in the heavens but to us as individuals where we are in the midst of life. We are all on a journey. Some of us have wild ideas that cannot possibly be true. Our journeys are like those of the three well-known characters in L. Frank Baum's children's book *The Wonderful Wizard of Oz* set in the mythical land of Oz who are in need and who have embarked on a very long, dangerous journey. The scarecrow has no brain, the tin-man has no heart and the lion lacks courage. They follow the road to the Emerald City where they hope to find the incredible wizard of Oz, the great man, who can help them, who can solve their problems and meet all their needs. After their long journey they finally arrive in the Emerald City. Alas, they discover to their absolute horror that the so-called great wizard is neither great nor a wizard. He is just a silly old man with a bald head who has no way at all of granting hearts and brains and courage.

The three sad characters come to realize that they cannot just step up to the counter and buy these things. Neither can they be had as gifts like presents under the Christmas tree. Such needs can only be met, fulfilled and discovered on the journey itself.

In 2011 the American Christian radio host Harold Camping predicted the world would end. More than 3,000 billboards popped up across the country and all around the world announcing Judgment Day (May 21) and the veritable end of human history (October 21). Both days passed uneventfully. Camping suffered a stroke and died two years later at 92. Parker D often said that some of these fellows were up and down like a yoyo and guys like Camping got "around like a button on a funny house door" (whatever that means). It sounded about right to me.

If one skins their eyes watching the skies for the second coming of Christ there is a good chance he will be missed altogether. Everywhere, at any moment, Christ comes again. To say that a second coming of Christ is expected gives the sense that perhaps he is scheduled to come once more only and until that time we must plod on. His second coming is nothing other than his presence in, with, and around his people. It happens on the journey; not in some special place. It happens wherever we are and does not, cannot, depend on who we are. Christ comes without warning and in that experience we must call out the same query as Saul of Tarsus did on the road leading to Damascus: "Who are you Lord?"

Who is that on the lakeshore? Who is that stranger on the road? Who is that one gesturing from the boat? It could be the biggest joke one has ever known. Alternatively, it might be the most decisive event one ever experiences. It could be the second coming of the Lord Jesus Christ.

Eagle Creek trail, Oregon

Ordinary Folk and Heavenly Hosts

Truthfully, I do not think I am anything special. There are times when I tell myself I am no good at all and I often wonder how galling it must be for people to see a fellow like me with enough nerve to mount the pulpit. I have heard many more eloquent speakers with better minds than mine. I have read books and writers that make me envious enough to merit classification among at least one of the medieval seven deadly sins. I once heard Billy Graham say that if he had to do it over again he would have spent a good many more years in preparation. Hindsight is generally 20/20 they say and as for now most of us are full of excuses as to why we cannot possibly do anything extraordinary. After all, we are merely ordinary people and certainly lack all the qualifications for being among heavenly hosts.

Even at my age I sometimes tell myself I am too old for certain tasks and projects. I hope it isn't true but I spend considerable energy trying to prove it is the case. But the tired argument, "I am too old" is entirely a specious one. Consider this. Cato learned Greek when he was 80. Sophocles wrote *Oedipus* and Simonides won the literary prize when both were past the age of eighty. Theophrastus did not begin to write his *Characters of Men* until he was over 70. Chaucer was 60 when he came to write the *Canterbury Tales.* Goethe worked at Weimar and did not complete *Faust* until he too was past the age of 80. Is it truly too late? Is one too old? At the age of 74, the Canadian Ed Whitlock became the oldest person to run a marathon in less than three hours finishing in two hours, fifty-eight minutes, and forty seconds. Margaret Ringenberg flew around the world at age 72 and at 79 competed in an aerial race from London to Sydney. Young Allan Stewart earned a degree from the University of New England in Australia when he was all of 91. Harry Bernstein was married to his wife Ruby for seventy years. When she died he took up writing to help deal with loneliness. He published his first book at age 96. Teiichi Igarashi reached the summit of Mt. Fuji after his 99th birthday while Frank Schearer, a retired doctor from Washington state, was still waterskiing at age 100. What precludes ordinary folk from joining with the heavenly hosts in the work of the kingdom of God?

The rebuttal is that age is wisdom and therefore one must be aged in order to truly accomplish something great for God or in life. Consider this. Benjamin Franklin was already writing for publication at the age of 16. George Whitefield was one of the world's greatest preachers by the time he was 22. D.L. Moody was preaching at 18 and Charles Spurgeon already had two years experience as a preacher under his belt by then. William Cullen Bryant wrote *Thanatopis* at age 18. Robert Southey was already famous by that age. John Milton composed one of his very best poems at the ripe old age of 22. Henry Wadsworth Longfellow became Professor of Modern Languages at age 19 and by the time he was 26 had become a well-loved poet. Robert Burns was a gifted writer at age 16 and William Gladstone belonged to the House of Lords at 23. Demosthenes was the greatest orator of all Greece at 25 and Solomon began a reign marked by wisdom and wealth when he was 18. Alexander the Great had conquered the known world by the time he was 32. Romanian gymnast Nadia Comaneci was only 14 when she became the first athlete in Olympic history to achieve a perfect ten in gymnastics. Victoria Van Meter became the youngest girl to fly across the United States when she was 11. Daisy Ashford wrote a bestselling novel that sold over 200,000 copies when she was 9. John Stuart Mill mastered the Greek language at age 7 and Mozart was all of 3 when he taught himself to play the harpsichord. And Bonnie Blair won five Olympic gold medals having begun ice skating when she was two years old. Is one too young? Is it truly too soon for one to plunge into the kingdom project?

If one is not too old or too young, then the argument will doubtlessly be raised that they lack the essential training or qualifications. It is a fact that God chooses ordinary people and these rather ordinary people are distinct for their lack of qualifications. Consider this. Adam was a good man but had problems with his wife. Noah was a splendid story of a resounding lack of success. He preached for 120 years and still had no converts. One does not need to say anything about his unrealistic building projects or his drinking. Abraham has been called the father of the faithful but his resume and reputation seems a bit more dodgy. While he was evidently trusting in God he was trying to work things out himself. He may never have slept with another man's wife but we do know that he offered to share his own wife with another man. He was also not above telling the occasional lie. Jacob was a thief. Joseph was a great thinker but he tended to brag and on top of that he had a prison record and had been accused of trying to seduce his boss's wife. He denied it, but they found his shirt in her bedroom. Miriam was a gossip. Her big mouth was a liability. Rahab worked in a brothel and her moral character was clearly under legitimate scrutiny. Moses was anything but a good communicator. He often lapsed into a stutter and embarrassed himself. On top of that he left one of his jobs abruptly over a murder charge. Hardly seems like a viable candidate for joining the heavenly hosts. David, on the other hand, appeared to have all the natural qualities and qualifications for leadership until the sordid tale came out of his illicit sexual affair with his neighbor's wife and his complicity in her husband's murder. All in all a most unsavory sort of chap. On top of that his armor did not fit. Solomon had similar positive qualities but the fact of the matter remains that he seemed more interested in women than in anything else and he collected them, literally, by the hundreds. Hosea did not collect women but he certainly couldn't choose them either and his wife's occupation would surely keep him out of any leadership or front line ministry capacity. Samson's hair was too long. Ruth was a suspect foreigner. Deborah had an interesting and successful curriculum vitae but gender would be an issue for some people. Does God actually choose women? Gideon doubted. Jeremiah was a likeable fellow but possibly emotionally unstable and pathologically negative. Amos was quite unpolished and tended to ostracise people. Jonah was a deserter who could not be trusted. John Baptist was particularly weird adhering to a strange diet, insisting on wearing rather odd clothing and his many eccentricities included spending lots of time wandering in the desert. Lazarus might have been okay but he was dead and smelled very bad. His sisters were still alive but hardly suitable. Martha was a worry-wart and young Mary seemed downright lazy. Zacchaeus was not only a sawed-off little runt he was also a crooked tax collector. Paul was somewhat short on tact and could be harsh in the way he dealt with people. John Mark clearly was no good. He had been rejected by St. Paul of all people. Timothy had ulcers or some other problem with his stomach. He would never be able to pass the physical. All of these were just plain ordinary people with hangups, problems, shortcomings and deficient qualifications. Yet somehow they all managed, in spite of their clear ordinariness, to do something extraordinary for God.

One might well argue that God used them in cases where there was no one else or during times of particular emergency. God would never have chosen them in different circumstances. For example, if God had a review panel and a selections committee none of these ordinary folk would have been appointed to God's extraordinary kingdom team or heavenly hosts. Consider this. A modern management consultant firm was asked to assess the twelve men chosen by Jesus to be his inner circle. The verdict was that the twelve men lacked the proper background, educational and vocational aptitude for the organizational enterprise envisioned by God. Fundamentally, they lacked a team concept. More specifically, Peter seemed to be emotionally unstable, had a bad temper and had been known to lapse into fits of anger during which time he cursed and swore openly. Andrew had no known leadership qualities. The two brothers, James and John, possessed no concept of corporate loyalty and even allowed their own mother to try and influence their standing in the company. This caused a significant level of discontent among the other workers. Beyond this, both had terrorist tendencies.

Thomas exhibited a questioning attitude that might undermine morale. Matthew, on account of his past, was regarded as utterly unsuitable. James, son of Alphaeus, had radical leanings. Bartholomew registered fairly high on the manic-depressive scale. Philip declined to wear the company uniform, Simon the Zealot appeared to be too single-minded to be of any value in managerial responsibilities and Thaddaeus was just a blank as though he had no past. Moreover, it goes without saying that Jesus himself, though popular, seldom stayed in one place for very long, was single, though there were rumors about his relationship with a certain girl named Magdalene, had a reputation for running into trouble with authority structures and was frequently seen hanging around with questionable characters in even more questionable places. One of this group was, however, quite qualified. He showed great potential, had ability and resourcefulness, possessed a keen business mind and had well-placed contacts. He was suitably ambitious and highly motivated. Judas Iscariot was therefore recommended for a senior position.

Too old, too young, too unqualified. Ordinary people became part of the heavenly hosts. The way was not smooth. It never is. The Kingdom of God is extraordinary in its ordinary nature and this is nowhere better seen than in the ordinariness of its constituents. Even then, many within the kingdom have no clue. Consider this. The following note was found in the seminary library at Princeton University.

> So Jesus took his disciples up on a mountain
> and began teaching them, saying:
> "Blessed are the poor in spirit,
> for theirs is the kingdom of heaven.
> Blessed are they that mourn for they shall..."
>
> And Peter, interrupting, said:
> "Should we be taking notes on this?"
> And Andrew said: "My pencil broke."
> And James said: "Will this be on the test?"
> And John said:

"The other disciples didn't have to learn this."
And Philip said: "I'm hungry."
And Matthew said:
"What relevance does all of this have to real life?"
And Thomas said: "Is it almost over yet?"
And several Pharisees passing by stopped to listen.
One asked: "What is your objective in this? Where are your plans,
your formulas, your thesis and antithesis?"
And Jesus wept.

The feast of all saints is celebrated on November 1 in the liturgical calendar. It is the time of year when we look around and remember the company we tend to keep. Most of them were just ordinary people too, stretching back two millennia. Who are these strange ordinary people? Ghosts? Heavenly hosts? This is how they are referred to in the book of Revelation. They are those people who fought a good fight, finished the course and kept the faith. Now they stand as angels around God's throne, wherever that is. They are for us the unseen community of the faithful who have gone before with all of their faults and foibles, shortcomings and shenanigans, guilt and greatness. These heavenly hosts allow us to draw on their strength not so much as heroes but as ordinary folk who gave what they had, when they could, from time to time, and God did something extraordinary with that. Whoever comes to Christ will never be driven away. No one whom God has entrusted to Christ will ever be lost. No one! Whoever walks with him remains with him for all eternity. Ordinary folk can trust the future for the future belongs to God and to the heavenly hosts.

In the name of the one who makes the ordinary extraordinary, we dare to say these things. Amen.

BLUE ICE, UNDERWEAR AND FENCES

Years ago the *Washington Post* newspaper carried a most intriguing story. It related how a farmer in Wisconsin was working in his field when all at once something fell out of the sky nearby. He went to investigate. Unable to determine what the object was, but convinced that it must be valuable or important, he chopped off a big piece of it, put it in his freezer and summoned the local authorities who came to the scene. All that could be concluded for certain was that the object was blue, pock-marked, frozen solid but when it thawed it gave forth a disagreeable smell. Scientists from a nearby college were called in and the inquiry continued. After a lot of handwringing and head-scratching, the mystery was finally solved. The mysterious frozen blue mass was determined to be blue potty fluid ejected from a passing air plane and frozen solid by the time it reached earth.

That's about how I feel in terms of my own religious heritage. Many of us can relate to the Wisconsin farmer. Mysterious gifts dropping out of the heavens or simply appearing in our backyards whether literally, spiritually or intellectually, most often prompts us to gather up as much of it as possible and protect it by placing it in our freezers. Many things come into our lives that fit neatly into this category. We feel compelled to preserve or continue that which comes to us whether by heritage or some sort of spiritual experience or "revelation." We assume that they come from heaven and therefore are of intrinsic value. That assumption should consistently be tested and re-examined and each of us needs to regularly take stock of what we have in our spiritual refrigerators and freezers. What are we preserving? Should we not sort out the values and priorities in our deep freezes and let some of them just evaporate and disappear?

This of course is not an easy thing to do. It is the loneliest feeling of all for no one else can truly participate in the de-frosting process. The task can feel like utter alienation. The enormity of the job can make one feel as though they are walking down an empty street in the middle of the night and the only sound one can hear is one's own footsteps. Change does not come easily for many of us. It is not something we gravitate towards. Change is not valuable to most of us. Few eagerly embrace it. There is of course something to be said for longevity, continuity and stability. But in terms of faith these things can often lead to spiritual suicide. There are those among us who simply refuse to change whether it relates to ideas, opinions, prejudices, theologies or habits. Some people are so conservative they do not even want to change their underwear. They steadfastly believe that their spiritual underwear is a gift from God, never to be touched, never to be examined closely and certainly never to be changed. Heaven forbid! Such spiritual underwear is well hidden behind and beneath our external veneer and masks. That is why it is called underwear. We all wear them, but no one can readily tell just what they look like. But God sees through our masks, past our façades and behind our external, spiritual clothing.

Spirituality, however, is no static matter. It is an adventure, a challenge. Authentic spirituality may have nothing in common with the church, established forms of religion or so-called revealed truths. God cannot be confined to any system for God is dynamic. Truth is not a set of principles to be memorized by rote and retained for one's own personal amusement or to quote at opportune times to prove one's point, however pious. There may well be absolute "truth" but it is out there. No one can lay hold upon it absolutely. The roads of life and faith are best travelled with honesty. Spirituality — past, present and future — can be predicated upon no less.

I once heard the story of an elderly woman who hired a man to put down a new carpet in her front room. The task completed, the man reached for his pack of cigarettes. Just then he noticed a bump in the center of the carpet near the middle of the room. The honest thing would have been to take up the carpet, retrieve the pack of smokes and put the carpet back down properly. That however would be too time-consuming. Looking around and feeling confident that no one else had observed the apparent oversight, the fellow took a two-by-four and gently tapped the bump until it was flattened out. Reaching his pick-up truck outside a few moments later two things happened simultaneously. First, he found his pack of cigarettes on the seat and at the same time the elderly lady came rushing from her house towards him exclaiming: "Excuse me mister, but have you seen my parakeet?"

It is difficult indeed to be serious about spirituality when we are collecting blue ice, refusing to change our underwear and spending time and energy tapping bumps out of our theological systems. Honesty and courage go hand in hand and are absolutely essential both for life and spirituality. Neither come easily or naturally but both are indispensable. We must be honest with ourselves and with God. We must be honest with our doubts. Doubting is an integral part of faith as Paul Tillich so eloquently put it. Doubting is not a sin. Doubting is okay. The strongest faith is the examined faith. Once faith is examined there may be courage to accept the road ahead, courage to accept the doubts and the courage to say "yes" to God, to new truths, to the ups and downs of the spiritual quest. But even then there may be loss.

In Quebec, the woodcutters working high up on the hill slopes many years ago devised a method of getting the cut trees down to the bottom of the hill quickly. They hollowed out a series of tree trunks and laid them end on end down the slope with water running through them. They would place the tree trunks in this shoot and send the logs hurtling to the bottom. At days end the lumberjacks would sit on their axe handles and slide down the same shoot as well. One day, one of the woodcutters did just that. As he reached the bottom his foot got stuck in a small hole in the hollowed out trunk. Just then he heard the warning call that a log was on its way down. He struggled frantically to free his foot but all to no avail. Just as the log was bearing down on him, he seized his axe, hacked his foot off and leaped clear just in time. He was crippled for the rest of his life but he was alive.

We may have to cut off some theological limb in order to gain the fullness of life. The question remains for each of us: Do we have the courage to cut? Or are we too conservative to change our underwear? Are we too enamoured with the blue ice to recognize its worthlessness and throw it away? If the baby is floating face down in the bath tub perhaps it is time to throw it out with the bath water. There is really no point in cultivating a corpse. Do we have the courage to throw the dead baby out with the bathwater? Do we have the sense to toss out the blue ice? Do we have the courage to cut? Do we have the integrity to change our underwear? Or will we just keep trying to tap all the bumps out of life while remaining infectionlessly insulated in our theological glass houses and ivory towers?

A Quaker working in the war-torn ravaged country of Poland just after the First World War along with Roman Catholics gave courageously of himself in helping to distribute food and clothing. He contacted typhus and died within twenty four hours. His colleagues wanted to bury him in their own cemetery as a sign of solidarity. This was, however, not permitted according to church law for he was not Roman Catholic. So the workers laid their friend to rest just outside the cemetery fence. In the morning it was discovered that the villagers had moved the fence just far enough to encompass the freshly dug grave. The brilliant American trial lawyer Clarence Darrow once noted: "The university has a duty to be the great storehouse of the wisdom of the ages and let students go there and learn and choose." There are however some fences that do not allow this. Education is not something that can be handed to students on a silver platter. That is indoctrination, not education. True spirituality is not a memorized catechism, it is the journey of, and a journey for, a lifetime. One attitude says we must be careful not to destroy faith. What faith? Blue ice faith? Is faith so fragile that any sudden movement sends it careening into a million pieces? Attitudes can either make or absolutely break the growth of spirituality. Attitude shapes values, ethics and doctrines either for good or for ill. These create expectations. Sometimes the world is indeed difficult to see clearly. Not because it is strange or unusual but because it is familiar. Familiarity can blind one. Ordinariness can stunt growth and limit horizons. A prisoner sitting in his cell one hot summer afternoon was given the opportunity to have anything he desired. He said he would like to have a double-dipped chocolate ice cream cone. The request was granted and the prisoner enjoyed his ice-cream. Once he had devoured it all the guard reminded him that he could have asked for the key and become a free man. Why do we so often settle for ice-cream when freedom is available? Perhaps it has something to do with the fact that too many of us have fridges chock-full of blue ice and we have not changed our underwear in ten years.

Our attitudes and values do create the shape of our spiritualities. It is always a challenge to avoid cultivating a spirityalty that has little or no problem filtering Christ through the attitudes of intolerance, hatred, bigotry and witch hunts. Too much of so-called spirituality throughout Christian history from the beginning down to the present thrives upon fanaticism and ignorance. This is a blue ice religion, to quote Darrow, which sets: "Man against man and creed against creed until with flying banners and beating drums we are marching backward to the glorious age of the sixteenth century when bigots [spiritual bigots] lighted fires to burn the men and women who dared bring any intelligence and enlightenment and culture to the human mind."

It is time to check our freezers, our underwear and our fences. No great truth whether spoken by Confucius, Buddha, Zoroaster or Jesus will ever be lost, for the greatness and certainty of moral principles survives long after the myriad forms, ceremonies, rituals and traditions have disappeared. Therefore, it seems right and fitting to throw out the blue ice, to change our underwear and move our fences. But where does this road and this approach to spirituality lead? It leads to God. It may well be a long and winding road that seems to lead nowhere and the road will go on and on so far ahead that no one can see where the turns and twists go, but in the end … God.

That is what faith is all about. Joyfully we praise the God of glory and the Lord of life. We must never forget that God is both. Life is gift. Seize it. Live it to the fullest. The discovery of authentic spirituality and God does not and will not come easily and without effort. There is always the possibility that we may not discover God at least in the way we hope or envision. That is a risk one must be willing to take, but it does seems like a risk worth running. As Blanche says in Tennessee Williams' play "A Streetcar Named Desire:" "Sometimes God is there, so suddenly." As people of faith we must count on that.

19th century Bible, Rhode Island

RED-LETTER EDITION IDOLATRY

"God said it, I believe it, and that settles it!" That's what the little plaque on the fridge in my boyhood home said. But what was it that God said, and what does it settle? These kinds of questions generally open the floodgates to theological terms and doctrinal innuendos that pulverize the questioner beneath a veritable deluge of compulsory concepts: "Inerrancy," "infallibility," "the Word of God," the "revelation of God," "God's only book," and so on.

I was always told by church people as a youngster never, ever, to put anything on top of my little leather-bound, red-letter edition King James Version of the Bible. (Incidentally, the KJV was the only true Bible.) This was the one God wanted everyone to use. At least that's the message I heard repeatedly. I never completely understood that cryptic prohibition about stuff on the Bible but I tried to obey the rule that is not quite as easy as it sounds when you're a kid. I once asked someone about it when I was eight years old and was told in a rather mysterious way that to put something on top of the Bible would be to dishonor God. I went away puzzled but I did my best to keep the Archie comics, the Hardy Boys, and the *Evening-Times Globe* off my KJV. After all, it would serve no good purpose to get God ticked off.

Somewhere along the way, the old KJV was replaced with the RSV and that translation has not fared nearly as well (in terms of keeping God happy). One copy is jammed between *The Oxford Dictionary of the Popes* and a Latin dictionary on my desk book rack. The other copy is far worse off. It rests beneath Thomas Merton's, *New Seeds of Contemplation*, Bultmann's commentary on John, and worst of all a copy of D.H. Lawrence's *Lady Chatterley's Lover*! According to those pious injunctions given to me as a youth, I should be cowering here in my chair as I behold this awful spectacle of desecration. Or should I?

I returned from church this morning a little more irritated than blessed. I had listened to one of the leading Christian voices in the country. His message had centered on the theme that we Christians need to live according to the Bible. I have no quarrel with that premise in general, at least as I understand his thrust. Something else profoundly disturbed me though and jarred me back thirty-five years in time to those days as a boy in the big old downtown mausoleum-type church. It sounded absolutely foreign and far away, even somewhat bizarre, to hear him say that the Bible had changed his life. He did not tell me to get my Greek Grammar off the Bible, but he was telling me that here clutched in his hand was a leather-bound magical potion; a theological alchemy – a true philosopher's stone! I was dumbfounded. Yes, this book had even transformed his sad life. He owed his new existence to it; his success depended on it; and he was going to be true to it until death did him in. The rhetoric almost sounded like some sort of morbid marriage pact. Here was a guy with a book of witchery! But he did not stop there, alas! but plunged on. He tried to prove that Jesus had taught the inerrancy of the Bible. I wondered if he had ever heard of anachronism. I also wondered which Bible he had in mind as the one without any errors. The one Emperor Constantine commissioned in the fourth century, the Latin Vulgate, the Wycliffite Bible, or the King James? He wound up his homily, not a moment too soon, by defining the essence of Christianity in terms of the dogmatic decrees of the virgin birth, the Bible as God's revelation, and the imminent return of Christ to earth. With a final barrage of rhetoric, he ended. For some it was with a tremendous bang. For myself, I regarded it as a fairly hollow whimper.

Do these sound like words of unbelief? If they do not, they should, for they are intended not simply as words of unbelief, but also as words of cynicism. Have we not finally checkmated ourselves by setting up alien authorities against God? In all of his sermonizing not a word was spoken concerning God's grace, mercy or love, the person of Christ, faith in such a person or the finished work of the cross. Instead, it was mumbo jumbo, impressive though it clearly was from an oratorical perspective, but mumbo jumbo all the same about books without errors of any type. As one who identifies himself as Christian. I must firmly dissent from such theology. Whether Scripture is inerrant or not is neither the question nor a pressing concern. The man on the hill is. Whether Mary was a virgin or not depends on whether you read Isaiah or Matthew. It is neither integral to my faith nor to the faith. The man on the hill is. Whatever your theology concerning eschatological matters is, cannot be made central and must therefore remain peripheral. What is central is the cross. We may look like fools in this faith and in such allegiance, but one must not forget him. He also looked like a fool on the cross, naked, scorned, dying. No book, bar none, transformed my life but the event that took place in that "fool" on the hill, in death, did. Let there be no doubt, books can transform. But the Bible did not transform me. The blood of Jesus Christ, the Son of God, did. One can be transformed by all kinds of books: The Qur'an, the Bhagavad-gita, the Tripitaka canons and scores of others. One has only to look at the zealots fighting holy wars in the name of Allah, Christ or some other god or religious leader. Such people have been transformed. I can honestly say that my life underwent a transformation after reading *The Freedom of a Christian* written in 1520 by a German monk named Martin Luther. It was indeed the "word" of God that liberated me from the bondage of works-righteousness. Does this mean, then, that Luther replaces Christ? Of course not. Nothing, not even the book that points to, and testifies of, Christ, must come between humankind and the man on the hill. "The strange new world within the Bible" is in reality beyond the Bible. It cannot be confined even to that august volume. God and God's word cannot be nailed down in any one place. For the word of God is like a passing thunderstorm that bursts here at one moment and elsewhere in the next.

Revelation is not a book or a doctrine. It is God in God's own self-revealing. That revelation occurs whenever humankind are moved to God by God through the power of Christ by faith alone. Somewhere in the second century of the Common Era, Christians decided to improve upon that. Amid controversy with a bunch of notorious fellows called the Gnostics, they devised what would become a criterion whereby right and wrong, truth and error, orthodoxy and heresy, could always be measured. This infallible standard became an instrument of legalism that essentially replaced the thunderstorm of God's revelation. At the time of the Reformation this criterion, the church, was attacked and overthrown in some measure. For a time it appeared that the Word in all its power would once again break forth. But alas, a new instrument appeared. The authority of the Bible was used to defeat the authority of the church. But then the Bible became another tool in the service of human pride. Thereafter, a true "believer" was now known as one who accepted the Bible in its many-splendored presentations. Not that the Bible in itself was bad but on the contrary, it was the way in which the Bible came to be used. That created the problem. Karl Barth summed it up quite well: "The Bible was now grounded upon itself apart from the mystery of Christ and the Holy Ghost. It became a "paper pope," and unlike the living Pope in Rome it was now no longer a free and spiritual force, but an instrument of human power."

Barth was right. Today, sitting in my usual place, I could see that clearer than ever before. He had prophesied and his words were being fulfilled before my skeptical eyes in church this morning. Perhaps it shall be necessary, if the Bible continues to eclipse the man on the hill, to pray for another Reformation, as Søren Kierkegaard suggested, that will do away with this "holy" book as effectively as Luther did away with the "holy" papacy. The Bible is not the Word of God. It points to the Eternal Word which, amid the stillness and silence, has leapt down from heaven into the midst of humankind (Wisdom of Solomon 18:14-15). The Bible is not the revelation of God. It does, however, point to that revelation which continually bursts through the mists of unbelief on every side. The Word that became flesh and dwelt among us, the Word that wound up as the "fool" on the hill is the transformer without compare and the power of God for salvation. According to Luther, the Word did it all: "I did nothing. And while I slept or drank Wittenberg beer with my friends Philip and Amsdorf, the Word so greatly weakened the papacy. I did nothing; the Word did everything." Was Luther here referring to the Bible? Absolutely not. A book could never have altered the course of history that decisively in itself but the man on the hill, the One who comes to us without a name, did. It is a terrible and dangerous error to replace Christ with the Bible. When "faith" is defined in terms of a book, rather than in terms of the living "Word," the focus of Christianity has been fundamentally changed. The Scripture as the Word is not the same thing as the Word-become-flesh. The truth revealed is the revelation, but the vehicle is not.

For some, however, the Bible is their security blanket. Like the small child who wails incessantly and refuses to go to bed without his or her "blankie," so some of us refuse to "do our theology" without our red-letter edition "blankies." Truthfully, it is far more difficult to live by the "foolishness" of the man on the hill than it is to mimic the literary charades of the Bible and repeat them inexorably to a constantly dwindling audience. But undue reverence for the book only produces bibliolatry, which, in the end, is but another cleverly disguised form of idolatry.

In a captivating prose narrative, George MacDonald, a nineteenth-century Scottish writer, and one of the most fertile influences on C.S. Lewis, tells the tale of a young British curate who had a remarkable dream. The young man dreamed that he was in the Armenian desert searching for the lost original manuscript of the fourth gospel. Finding the isolated convent where he believed the manuscript to be, he worked his way deeper into the recesses of the complex and at length entered a room where he found the book on a table.

> Oh! how my heart beat! How my eyes would dwell upon every letter formed by the hand of the dearest disciple! Bending with awe, I stretched my hand to lay it on the book. But before my hand reached it, another hand, from the opposite side of the table appeared upon it – an old blue-veined, but powerful hand. I looked up. There stood the beloved disciple! His countenance was as a mirror which shone back the face of the Master. Slowly he lifted the book and turned away. Then I saw behind him as it were an altar where a fire of wood was burning and a pang of dismay shot to my heart, for I knew what he was about to do. He laid the book on the burning wood, and regarded it with a smile as it shrank and shrivelled and smouldered to ashes. Then he turned to me and said, while a perfect heaven of peace shone in his eyes: "son of man, the Word of God lives and abides forever, not in the volume of the book, but in the heart of the man that in love obeys him."

The Word of God lives – and abides – forever, forever, and always in all places. Not black on white, or even red on white, but in the holiness of the naked who follow the naked Christ.

I am convinced that God does not care whether Bultmann sits on the RSV, Calvin on the NIV or W.H. Auden on the KJV. What God does care about is the Word becoming flesh yet again in our very lives. Nonetheless, as we plunge frenziedly into our quest for truth we may take comfort in the knowledge that our ardent striving after God is indeed aided by the map of the book we call the Bible. It is a means, but not the end, to a contemporary incarnation, seen first in the paradox of the man on the hill.

I am running free again through the tall grass in the backyard on a Sunday morning over fifty-five years ago. Clutched in my chubby hand is my black, red-letter edition KJV. I have kept the dust off of it over the last week and kept Frank and Joe Hardy underneath it. I wanted to please God. Now, thirty-five years later, with that same black book before me, (Merton, Bultmann and others still atop it) I have learned something more important about the Word, God's revelation and the man on the hill. I have learned that the man on the hill is both the point of arrival and departure, and that the Word which is becoming flesh within me is indeed that same thunderstorm as of old – God with us! And today, like that small lad in the huge church with the puzzled look, I want to know him, knowing full well that even if Christendom is finished, Christ lives.

Morskie Oko (Eye of the Sea) Lake, Mięguszowiecki Summits, Tatra Mountains, Poland

Bruneau Canyon, Southern Idaho

The Traveller, Christchurch, New Zealand

ODE TO THE HERETIC

By the time the Chalcedonian church fathers retired from their conciliar business in the year 451, orthodoxy had achieved maturity. The dogmas of Nicaea, Constantinople, Ephesus and Chalcedon had coalesced to create a non-negotiable line of distinction between the forces of right and righteousness, on one hand, and the servants of error and iniquity, on the other. The forceful and resounding Athanasian Creed was the final plank in the house of patristic orthodox authority.

And "whoever will be saved" must of necessity hold to this faith. The one "therefore that will be saved must think thus." "It is necessary to everlasting salvation" to adhere to this "faith, which except [each one] believe faithfully, [they] cannot be saved."

Thus the wheel of the ecclesiastical world rolls ever onward crushing the dissenter, the conscientious objector, the disbelieving believer, the reluctant unbeliever, and the heretic. The path of truth and godliness is strewn with the remains of the resisters and stained with their blood. The wheel rolls onward and their mangled bodies hang upon it for all of time and eternity through each unending revolution. These are the martyrs:

Cerinthus chasing the ghostly apparition of the docetic Christ,
yet pausing to hurry out of the bathhouse
in pursuit of the disappearing Apostle John.
Marcion clutching his slim version of the Holy Scriptures.
Montanus with his women
proclaiming the final word of prophetic insight.

"Whoever has an ear, let that one hear what the
Spirit is saying to the churches."
Origen filling out his divine cross-word puzzles
before committing that senseless deed.
Sabellius holding up his God of the many faces.
Paul of Samosata accompanied by his anti-Trinity singing women.
Mani crucified in the Gnostic nether world
between the Light and the Darkness.
Arius singing his song: "There was a time when the Son was not"
in the face of the thunderous Athanasian storm.
Didymus the Blind remembering everything he heard especially heresies,
though it was said he saw God
from the time when he was four when he lost his eyes.
Nestorius with his God-bearing man.
Eutychus surrounded by the so-called Robbers of Ephesus.

These are the witnesses, the losers, the powerless. Their footsteps have ceased to echo, their words have fallen silent, their pens have slipped from nerveless fingers. And the wheel rolls on, their mangled bodies still clinging to it giving the weary wheel its ultimate impetus, motion and momentum. This is the wheel of truth. This is the wheel of heretics and heresy. More than that: "This is the Catholic faith. Unless [one] keeps it in its entirety inviolate, [they] will assuredly perish eternally."

Those who do not so believe will be damned to the fires of hell forever in the Name of Jesus and to the praise of God.

In the Name of the Father, the Son and the Holy Ghost. Amen.

King of the Castle and the Dirty Rascals

The early church father John Chrysostom (+407) taught that unless the Holy Spirit prepared the heart and mind of the preacher, he spoke in vain. And unless the Holy Spirit prepared the hearts and minds of the congregation, they listened in vain. Now may the Holy Spirit prepare our hearts and minds. In the name of God – Creator, Redeemer, Life Giver. Amen.

In John's gospel for today (18:35) the Roman official Pontius Pilate asked Jesus a question: "What have you done?" The query implied some form of subversive activity. Today we mark the end of the year. Not the end of a fiscal year, or a calendar year, or the solar year, or an agricultural year, but the end of the church year. And what shall be the last word? Last words are important or at least important opportunities. The last word on this occasion is important because next week we start all over again, a new year in the church calendar. Advent has come again.

There are two repeated themes in the lectionary readings for this Sunday. One is water which is referred to five times in Psalm 93. The other is fire which is noted three times in Daniel 7. All three synoptic gospels – Matthew, Mark and Luke – record John Baptist saying: "I baptize you with water, but one more powerful than I is coming. He will baptize you with the Holy Spirit and fire." But there is also another even more pervasive and unavoidable theme in each of the four passages. That theme is royal power or kingship. In this context it means Jesus, truth claims, and social application. Some people don't want to talk about it. In certain Christian circles this last Sunday in the church year is called "Christ the King" in some liturgical calendars. The tradition is not ancient. "Christ the King Sunday" goes back only to 1925 when Pope Pius XI announced in an encyclical a new feast that became known as Christ the King. This new feast is celebrated in the Roman and Lutheran Churches and unofficially in some Episcopal parishes, but it's not mentioned in the Episcopal calendar of the church year and it is not celebrated in many churches.

Christ the King is the last Sunday in "Ordinary Time," the name given to that long period between Pentecost and Advent. Here at the end of ordinary time we are presented with something rather extraordinary. A king! This might strike some of us as rather peculiar because politically Americans don't resonate very well with the idea of a monarchy. After all, America's history includes the idea of freedom from the British monarchy and King George III. I was born in Saint John, the oldest incorporated city in Canada. If you know your eighteenth-century history you may recall that there were people in the American colonies who had no desire to separate from the British monarchy. They wished to remain loyal to the crown and became known as "Loyalists." So they left revolutionary America and sailed north. They landed at what was later known as Saint John. And the city from that time to the present has been known as the "Loyalist City." It was before my time. I had no opinion. Queen Elizabeth II came to the throne in 1952. I was always somewhat puzzled by visits to Canada by the royal family but I never saw them until 1991 when I chatted with Prince Charles at Cambridge over drinks and nibbles.

Americans may have little use for political monarchies but there are quite a few kings in popular culture and in American cultural memory. People call their dogs and horses "king." The "king" of rock and roll is Elvis Presley. Michael Jackson has been called the "king" of pop. If you prefer a different kind of music you might listen to B.B. King. At one time you could turn on the television and you might see the animated show "King of the Hill," or see who Larry King was talking to. Children loved Simba when he became the Lion King. One of the Hollywood blockbuster films of two decades ago was Tolkien's, "Return of the King" and one of the best known figures in cinema history is King Kong. How about literature? There is the King James Bible or Stephen King. You choose. What about history? There's King Arthur of the medieval legends. David Crockett was elected in 1827 to represent Tennessee in the United States House of Representatives but was later known as the "king" of the wild frontier. And people in the American south in the nineteenth century knew all about King Cotton. Martin Luther King became one of the most visible American cultural icons in the twentieth century. Roy Rogers was the king of the cowboys. The Los Angeles Kings are a professional hockey team while the NBA has the Sacramento Kings. The fascinating artifacts and treasures belonging to the Egyptian King Tut who died more than 3,350 years ago are on display right now in San Francisco. King Bhumibol was the world's longest serving head of state and the longest reigning monarch in Thai history with a rule that spanned 70 years. If you want some unhealthy food there is Burger King just down the road. Some of us have played games featuring kings. When I was a small boy growing up in Canada we had a game we played in the winter. There was always a lot of snow and the snow plows would come into the school yard and push the snow back so the teachers could park their cars. There would be huge piles of snow, easily five feet high. We would divide into teams of three or four and see who could retain control over the pile of snow. Those on top would taunt the other kids with a little song that went like this: "I'm the King of the castle and you're the dirty rascal." The other teams would charge and a great struggle would ensue for control over the snow pile. When the bell sounded to end the recess whoever happened to be on top of the snow pile could claim to be the "kings in the castle" while the vanquished teams lying on the snow and ice at the bottom were just the "dirty rascals."

Cultural motifs aside, there is a need to reconceptualize the idea of kingship away from the school yard frolics. Do we need a king? Do we even want a king? As pointed out, kingship is a concept without much currency in contemporary culture. The term might be replaced but the content is perhaps important enough for us to consider retaining. Kingship is not just about power. It is a concern for the well-being of all people. A theology of kingship at its very best calls the king to address issues of justice and righteousness, to use and administer public power for the sake of the weak, the powerless, those afflicted by injustices and all peoples marginalized by strident power plays that sometimes create havoc in our world. This idea of kingship is somewhat like the famous tenth-century Bohemian monarch – Svatý Václav – whom we all know as "Good King Wenceslas" from John Mason Neale's nineteenth-century Christmas carol. He is the servant king who comes not with crown and scepter riding on a flashing steed as a conqueror, sword in hand, but rather as one with hope and love as a servant. He comes not to dominate but to reconcile; he comes not to exclude but to give and to include. The good news of Christ the King must again be proclaimed at the center of the world. Perhaps it is time to stop romanticizing the kingship of Jesus. Listen to the echo of the question posed by Pontius Pilate so long ago: "What have you done?"

In the first century claims of kingship were subversive. You could get killed for making such audacious claims. Today the idea is blasé. Here is our challenge: How does the text retain its counter-cultural edge for us? One other thing is striking about the gospel lesson. Jesus says: "Everyone who belongs to the truth listens to my voice." On the face of it the statement is not politically correct, is not socially proper, and is not even, in a post-modern social world, reasonable. Does this mean that only Jesus speaks truth? I don't think so. No great truth, regardless of its source, can ever be lost for truth is eternal. This is not about religious territorialism. Christ is my center but Christianity is not my limit. So if one is truly interested in truth, then one will listen to truth wherever it is proclaimed. But what is truth? Alexander Solzhenitsyn once wrote: "One person speaking the truth has more power than an entire city living in falsehood." Truth! Do we really want to know what it is? There is serious risk. It might shake us to the core. Do we want the burden of bearing truth, of knowing truth, or speaking truth? In the film *A Few Good Men* Tom Cruise is a US Navy lawyer involved in a court-martial procedure. At the height of intense and electrifying examination of a witness, Cruise shouts: "I want the truth." The witness, Colonel Jessep, played by the inimitable Jack Nicholson snarls back: "You can't handle the truth." You see truth is often demanding and dangerous. Sometimes it can also be quite deadly. What is truth? The Christian message, historically, is clear: Jesus is truth. He speaks it. More than this he embodies it and more than that, he lives it. Truth is not doctrine. Truth is a person. If we are Christians then we have to deal with Jesus. And then the Pontius Pilates of the world are likely to say: "What have you done?"

There are preachers and priests who admit they avoid mentioning Jesus in sermons for fear of offending people in their audiences. I think such preachers and priests should seek alternative employment. We live in a world so afraid of offending or of being offended! Christ does not appear to have given such considerations much currency. His work and statements seem directed at comforting the afflicted and afflicting the comfortable. It comes down to this: Are we Episcopalians or are we Christians? Are we followers of Jesus or just secular people who happen to go to church on Sundays? I wonder what would happen if 535 men and women in Washington D.C. – most of whom say they are Christian – decided to place Christ the King at the center of their policy-making decisions? What would happen? Somebody would likely be heard to say: "What have you done?" One hundred years ago G. K. Chesterton put his finger on the issue when he wrote: "The Christian ideal has not been tried and found wanting. It has been found difficult; and left untried." There is a rather substantial difference between Christ and the structure that men and women have built around him. One should not confuse the two. For as Martin Buber once noted: "Nothing is apt to mask the face of God so much as religion." And it is easy to confuse motion with progress.

If Christ is King it seems prudent to ask what relevance do the teachings and ethics of Jesus have on issues facing our communities? How does the teaching of Jesus affect the current debate on health care, on the inequities caused by poverty, and the problems of unemployment? What place do the ethics of Jesus have on prevailing social policy, on issues of war and violence? How does the kingship of Christ come to bear on the economy, on the justice system and our exploding prison populations? Does Christ the King figure into U.S. foreign policy? Is the kingship of Jesus relevant in the values held by every person who claims to be Christian? Do our private agendas come under the purview of the teachings and ethics of Jesus? Where is Christ the King when American soldiers are taught to hate and when tried in court for atrocities against civilians testify that they were taught to hate by a nation that professes to be Christian? A recent American president publicly announced that Jesus was his favorite philosopher. The statement is easy to make but where do we find evidence of the kingship of Jesus in the policies of that administration? Where does Jesus stand in an economy that favors all too few? Or could it be that when thinking of these questions we are forced to concede that we are implicitly saying yes to the reign of post-modern Caesars? If so, our actions and values may constitute things that actively diminish the reign of Christ.

One often searches in vain for a serious debate about what it means to confess Christ the King in a world of violence. Christianity does not mean resignation to a future of one pre-emptive war after another after another. The ethics of Jesus do not condone turning a blind eye to politically motivated torture and massive civilian casualties. Confessing Christ is the central task of the church and this becomes ever more urgent when that confession is co-opted by competing claims and the intrusion of post-modern Caesars into the porches of contemporary religion. An appalling theology of war, articulated in the highest circles of American government, can also be found throughout churches in America. Peculiar language defining America as a righteous empire has found its way into Christian discourse and the uses are not occasional.

The roles of God, church, and nation are increasingly confused with narratives of a global American mission and conviction about a divine mandate to rid the world of evil. The danger today is political idolatry exacerbated by the politics of fear. Jesus Christ, as represented and attested in Holy Scripture, is not bound to national boundaries or identities. Those who confess the name of Christ are found throughout the earth. Allegiance to Christ must take priority over national identity. Whenever Christianity compromises with empire, the gospel of Christ is discredited. It is imperative and consistent with the teachings and ethics of Jesus that his followers must reject the idea that any nation-state should ever be described with the words: "The light shines in the darkness and the darkness has not overcome it." These words, found in Scripture, apply only to Christ. No political or religious leader has the authority to twist them into justification for war or political advantage. The ethics of Jesus demand a total rejection of the doctrine that a war on terrorism takes precedence over ethical and legal norms. If the kingship of Christ is properly recognized than many practices sit at variance with the ethics of Jesus. These include torture, the deliberate bombing of civilians, and the use of indiscriminate weapons of mass destruction. And here is the litmus test: The distinction between good and evil does not run between one nation and another, or one group and another. It runs straight through every human heart. Christ is either authoritative for Christians, or he is not. The lordship of Christ cannot be manipulated by any earthly power. The words of Jesus may not be distorted for political or propagandistic purposes. No nation, no state, no political power, may usurp the place of God. Jim Wallis made the case cogently. One might expect that this message would be *de rigueur* for Christians. Definitely not so. When a Minnesota pastor challenged the illegitimate connections between patriotism and the gospel, 1,500 church members rose and walked out. Do we not hear the words of Pontius Pilate once more: "What have you done?" What has Jesus done, and what shall we do with him?

Pope Pius XI's encyclical *Quas primas*, paragraph 33, of 11 December 1925 says if Christ is King and "if this [kingship] embraces all people, it must be clear that Christ must reign in our minds, Christ must rule in our wills, Christ must reign in our hearts, Christ must reign in our bodies and in our members." Does he? The Collect for Proper 29 reads in part: "Mercifully grant that the peoples of the earth, divided and enslaved by sin, may be freed and brought together, under the most gracious rule of Christ." But the question is this. How far will we go with this fellow Jesus? To the limit of our political allegiances? To the extent of our economic comfort? To the border of our social ideas? Or, to the cross? It is a question that can only be answered by each individual and by each community of Christians.

Peter Abelard's reinterpretation of Redemption was one of the great new ideas of the twelfth century. Abelard argued that the Incarnation – God in the human form of Jesus – was successful not because it satisfied curious notions of divine justice, not because it provided an adequate substitution, not because it paid a ransom to the Devil, but because it demonstrated the example of love. There's a thought worth pondering.

I think the message of a King of love is a wonderful thing to announce at the end of the Church year. We shall gather at the table of the Lord shortly to be reminded of God's love for all humanity in Christ. Then we shall gather around tables downstairs to celebrate "Thanksgiving." And what better thing to be thankful for at the end of the church year than that the reign of Christ continues – that he is not an absent king in a faraway castle and that we are all just dirty rascals – but that we are accepted. In the name of Christ the King, we dare to say these things. Amen.

A Drama For All Seasons

When Jesus had spoken these words, he lifted up his eyes to heaven and said: "Father, the hour has come; glorify your Son that the Son may glorify you, since you gave him power over all flesh, to give eternal life to all that you have given to him. This is eternal life, that they know you the only true God and Jesus Christ whom you have sent. I glorified you on earth and accomplished the work which you gave me to do. Now, Father, glorify me in your own presence with the glory which I had with you before the world was made. I have declared your name to the people which you gave me out of the world. They were yours and you gave them to me and they have kept your word. Now they know that everything that you have given me is from you for I have given them the words which you gave me and they have received them and know in truth that I came from you and they believe that you sent me. I am praying for them, I am not praying for the world but for those whom you have given me for they are mine. And now I am no longer in the world but they are in the world. I am coming to you. Holy Father keep them in your name which you have given to me that they might be one even as we are one. I in them and you in me that they may become perfectly one so that the world may know that you have sent me and have loved them just as you loved me."

John 17:1-11, 23

Clergy are like manure. Spread thinly over the land they are very good. But put them in a heap and…phew! The drama of Christianity is not about clerics or important people necessarily. Rather, it is a drama made up of ordinary people in the midst of ordinary life. There was a fellow named Jake who was crossing a frozen river. Fearing that the ice might not be thick enough to sustain his weight, he got down on all fours and carefully began edging across the frozen surface. All at once he heard a great rumbling sound. He thought it was the end. Then suddenly a team of horses pulling a wagon went careening past him. The people on the wagon peered down at him as they passed giving him very odd stares.

He got up somewhat sheepishly. That was a drama that did not turn out so well for Jake. But the drama for all seasons engages the hearers and the viewers on all levels and turns out well in the end.

This drama has three major themes: First, witnesses of power (verse 23), Christ glorified in us (verse 10) and the idea that all would be one (verse 11). This drama for all seasons has to do with truth, revelation and with stories. The divine drama occurs in the stories of our lives. If God is not present in those stories we might just as well give up the whole business. The seventeenth chapter of John's gospel is part of the High Priestly Prayer of Jesus. It is not much of a story. There are no names, no main events, just some pious prayer language. So in order to understand what is going on in the text we need to look at the whole book.

I suggest that this text functions as a key to the entire fourth gospel. Imagine we are all sitting in a theatre. I'll briefly narrate the drama of the Johannine gospel and you try to imagine the drama, the story, the play, taking place on the stage before you. We begin with the transcendent Logos; the Word made flesh. From the desert the Baptist cries: "Behold the Lamb of God." The man Jesus, the lead role, appears, providing drinks for everyone gathered. Nathaniel sits under a fig tree in a cloud of skepticism. Nicodemus hurries past in the darkness. A Samaritan woman pauses at Jacob's well. A lame man lies by the Pool of Bethzatha near the Sheep Gate for thirty-eight years. Crowds throng the shores of the Sea of Tiberius. Lazarus staggers out of his tomb. Judas leans back at the table with his money bag. The bare feet before dinner and the one who stoops and washes them all. Impetuous Peter hacks off the ear of an enemy in the Kidron Valley. Pilate in the judgment hall asking that immortal question. Christ at Golgotha, crucified between two crooks. Mary Magdalene with the presumed groundskeeper in the garden. Dishevelled fisherman exhausted after a hard night's work. Thomas doubting to the end, yet falling to his knees to declare his faith in the crucified, risen, one. Even the various minor players add a sense of the profound. It is quite impossible to simply watch the drama or just be a spectator.

The drama does not end with John. It continues. Will we watch the drama as spectators or will we participate in it? Will we be witnesses of power, glorifying Christ, and questing for unity, or will we be like those who stay on the sidelines? Are we hooked on mediocrity, or on being spectators? Or are we prepared to get in the dressing room and then out onto the stage as participants in the drama for all seasons? Those men and women in the fourth gospel were the actors then. There have been more modern players: Schweitzer, the murdered Romero, Bonhoeffer and many more besides. Still it is quite easy to sit back and great is the temptation to recline in comfort and watch the acting of others. The drama for all seasons does not happen only in churches or in sacred space. Instead it continues everywhere in all places and each one may contribute in imaginative ways. It can occur wherever men and women embrace faith honestly. The mystery unfolds when people of faith act accountably.

Once upon a time a preacher got up on a Sunday morning. It was a magnificent day and all of a sudden he was overcome by a desire to play golf. He rang his assistant pastor and told him something had come up and asked if the younger man could handle the duties at the church. His assistant assured him he could take the service telling the pastor "I hope whatever has come up will turn out okay for you." On the golf course the preacher went par on the first hole. He birdied on the second. At the third hole he hit a long shot to an elevated hole. It looked like a good shot but the ball was lost in the morning sun. When the preacher got up to the hole and looked around for his ball he found it in the hole. The preacher was elated. Three holes: par, a birdie and a hole in one. "Wow. Am I cruising today." Just then he heard a quiet voice: "But who are you going to tell?"

Who are the actors and actresses today? Luther taught that the Word of God was like a thunderstorm. We would all do well to simply lower our theological umbrellas and allow ourselves to be drenched in the deluge of the ongoing divine drama. To stubbornly insist on standing under our umbrella is tantamount to getting into the shower wearing a raincoat. It is meaningless.

The drama has witnesses. The story must be told continuously, and also lived, and young and old alike may write their own verses and add them to the evolving story of God's drama for all seasons. This drama calls us to be witnesses throughout the world; witnesses in our world. In order to be effective witnesses we must know the story intimately. We must know the details. Without a basic existential knowledge it is difficult to join the chorus. The only way to get it straight is to be an actor, with the proper script, in the midst of the drama. There is no need to memorize lines to be in this play. The only way to know is to be.

Thomas has been mentioned. Regardless of the naysayers the strongest faith is the examined faith, or as Paul Tillich once said: "Doubt is an integral part of faith." So it is quite okay to doubt but stay involved in the drama. Jesus says that he is glorified in them. In other words that motley crew in the fourth gospel glorified Jesus. The motley crew here today who are trying to be part of the drama for all seasons also glorifies Christ and does so whenever the story is told, whenever the power is witnessed to, and whenever one lives in the drama that plays in every season.

Then there is that haunting line: "That they all may be one." Among the most grievous tragedies in the history of the church has been the incessant fragmenting of the body of Christ. In this drama there must be an end to individualism, division and self-centeredness. There cannot be unity if all we want is the window seat or the lead role. One man and one woman shows will destroy the drama. But a common participating in the on-going story of the Spirit may bring us nearer to the reality of being one.

The drama moves through the freshness of spring, the heat of summer, the colors of autumn, and the cold of winter. One can be involved in that movement or one can sit in a pew, stand under an umbrella or refuse to act until the lead role is assigned. Whatever we choose to do, the powerful play goes on and there is still opportunity to contribute. The drama for all seasons is the drama of Christ and it is an inclusive one. A newcomer arrives in heaven and is shown about by St. Peter. As they round a corner Peter whispers: "Keep your voice down here as we pass through this corridor. The Pentecostals are in here and they think they are the only ones to arrive." The drama for all seasons is not a Pentecostal drama, it is not a Catholic drama, it is not a Baptist drama, it is not even a Lutheran drama. It is the drama of Christ. The story of the fourth gospel is a drama, which after all the scenes have ended and the props are empty and bare, transcends even itself. For even Christ surrendered to the cross to make the point that nothing, not even himself, was an adequate substitute for the reality of God. There is more to God than the historical person of Jesus Christ.

What is the meaning of it all? This drama, in terms of our participation, is contingent upon an encounter with God; an event that may break through all barriers at any time and in any place. That encounter with the Christ of the cross is the key moment that allows each of us to participate in the drama, the powerful play that goes on and on. For that experience, that learning, and that story is the continuing drama of all seasons for all seasons.

High desert trail, southwest Idaho

Intrepid Mountaineering

Travellers, Pilgrimages and the Journey of the Red Knot

In 1984 the British rock music group "Alan Parsons Project" recorded a song called "The Traveller." It goes like this.

> The traveller is always leaving town
> He never has the time to turn around
> And if the road he's taken isn't leading anywhere
> He seems to be completely unaware
> The traveller is always leaving home
> The only kind of life he's ever known
> When every moment seems to be
> A race against the time
> There's always one more mountain left to climb
>
> The traveller awaits the morning tide
> He doesn't know what's on the other side
> But something deep inside of him
> Keeps telling him to go
> He hasn't found a reason to say no
> The traveller is only passing through
> He cannot understand your point of view
> Abandoning reality, unsure of what he'll find
> The traveller in me is close behind

Advent is the beginning of the Christian calendar. It is a time of keen anticipation. It is a time of great expectation. The word advent means coming. But it also means going. The question is this: What is coming? What is it that we expect? Naturally, the answer is Christ. But also implied in this season of Advent is the idea of going and where are we going? We are going to Bethlehem. Where is Bethlehem? What is Bethlehem? And how far is it to Bethlehem? Today, modern Bethlehem is a Palestinian city in the West Bank, five miles south of Jerusalem, with a population of about 30,000. It used to be 90% Christian but due to illegal Israeli settlements taking over land formerly owned by Christian families that population has declined to about 30%. There is no point in going to that Bethlehem. Moreover, that Bethlehem has nothing to do with Advent. Where are you going this Advent, and how are you getting there?

Every year, there is a fantastic journey in the western hemisphere. It is the journey of the red knot from the islands of northern Canada to Tierra del Fuego on the southern tip of South America. The red knot is a bird, a sandpiper, that twice a year visits the U.S. Every year the red knot flies over 18,000 miles, from northern Canada to South America stopping off on the beaches of the Delaware Bay and Cape Cod. While it is winter here, the red knot feeds on the sunny beaches of Tierra del Fuego. In February as the southern hemisphere summer is coming to a close they start their journey north. They fly over the coast of Argentina, across Brazil stopping occasionally for sustenance. They know exactly where to find food. Each year they stop at the same stretches of sand and marsh. Reaching the northern shores of South America at Guyana and Suriname they strike out across the Atlantic on a weeklong nonstop flight which by mid-May brings them to the marshy shores of the Delaware Bay just as horseshoe crabs are laying millions of eggs. Here they rest. A single red knot might consume 135,000 horseshoe crab eggs. Refreshed and ready to go they take off once more on a nonstop flight to the Canadian archipelago islands north of Hudson Bay. Here in the northern hemisphere summer they mate and breed. The female red knot lays four eggs which she and her mate take turns incubating. By July, the adults abandon the little birds and head south. The young birds fend for themselves until late August and then they (alone and without any apparent guidance) begin the 9,000 mile journey to Tierra del Fuego to join their parents. They will come back to Canada the next year to mate and breed and the journey repeats itself year after year after year.

What is amazing about the red knot is this: Without a guide or previous experience the little red knot can fly 9,000 miles along the same migration route, stopping at the same places, and arriving at the same destination. How do they do it? How can they make their way along a route they have never travelled before to a destination they have never seen? How can they fly without error over vast stretches of featureless sea? How can the red knot accomplish such an epic feat of navigation? It remains something of a mystery.

The prophet Isaiah (40:1-11) speaks boldly of "preparing the way of the Lord." He speaks of the frailty of humanity. Flowers bloom and blossom and we admire their beauty in the spring and summer time. But then they fade, wither and die. We are just like the flowers of the field. We blossom and then we wither and soon we shall die. We are fading already. Do you doubt it? Look at a photograph of yourself taken 10, 20, 50 years ago. Need I say more? The grass withers, the flower fades, there is no remedy. It is inevitable. But Isaiah also speaks of the intervention of God: God comes with power, and in the role of a shepherd God feeds the flock, gathers the little lambs, carries them, gently leads the mother. How? And the "way" is not easy. Isaiah writes of wilderness, desert, valleys, mountains, uneven ground and rough places! Prepare the way of the Lord. What does this mean?

The writer of II Peter (3:8-15) asks what sort of person ought you to be? He or she then speaks about "waiting for, but also hastening the coming." What does this mean? We wait for newness. We wait for the reign of righteousness but we are told that while we wait, we should strive! What does it mean to strive? The gospel of Mark (1:1-8) tells us this is the beginning of the good news. We find another reference to preparing the way of the Lord. We hear of this man named John who claims there is a baptism of the Holy Spirit. I want to return to this idea in a moment. To repeat: Advent is not simply a time of waiting. There are seventeen references or words to movement in these texts: Way, highway, get you up, lead, turn, pathway, hastening, strive, going out and coming.

The gospel of Mark refers to the baptism of the Holy Spirit. The word "spirit" (*pneuma* in Greek), means a current of air. Air is essential for life. Take the oxygen out of this room and in a few minutes we would all be unconscious. In a few more minutes we would all be dead. Baptism in the Holy Spirit implies transformation, the energizing power of God. John says, I indeed baptize you with water but there is another who will immerse you, surround you and fill you with the breath of life. That current of air revives withering grass. It re-energizes fading flowers. It fills pilgrims with life for the journey. Baptism in the Holy Spirit is what enables us to make it to our Advent destination which is Bethlehem. On our way to the spiritual Tierra del Fuego, the Holy Spirit is the built-in GPS.

St. Augustine once famously wrote, you have made us for yourself and our hearts are restless until they find rest in thee. There are two kinds of people in the world: Those in the pasture and those on the pathway; those who are settlers and those who are pilgrims. Pastures are limited and confining. Pathways can go ever on and on. Settlers have reached the end of their road; pilgrims keep going.

From the European Middle Ages, right down throughout history to the present, people have gone on pilgrimages. One of the principal medieval journeys was the spiritual pilgrimage "El Camino de Santiago" (the way of St. James) to the famous medieval shrine of Santiago de Compostela (in northwest Spain near the Atlantic Ocean), where many believed the relics of St. James the Apostle were interred. Pilgrims have taken this journey since the eleventh century. Four major paths from France beginning at Arles, Le Puy, Vézelay and Tours converged on the Pyrenees, crossed into northern Spain and followed west to Santiago. It was so popular that a guidebook (the *Liber Sancti Jacobi*) was prepared in the twelfth century. From the Pyrenees to Compostela is about 500 miles. The journey is called pilgrimage, the *camino*, the way. People make this *camino* for different reasons. Many people had little idea of what they were in for or where they were really going. Along the way the pilgrim meets many other people, encounters challenges and must deal with adversity. The *camino* is a time for confidences, listening, and seeing oneself, others and the world through new eyes. The journey is rigorous, with many obstacles from lack of sleep to being robbed to very sore feet, but it is a transforming journey toward freedom. Like the "Alan Parsons Project" traveller, the pilgrims are on their way seeking the fulfillment of their hopes, healing for their pain, and they learn so much. Everyone has their own reason for undertaking the *camino*. They receive their diplomas at the end, and realize they had all that they needed because they just needed "to be." They were all broken in some way but the *camino* is learning to accept that we are not perfect. So many make the *camino* and they start together and then separate on the walk and then come together in the evening to share food, wash clothes; to share life with others – the greatest journey. The *camino* shows us that we are community and that when we share everything we are nourished. The pilgrimage also teaches us that we are not alone. The *camino* is a spiritual and a familial journey. How far is it to Bethlehem this Advent? Christ has come once as a child. He comes again. Not in the heavens but to us as individuals where we are in the midst of life. We are all on a journey.

For Christian pilgrims travelling through the season of Advent, the many roads lead to another kind of Bethlehem. The journey through Advent brings us into confrontation with the good news of Christ's coming. It forces us to look backwards to the historic birth of Christ but also calls us to look forward to his coming again in the hearts and lives of people everywhere. Two millennia ago the announcement of the way to Bethlehem was made in a most curious fashion illustrated by a half-naked, loud-mouthed, apparent lunatic stalking the deserts of the ancient Near East. This was a rather strange figure roaming the Judean wilderness, wild, uncouth, but sent from God. His name was John. He came to help prepare the way of the Lord and to make an important announcement about what he called the baptism of the Holy Spirit.

Between 1917 and 1928 there was a worldwide epidemic of encephalitis lethargica. Five million people were affected. Some of the victims were left in a catatonic state unable to speak or move for decades. Dr. Oliver Sacks, professor of neurology and psychriatry at Columbia University, worked with some of these affected patients. In 1969 Sacks discovered the beneficial effects of a new drug on his patients. They awoke. His account was made into a film thirty years ago called *Awakenings* starring Robin Williams as Sacks and Robert De Niro as Leonard (one of the patients). In his adjustment to new life, Leonard becomes romantically interested in Paula, the daughter of one of the other patients. Alas, the effects of the drug L-dopa are temporary and soon Leonard's tics become more prominent and he shuffles when he walks. Soon he begins to suffer full body spasms and can hardly move. Soon he will return to his catatonic condition. Paula comes to see him one last time. Just before she leaves, they dance. Leonard is shaking pretty badly. But as Paula holds him the tics subside, the spasms stop, and the shaking leaves. It is a moving scene. I wept when I first watched it. But then the dance ends and the tics return, the spasms take hold of Leonard, and the shaking is uncontrollable. Leonard shuffles to the window, his body possessed by spasms and he watches Paula leave. Soon, Leonard is no longer awake. The dance was profound, moving, but like all dances it had to end. By contrast, the baptism of the Holy Spirit lasts forever.

After the vigil, the hoping, personal preparations, anticipation, after the long journey through Advent, we finally arrive at our contemporary Bethlehem. There are "wise men" and fools, saints and shepherds, kings and crooks, all making their way to Bethlehem, following the *camino*, just like you and I. What do we find? Just a small cave, perhaps a barn. A few animals, a bewildered carpenter named Joseph who was not quite sure whether he ought to be proud or embarrassed, a young mother named Mary and a manger. Lying amid a farm-like scent in that manger will be a child. According to the Christian faith, the child lying there is much more than a new-born baby. The Nicene Creed sums it up this way: "God of God, Light of Light, true God of true God…who for us…came." So this is Bethlehem.

Jesus said to the English medieval mystic Julian of Norwich: "This I am. I am what you love. I am what you enjoy. I am what you serve. I am what you long for. I am what you desire. I am what you intend. I am all that is." How far is it to Bethlehem? This Advent, Bethlehem is wherever men and women receive him. Bethlehem is the end of every sincere search for Christ. Bethlehem is everywhere and nowhere. Bethlehem is God with us, revealed in us. When one reaches that ancient town one can sing the medieval hymn: "Rejoice, rejoice, Emmanuel shall come to you, O Israel."

Baptism in the Holy Spirit is the energy needed to find our way through the wildernesses and deserts of our lives like the red knot. God's spirit is the force that carries us through the valleys and mountains of our pilgrimages to Santiago. The Holy Spirit is the transformation needed for the uneven ground and rough places the traveller always encounters. It is what enables each of us to complete the *camino* and arrive at our destination which during Advent is Bethlehem. Baptism in the Holy Spirit is the never-ending dance that causes all of our spasms to cease and our shaking to subside.

In the name of the one who meets us on the journey and who baptizes us with the Holy Spirit, we dare to say these things. Amen.

Columbia River Gorge

Partridge Island, Canada

LETTING GO OF THE RICE

It is important to know when it is time to let go of the rice. I once read a story about the alleged South Indian Monkey Trap. This was a clever innovation enabling hunters to capture monkeys. They hollowed out a coconut shell, put some rice inside, and then chained the coconut to a tree. Pretty soon a monkey would happen by and his curiosity would cause him to inspect the shell. Finding rice therein the monkey would thrust in his hand and take a fist-full of the rice. The hole was large enough to admit the hand but small enough to prevent a fist full of rice from escaping. The hunters begin to close in. Seeing their approach, the monkey tries to force the fist-full of rice out of the shell. He should open his hand and save his life but at that moment the rice seems more important and thus, unable to relinquish his prized rice, the monkey is slain. Is the fate of the poor monkey not an allegory of misplaced values that confront us every day?

I saw "Allen's axiom" printed on a cereal box when I was boy. It is too often ignored: "If all else fails, read the instructions." Christianity has failed. Perhaps those identifying with the Christian faith should read the instructions again, for the first time. What is it that God requires? In the Hebrew Bible (Isaiah) we find that God acknowledges that people want to do what is right. The people say: "We fast and you don't see it," and "we practice our religion and you take no note of it." God says this is true and that's because the problem is that the religious observances have become corrupted. Yes, the ritual is observed but the essential transformation is missing. God demands more than sterile posturing, or "mortifying the flesh," or "bowing heads quickly," and spreading out sackcloth and ashes. Having observed all of this, God says: "Are you serious? Do you really think that's what I want?" If we put this ancient narrative into modern Episcopalian terms (for example), then God is saying the same thing about the *Book of Common Prayer*, the weekly celebration of the eucharist, the defined liturgy, and all the fuss about bishops. The people, whether ancient Hebrews or modern Christians, take pleasure in their religious practices. But God is not impressed with religion. Instead, we seem to get a dismissive message: Forget the ritual. Forget arrogant theological dogmatics. Stop going through extravagant exegetical gymnastics trying to get your precious doctrine just so. Give it up and instead, act!

I was once asked to teach an introductory course in theology at a seminary. I suggested to the students that it would be a good idea to think carefully about language and how we framed our theology. I required them to use inclusive language and this applied also to how we spoke and wrote about God. Judging from the vitriolic reaction, you might have presumed I had encouraged them to engage in the grossest forms of licentious degradation. Formal complaints were filed with the administration charging that I was not teaching the faith but attacking it. Taken literally, this meant that these well-intending students were convinced that God was truly male! Twenty-six students had begun the journey with me that semester. Twelve finished the course but two of them failed to achieve a passing mark. It was a resounding failure. Perhaps I should have suggested to these seminarians gearing up to lead churches and take on leadership roles in Christian ministry that it was high "time to let go of the rice!" Let me put it another way. "Every day, according to the UN World Food Program, almost 16,000 children die from hunger-related causes. That's one child every five seconds." Many people don't give a shit! In fact, many find it more shocking that I used an expletive in the pulpit than they do about children dying of hunger. How can the use of a four-letter word be more grim than the deaths of 16,000 children every day from hunger? It would appear that it is well past the time to let go of the rice. What does God want? What does Scripture say about what God desires? If we follow the Isaiah text, we find an emphasis upon liberation for the disenfranchised, the down-

and-outs, poor slaves, hopeless prisoners, the hungry, the homeless, those lacking proper shelter from the cold, and so on. Then of course there is that marvelous declaration of just what God is looking for in humanity: Always do justice, love mercy, and walk with God in humility (Micah 6:8). Anything less, is a mere grasping of rice. I once overhead a conversation in a seminary library. The subject was about ministry to those unable to leave their homes. The librarian thought this was a very good idea but sadly declined to be involved noting that to take up the opportunity she would have to miss prayer meeting.

Another important matter has to do with the idea of faith itself. Here we find that it is more useful to be doers of the faith rather than believers of a faith. The emphasis is neither on worship nor on doctrine, but on ethics and more specifically on the ethics of Jesus. It is useful to take another look at first principles. The idea of faith for many Christians is a synonym for belief. It may be useful to think of faith as being, not just believing in this, or that, or the other thing. Further, faith is not a system of belief based on certainty. Instead, faith is a relationship; faith is a conversation. It might be pertinent to ask: What do you believe? This is not to suggest that the Christian faith is centrally about being believers in the sense of giving intellectual assent to propositions. Nowadays, we hear people asking: What is your position on the doctrine of...? By contrast, the early church had no creeds at all and was simply called "the Way."

Theology can be liberation or just a coat of mail. In December 2010, St. Joseph's Hospital and Medical Center in Phoenix lost its certification from the Roman Catholic Diocese of Phoenix because it allowed the abortion of an eleven week old fetus in order to save a woman's life. Bishop Thomas Olmsted excommunicated a nun who served on the hospital's ethics committee. Doctors were convinced the risk of death to the prospective mother was 100%. The Hospital Ethics Committee said: "The goal was not to end the pregnancy but to save the mother's life." It is time to let go of the rice. As he died at the stake in Geneva in

1553, at the hands of John Calvin and other Protestant defenders of truth, Michael Servetus cried out: "Oh Jesus, Son of the Eternal God, have pity on me." Pastor William Farel, who stood witnessing the event, remarked that Servetus might have been saved if only he had shifted the adjective and confessed Christ as the eternal son rather than as the son of the eternal God. Is salvation predicated on adjectives? Is acceptance by God a matter of correct grammar?

The person of Jesus must also be taken into account. Albert Schweitzer said that Jesus often comes without a name and speaks to us a simple message: "Follow me." Those who obey, discover who Jesus truly is. But Schweitzer has been considered a dangerous heretic and so pastors and theologians sat in their comfortable offices in Europe writing critiques of him while he built a hospital in French Equatorial Africa and healed the sick. Whose fists were most likely filled with rice? Schweitzer or his detractors? Even today, Jesus is saddled with the baggage accumulated by his followers. For example, what does Scripture tell us about what Jesus said about sexuality? A search reveals he said nothing. What does Scripture tell us about Jesus on the question of homosexuality and gay marriage? Nothing. What did Jesus say about abortion? Nothing. What about prosperity as a sign of God's favor? Once again, nothing. Yet some of these themes are fodder for millions of Christians and Christian identification. What is the price of rice these days whether in China or in your neighborhood? How can one determine the value of rice and how can one know when to let it go?

Perhaps the most famous discourse of Jesus, the so-called "Sermon on the Mount," is striking for many things not least among them the lack of a single word about what to believe, but plenty of words about what to do. The kingdom of God remains a key central theme. Perhaps one should forget celebrating Christmas and instead live the incarnation. Should Christians forget about celebrating Easter and instead live it? By contrast, the Nicene Creed does not include a word about doing. There are only words to believe. The Sermon is intended to transform the world; not affirm something theological or religious. It can be argued that the Sermon is an embarrassment to Christianity. The Catholics historically have placed the burden on the professionals, the demands of the Sermon have either been circumvented or fulfilled vicariously by the saints. Protestants laud the Sermon but say it's not what Jesus really meant, or it's impossible, and in any event the practice of it has been lost beneath the libraries of commentaries that try to interpret, but fail to implement, its broad thrust. So, instead of practicing the Sermon, we choose to recite the Creed. We pay more attention to theologies about Christ, than we do to the practices and ethics of Jesus. Following the way of Jesus has been overshadowed by believing in Christ. There is a deep irony in all of this: Christians worship Jesus but often do not live according to his teachings. It is worth considering that perhaps it is not knowledge but practice itself that is transformative. According to Albert Schweitzer, the great enemy of morality and ethical action has always been indifference.

In 1928 a case came before the courts in Massachusetts. The facts were these. A man walking along a boat dock tripped on a rope and fell into the water. He could not swim. He screamed for help but his friends were too far away on another dock to give any assistance. A few yards away was a young man sitting on a deck chair. He happened to be an excellent swimmer. However, he made no effort to help the desperate man in the water and sat there watching silently as the poor fellow drowned. The family of the deceased were extremely upset at the display of callous indifference and sued the man at law. They lost. The court somewhat reluctantly ruled that the man on the dock had no legal responsibility to attempt to save the drowning man's life. The Sermon reflects an ethos suggesting one should not just fulfil the letter of the law, but engage in the obligation of heart, spirit, as well as deed. The law of God implies transformation in thought, word and deed.

One of the massive changes that occurred in Christian history were the Reformations. There are polar views on whether this major event was good, bad, or indifferent. Irrespective of one's view, there may be some value in striving for a New Reformation. Is it not time to get beyond Protestantism? Western Christianity has been made up of Roman Catholicism, Protestantism, and the "middle way," a term and concept generally favored by the Anglican/Episcopal communion. Critics of contemporary Christianity argue that each iteration is spiritually bankrupt. If that be true, even in a limited sense, how about a new way? How about getting back to "the Way?" Five hundred years ago, Luther was motivated about reform in doctrine and many other reformers were concerned with various aspects of corruption that had infiltrated the church. The new reformation surely must be about recovering "the Way," understanding faith as praxis, not as intellectual assent. A new reformation might consider an emphasis on ethics rather than doctrine, on truly following Jesus rather than worshiping an idea. How much preaching in contemporary Christendom is true to the gospel? Being honest about Jesus will disturb some people and will distress others and it ought to. The question is not principally about correct doctrine, but whether we should show mercy and justice to all those who do not possess what might be regarded as orthodox ideas.

What are you and I willing to give up to follow Jesus? Wilbur Rees once suggested he did not want to get rid of God altogether and instead would like to buy three dollars worth of God. Pastor Rees did not want too much of God, certainly not enough to transform his soul or disturb his sleep, but would take the equivalent of a cup of warm milk, or just enough to carry him into a brief slumber in the sunshine: "I don't want enough of God to make me love a black man or pick beets with a migrant. I want ecstasy, not transformation. I want the warmth of the womb, not a new birth. I want a pound of the Eternal in a paper sack. I would like to buy $3 worth of God, please." Jesus neither said: "Blessed are they who believe" nor "Blessed are they who form doctrines." The church that emphasizes doctrine at all costs distorts the gospel, and ignores the ethics of Jesus, is a church that facilitates evil and should not be tolerated. Perhaps this is the basis of meaningful reformation and also indication of when it is time to let go of the rice. Where do we go from here? Perhaps a new set of questions might take us away from the rice inside the coconut shell. So, don't ask "are you a believer?" but do ask: "Are you a follower of Jesus?" Don't ask: "Are you saved?" but do ask: "Are you able to drink of this cup?" Don't ask: "Do you love Jesus?" but instead ask: "When is Jesus a disturbing and transforming presence in your life?" Formal statements of faith are limiting. For example, the Apostles' Creed tells us that Jesus was indeed "born of the Virgin Mary, suffered under Pontius Pilate." Is it not striking that from birth to death, the life of Jesus is reduced to a comma? We find pretty much the same thing in the Nicene Creed.

The Mennonite theologian Clarence Bauman pointed out that for a long time it has been noted that the Sermon on the Mount was widely admired but less affirmed for its meaning. The eighteenth-century German painter Julius Schnorr von Carolsfeld executed his *Der Bergpredigt* [The Sermon on the Mount] in 1860. At the edge of the crowd, Carolsfeld included a perplexed looking Roman soldier holding a sword listening to Jesus. This underscores the cognitive dissonance between the idea and the practice of the Christian faith. Can one hold onto swords and take seriously the prince of peace? The call of the gospel is for deeds, not creeds. The latter may only be something that traps the believer in a hollow coconut shell. Medieval crusaders sang hymns about the gentle Jesus and then waded through bloody streets in Jerusalem, praising him as they smashed the heads of children. Surely it is time to let go of the rice.

The second-century bishop Irenaeus once said: "The glory of God is a human being fully alive and full humanity exists in seeing God." What does that mean? Perhaps it means being in a place of existence where God says to you and I: "Here I am." The Hindu Swami Prabhavananda concluded: "We cannot bring peace until we realize our oneness with God and all things." It is impossible to be one with God until we are willing to let go of the rice. Life is precious and eternal life even more so than all of the rice in China. Just let it go. We must center our whole mind upon God, and then, extending our arms to everyone, embrace all in the love of God." God says: "Here I am." An eighth-century hymn of the western church proclaims that God is love and where true love is, God is also there: "Ubi caritas et amor, Deus ibi est." Salvation is "light" and "healing" and the everlasting presence of God. Surely letting go of the rice is worth all of that.

Hanging man, Prague

The Seven Last Words of a Condemned Man

It is more than 600 years since Jan Hus perished in the flames of the stake not far from where we have gathered today. In Christian tradition, special significance has been attached to the seven last words of Jesus spoken from the cross in the moments before his death. Entire books have been written about those last words. Sometimes last words are profound or memorable simply because they are last words and there will be no more. Let us look at some of Hus' last words. They reflect important issues of faith and his commitment as a witness to Christ.

What did Hus say? Do these words have relevance for those of us today who remain on pilgrimage? On Saturday morning, 6 July 1415, around 6:00 a.m., Hus was brought from the Franciscan prison to the cathedral in the German city of Constance where the great men of Christendom had gathered. Mass was sung. A sermon was preached against heresy. The court trial continued. Legal briefs were summarized. Articles of accusation against Hus were read out. He was found guilty as charged.

As Hus was forced to submit to the humiliating ritual of stripping and shaming he spoke the first of his notable last words: "Lord Jesus Christ, forgive my enemies for the sake of your mercy." The key words include "forgive" and "mercy." On the latter, we are helpfully reminded of the "comfortable words" of the prayer of humble access that appears in many Protestant Eucharistic liturgies where we hear the words: "You are the same Lord whose nature is always to have mercy." If it is characteristic of Christ to be always merciful, then exceptions cannot be made when the faithful are under attack or suffering duress. Instead of cursing his enemies, Hus asked God to forgive them. Hus asked God to overlook their sins. Hus took the extraordinary step of asking God to look the other way. His detractors in the cathedral openly mocked him when he asked for mercy on their behalf. Perhaps they did not feel they required divine mercy but Hus urged it anyway.

Hus was defrocked from the priesthood in an elaborate ceremony. This ritual culminated with seven bishops removing the Eucharistic chalice from his hands while declaring: "O cursed Judas, we take away from you the cup of redemption." In reply, Hus spoke the second of his notable last words: "I trust in God." Faith is not wishful thinking or optimism. Faith is trust. Jan Hus reflected this when he replied to the bishops: "I trust in the Lord God Almighty that he will not take away from me the cup of redemption." The bishops agreeing with Hus' conviction as a heretic consented to his expulsion from the church and considered him excommunicated. Jan Hus was then expelled from the church and cast outside the realm of salvation. Hus' response was to declare he trusted in God. Roman authorities crucified Jesus along with two criminals and in so doing cut them off from human society. One of the condemned asked Christ: "Remember me when you come into your kingdom." Jesus answered saying that on that same day the criminal would enter the kingdom of God. Like the damned criminal at Calvary, Hus asked to be remembered, affirmed his trust in God, and eagerly anticipated drinking from the cup of salvation that same day. Witnessing to the faith means trusting in God. It means believing that nothing can separate us from the love of God.

Multiple curses were applied to Hus as he was expelled from the church. The ritual reached its climax when the bishops declared: "We commit your soul to the devil." In reply, Hus spoke the third of his notable last words: "I commit my soul to Jesus Christ." Legal appeals exhausted, a five-year court case now at an end, facing execution, Hus could not do more than repeat the words of his crucified Lord who said: "Father, into your hands, I commit my spirit." This is neither mere resignation nor defiance. It is instead an expression of faith and total commitment to the values by which Hus had lived. Jan Hus tells us initially he desired a career as a priest in order to have a good life. That did not matter once he reached Lake Constance and the moment of truth.

Seventy years ago, Viktor Frankl made an important observation. He said: "Everything can be taken from an individual except one thing: The last of the human freedoms – to choose one's attitude in any given set of circumstances, to choose one's own way." Short of denying the courage of his own convictions or personal integrity, Jan Hus could do little that early Saturday morning in the Cathedral of Constance except to exercise the last human freedom that was choosing his attitude, choosing his own way. Faced with the loss of all things, Jan Hus chose faith. He chose trust. Hus chose to place his life (the one in this world as well as the one in the next) into the hands of God. He chose his own way which ultimately was to choose God: "I commit my soul to Jesus Christ."

The authorities led Hus from the cathedral. Almost the entire city population accompanied Hus to death. The procession wound its way through narrow medieval streets, past piles of burning books, to a field outside the city walls. Today the place is marked by a large boulder in a quiet neighborhood. Faced with the wooden stake and the enormity of the moment, Hus declared the fourth of his last notable words: "I am willing to die for the gospel of Christ."

What are we to make of such resolve? His accusers claimed he was contumacious. Others argued he was impervious to reason. Still more asserted he was filled with pride and arrogantly believed that he alone understood divine truths. It is not possible to psychologize Hus from a distance of 600 years. What we have are his words, reliably attested, confirming his willingness to lay down his life in defense of truth. "Truth" is a slippery concept in our postmodern world of relativism where all claims are treated as equal. Along with concepts such as "sin" the idea of "truth" is unfashionable but theologically indispensable. Were he alive today, Hus would be immune to such arguments. The gospel was truth. The person of Christ was truth. To these realities Hus was committed absolutely. Badgered to recant, harassed to submit to lesser authorities, and forced to the stake, Hus declared he could not retreat from these principles. We find in his resolve an echo of a letter composed in a Roman prison 1500 years earlier by St. Paul: "I am now at the point of being sacrificed. The time of my departure is at hand. I have fought a good fight, I have finished the course, I have kept the faith." Jan Hus was prepared to die for something greater than himself, something surpassing his own personal historical relevance, something that was of eternal value.

Hus was fastened to the stake and a sooty chain was wrapped around his neck. Time was running out for Jan Hus. With perhaps only the executioners close enough to hear, Hus declared the fifth of his notable last words: "I am not ashamed." This was a public execution. This was the result of committing the crime of heresy. Hus had ascended the ladder of professional success, he had long occupied the pulpit of an influential church, he had attained the chancellorship of a prestigious university, he had been honored at the courts of kings. Now he was an outcast, excommunicated, convicted of serious offenses. He was the subject of humiliation, and public ridicule. What did he have to say now? His words echo St. Paul: "I am not ashamed of the gospel. It is the power of God for salvation to everyone who has faith."

The Middle Ages are often characterized as heroic when knights rode with honor and kings strove against adversity to establish justice and equity. A near-naked man tied to a stake is not heroic. It is shameful, dishonorable, and certainly nothing to take pride in. Shame might be understood as the proper response at failing to achieve and maintain social expectations. It implies both a loss of honor as well as self-esteem. Shame, embarrassment and abject humiliation are emotions one might associate with the indignity of being burned alive at the stake. But faced with this predicament, Jan Hus simply declared: "I am not ashamed."

Hus may not have been ashamed, but did his confidence waver? Two wagons filled with wood were unloaded and the wood was piled up to his chin. Straw and pitch were added and now the moment of truth. The imperial marshal encouraged Hus to save his life: Recant or else! Live or die! Yes or no! There must have been a pregnant pause at so solemn a moment when life has so little time left to run. Eyewitnesses say Hus barely paused when he spoke loudly so that many could hear the sixth of his notable last words: "God is my witness that the focus of my preaching was to turn people from sin. In the truth of the gospel I am willing gladly to die today." There could be no turning back. One of the tragedies of the great Council of Constance was that Hus insisted upon dying. But the price for life was one that proved too high for him to pay. He could not possibly relinquish his understanding of truth even if that commitment should cost him his life. The courage of conviction always requires a great deal. There are different ways of dying but the cost of true discipleship demands everything, not simply what is convenient or disposable.

The practice of the faith in private, in comfort, or in well-ordered places of religion seldom exacts more than sore knees or tired feet but the cost of commitment may require martyrdom, a concept that is not simply confined to the dusty annals of church history or stories of men and women from long ago and far away. Foundational Greek Christian texts make little distinction between witnessing and martyrdom. To bear witness is to attest to something, to assert credibility, or to provide assurance. To give testimony is to declare something to be true or to confirm something one has seen. Hus called God as his witness. He publicly enjoined God to give testimony. There is a cost to discipleship and a price associated with integrity and conviction. On the morning of 6 July 1415, Hus was called upon to pay the price. He did not call his friends, he did not make appeal to his students, he did not summon his colleagues. He did not solicit any of the world-renowned theologians of his time. Instead, he nominated God as his star witness, the only one whose testimony could not be impeached.

Upon hearing these words, and knowing that nothing could dissuade Hus from the grim course he had chosen, the pyre was set ablaze. The seventh and last words of Hus repeat a traditional hymn: "Christ, son of the living God, have mercy on me." At the end, Hus did not rely upon himself. He did not shout theological claims from the fire. He did not insist that he had been correct. He did not take that last opportunity to vilify his detractors. Instead, Hus threw himself on the mercy of God. He had been judged by the Archbishop of Prague, the papal court, and by the Council. Hus preferred the judgement of God that sees from an eternal perspective, possesses unblemished clarity, and is tempered both by justice and mercy: "Christ, have mercy upon me."

More than a century ago, the Scottish thinker George MacDonald said mercy and justice were the same thing. He argued that one could not have justice without mercy and mercy could not be had without justice. Hus may have held a similar understanding. In his dying words amid the flames, Jan Hus asked God to take pity on him. In his last words he admonished everyone to take comfort in God's unlimited mercy. The last words of Hus reached a climax when the flames overpowered his strength and he was gathered unto God. The first of his last words, noted earlier, asked mercy for his enemies. At the end, Hus asked mercy for himself. The last words of Jan Hus prompt several questions. First, who is Christ for us today? Second, what does it mean to take Jesus seriously? Third, is truth something to be protected or explored? For the Christian, Jesus remains the moral conscience that condemns the inhumanity of post-modern civilization; the thought paralysis that often yields the tyranny of the majority; its spiritual bankruptcy, and its neglect of the Kingdom of God. What does it mean to confess faith in Christ in our world today? For Jan Hus, it meant giving witness unto death.

Sixteen and a half centuries ago, St. Ambrose (who was born in Trier) declared: "If we must give account for every idle word, let us take care not to have to give account for every idle silence." Silence is betrayal. Where is the serious debate about what it means to confess Christ in a world of violence? Should Christianity passively accept pre-emptive wars? Faithfully confessing Christ means ever resisting militarism and nationalism. Theologies of war, emanating from the highest circles of world governments, continue to seep into our churches. The kingdom of God must not be aligned with the "righteous empires" of the world. Security issues facing our nations do not allow for easy solutions. But God's truth cannot be controlled by government or church. The church must be wary of allowing the gospel to be taken over by Washington or London. What faithful Christians must do is follow the example of Jan Hus and construct a new confession of Christ. Commitment to Christ must take priority over national identity as well as church affiliation. Whenever Christianity becomes linked with empire or controlled by denominationalism, the gospel of Christ is discredited. The distinction between good and evil does not run between one nation and another, or one Christian group and another. It runs straight through every human heart. Hus understood this. Jesus Christ is either authoritative for Christians, or he is not. The lordship of Christ can never be subordinated to any earthly power. His words, his ethics, and his acts, may not be distorted for propagandistic purposes. No nation may usurp the place of God. No Christian community may presume to possess Truth entirely or exclusively. Once again, Jim Wallis is prophetic.

In 1520, Martin Luther received a letter posted from Bamberg. In that correspondence we find the comment: "Jan Hus has come to life again, after having been dead so long. He is not dead; he will live as long as truth lives." And what is truth? That was the question at Constance 600 years ago. Hus said Christ was truth. Hus was a witness unto death. His faith and his witness, reflected in his last words, caused some to declare that Hus was "a burning candle in a gold chandelier" shining the light of truth in the dark places of the world. Another eyewitness challenged his readers thus: "Let us clothe ourselves with the spirit of that courageous man." But now let us give Jan Hus the last word: "Therefore faithful Christian, seek the truth, listen to the truth, learn the truth, love the truth, speak the truth, adhere to truth and defend truth to the death. For truth will set you free."

Gottlieben path, Switzerland

Camel train, Outback, Australia

WHERE THE ROAD NARROWS

On either Friday, 16 March, or on Saturday, 17 March 1912, Robert F. Scott made the following entry in his personal journal near the end of a doomed expedition to the South Pole:

> Should this be found I want these facts recorded. Oates' [Captain L.E.G. Oates] last thoughts were of his Mother...We can testify to his bravery...He did not – would not – give up hope till the very end...He slept through the night before last, hoping not to wake; but he awoke in the morning – yesterday. It was blowing a blizzard. He said, "I am just going outside and may be some time." He went out into the blizzard and we have not seen him since.

One of my professors in seminary did his graduate work at Union Theological Seminary in New York City. Among his teachers had been the late famous Reinhold Niebuhr and Paul Tillich; theologians who taught at Union in those days. Each had a different view of death. As death approached, Niebuhr spoke of his regret at the brevity of life and wished death could be avoided. On the other hand, Tillich saw death as an opportunity for new explorations and anticipated his own death with almost a sense of excitement.

We are all born into this world. Some of us will live only a short time. Others will live for a very long time (at least in human years). Most of us will last somewhere in between. While the longevity of our existence will always be in doubt, there is no doubt concerning our final end. Dying is as inevitable as the rising sun. Indeed, it is part of living. One need not seek death for death has a way of finding each of us no matter where we are. One should try to seek the pathway that allows death to become fulfilment. Most of us dislike the thought of death, and many, especially the young, scorn the very idea. The way is broad, this way we trod, but sooner than we can imagine a bend appears up ahead; the place where the road narrows. Clarence Darrow once wrote: "What we call Time rolls on its course, and in the twinkling of an eye turns the puppets into oblivion regardless of how wildly they shout that the multitude may know that they are here." Death is the final bridge that each of us must cross. We come to it at the place where the road narrows. It spans the yawning chasm of nothingness between this life and the Great Unknown. And it really is the Great Unknown. No amount of speculation or theologizing can make it anything else. St. Teresa of Avila in the sixteenth century referred to life as a second class hotel. The difficult thing, Malcolm Muggeridge wrote, is trying to explain how the nearness of death makes what is left behind, life itself, so appealing. "Checking out of St. Teresa of Avila's second-class hotel, as the revolving doors take one into the street outside, one casts a backward look at the old place, overcome with affection for it, almost to the point of tears."

Yet, many feel it is not the end. Dietrich Bonhoeffer had just finished preaching his last sermon in the prison at Flossenbürg in April 1945 when the guards came to get him to take him to the gallows. His last words were these: "This is the end, but for me it is the beginning of life." As they stood in the roaring flames at Oxford in October 1555, Hugh Latimer turned to Nicholas Ridley and admonished his friend: "Be of good cheer, Master Ridley, and play the man. We shall this day light such a candle by God's grace in England, as I trust shall never be put out." Two nights before Karl Barth died, his biographer Eberhard Busch recounts how Barth sat before his open window in Basel at 1:15 a.m. in the middle of winter singing very loudly out into the night of the great comfort there is in knowing that Christ is coming with great joy.

To face death with trepidation is no disgrace. Whether you can, like Jacob, gather your feet up into the bed and simply give up the ghost, or whether you fight on to the finish with your boots on and your guns blazing, is without significance. The question is, into whose hands will you commit yourself? Writing from the Franciscan prison in Constance just before his death in 1415, Jan Hus, knowing full well that his time was drawing near, took a stand upon hope.

> O, most kind Christ, draw us weaklings after yourself. Unless you draw us we cannot follow you. Give us a spirit of courage that we may be ready and if the flesh is weak, may your grace go ahead of us at this time and hereafter. Without you we can do nothing, especially not to go to a terrible death on your account. Grant us a strong spirit, a heart without fear, a proper faith, a firm hope and perfect love in order that we may be able to give our lives for you with patience and joy.

Paul claimed to have fought a good fight and Jesus willingly embraced his fate in the place of The Skull. John A.T. Robinson, it was said, was remembered by more people at Cambridge for his last sermon in 1983 when he stood before a full house, while he was himself dying, and spoke about the reality of God in his cancer. "We are beggars. That's the truth." These were the last words to come from the prolific pen of Martin Luther. Yet even as beggars in the hour of death, the riches of Christ, in the fullness of life, surpasses all measure of great poverty.

> Farewell to you and the youth I have spent with you
> It was but yesterday we met in a dream
> You have sung to me in my aloneness,
> and I of your longings have built a tower in the sky
> But now our sleep has fled and our dream is over,
> and it is no longer dawn
> The noon tide is upon us and our half waking
> has turned to fuller day and we must part.
> If in the twilight of memory we should meet once more
> We shall speak again together
> And you shall sing to me a deeper song
> And if our hands should meet in another dream
> We shall build another tower in the sky.
>
> Kahlil Gibran

Death is but one final opportunity to live in the example of Christ. The process of dying can either be a hideously traumatic affair, or it can be the very apex of life. John A.T. Robinson's doctor told him he had six months to live. Indeed, Robinson died almost six months to the day. A friend later expressed his perception of the bishop's death. "I loved him also for the manner of his dying, and will always be thankful for popping into his rooms just as he was leaving Trinity for the last time, and being able to pack him into his car, and bid him farewell. He faced death with his customary intelligence and drive, exploring all avenues."

Life is ever drawing to a close, somewhere, for someone. Even the very thought gives one the feeling of an obituary carved on a marble stone. The passage of time is perhaps the most incredible phenomena in life. The irretrievableness of both human history and time boggles the mind. When over three quarters of a century had passed in his life, the famous criminal lawyer Clarence Darrow reminisced. "And yet, I cannot realize that I am old, and that the sun has so quickly passed from the morning over the meridian, and is now already rapidly sinking behind the clouds. Where can the long day have gone? It has only been a short time since I started on the journey with all the world before me, and immeasurable time for the journey I was to take; and now the pilgrimage is almost over and the day is nearly done."

Sooner or later we shall all stand at that point in time where Darrow stood, the place where the road clearly narrows, and we shall witness the twilight of our own "day." The question then, is not what profound words we can say. Nor is it a time to fret over what has been done or left undone. It is far too late for that. There is time only for life's last act: To die. The only question is God.

One of the best known songs performed by the British comedy troupe Monty Python is the catchy tune "Always look on the bright side of life."

> Some things in life are bad
> They can really make you mad

Other things just make you swear and curse
When you're chewing on life's gristle
Don't grumble, give a whistle
And this'll help things turn out for the best...
If life seems jolly rotten
There's something you've forgotten
And that's to laugh and smile and dance and sing
When you're feeling in the dumps
Don't be silly chumps
Just purse your lips and whistle, that's the thing...
You'll see it's all a show
Keep them laughing as you go
Just remember that the last laugh is on you.
Always look on the bright side of life
Always look on the bright side of life.

The bright side of life is God. Life is the gift that enables each of us to reach the Kingdom of God. Sin, death, and hell do not get the last laugh. That belongs to Christ who defeats all.

The Last Laugh

Eliot Glacier, Mt Hood, Oregon

WISHFUL THINKING

Wishful thinking! The Christian faith is built upon wishful thinking. Things like grace, truth, and the hope that there is a higher power is wishful thinking. That our lives matter, that ultimately all shall be well, that there is truth and justice somewhere, and that when all is said and done we shall be saved or rescued from everything that takes away from all that we were intended to be, is wishful thinking. Wishful thinking is at the heart of the dreams that cause us to live and move and have our being. And there is nothing wrong with such wishful thinking. I myself hope for these things.

The trouble with Bible stories is that we've heard them before. We've heard them so often we've stopped listening. I think we need to hear them again, perhaps for the very first time. As I read and re-read and ruminated on the four set liturgical texts I began to see a definite pattern emerging, and a disturbing pattern. A responsible sermon on these texts means challenging the texts (hopefully with humility) but also, and just as importantly, to try and point the way forward, to the next level, to the next experience of grace. I want to be honest with the texts, honest with you, and true to myself. So I want to share with you two readings of these texts. **Part One!**

In the first narrative (Genesis 32: 22-32) we read about a nocturnal wrestling match on the banks of the Jabbok River. It is a curious story. The unidentified wrestler (who is simply called a man) must either be a human, or a supernatural being (i.e. the numen of the place, like the troll in the tale of the three Billy Goats Gruff, or an angel), or Yahweh. If it is the latter, how is it that Jacob prevails? If it is Yahweh, why does the breaking of day cause concern to the mysterious wrestler? Is this

Dracula whose powers are lost or diminished in the light of day? It raises the obvious query of whether humans can really wring a blessing out of God. Jacob's name is changed to Israel and Jacob's opponent makes a run for it just in the nick of time.

We are at a disadvantage because the context (background) of the story is missing. Digging a bit deeper we learn of a conspiracy hatched up by the naughty Rebekah to have her son Jacob deprive his twin brother Esau of his birthright, to deceive his old father Isaac and to secure the paternal blessing. There are blatant lies when Jacob says to his father: "I am Esau" and reaffirms that deception: "Yes, I am Esau" and this is followed up with shocking blasphemy when Isaac wonders how Jacob managed to find game so quickly Jacob says: Oh "the Lord your God granted me success!" Twenty long years pass slowly. Now Jacob – the dishonest, lying, cheating, unethical fellow – is about to get his much-deserved comeuppance and he begs God to deliver him and we wind up with this entertaining but preposterous wrestling match tale!

The text claims that Jacob wrestled all night. Did they take breaks? Who is he wrestling with? Why does Jacob not press the guy on his identity? Where are the women and the children all this time? How did Jacob manage to get the upper hand? We do not know the answers to these queries. Then he forces a blessing! And either Jacob or the story-teller concludes that Jacob had seen God face to face. The text suggests that neither wrestler knew the identity of the other. Why ask for a blessing from a stranger? Jacob is lamed. It is worth considering that our scars perhaps remind us that the past was real. The name of the place is called "Penuel" which means "the face of God." This may have been wishful thinking on Jacob's part.

The second text from Psalm 121 also seems to me to be wishful thinking. Despite the assurances of the writer, my feet are moved. There is often no shade, sometimes evil does prevail. Sometimes I am not safe. I have lived far too long and known too many people whose feet have involuntarily been moved and sometimes into the most appalling of circumstances. There are some of you sitting here today who have not been shielded from the blazing heat of the sun (in antiquity the moon was regarded as a source of diseases); still more who have not been preserved from evil; and far too many who have not been kept safe and through no fault of their own. So where is God? And what are we to make of these declarations?

In 2009, 54 year old James Bain was released from a Florida prison after serving 35 years for the rape of a young boy. He was 19 years old when he went to prison. The problem is Mr. Bain was not the perpetrator. DNA analysis conclusively excluded him and he is only one of at least 259 recent cases wherein men have been exonerated from crimes they were convicted of and in some cases served decades behind bars. And in some of these cases we have discovered clear systemic institutional injustice in the offices of District Attorneys. What do we say to those people whose feet have not been kept steady, who have been burned by the sun, whose fragile lives have not been spared from evil, who exist perpetually in danger?

The Psalm does not, for many people, reflect reality, but rather expresses hopefulness. There is prayer, and pious longings, rather than promise in this verse. It is wishful thinking. It seems impossible to make absolute claims for these expressions of hope. Clearly the sentiments in the Psalm are untrue for many people. Some wish to see all of this as fulfilled in eternity not in history. The Psalm suggests intelligent design in the universe. Yet most of the universe is hostile to life. In many of the historical narratives of the Hebrew Bible, Yahweh is often a dangerous, irritable, angry, capricious and violent deity. The central question posed in Thornton Wilder's Pulitzer Prize winning 1927 novel *The Bridge of San Luis Rey* is: "Either we live by accident and die by accident or we live by plan and die by plan." That thesis statement can be applied right here. The Psalm suggests design, sometimes reality indicates otherwise. What do we do?

The epistle reading (II Timothy 3:14-4:5) makes bold claims about Scripture that some find very comforting. But are the words to be equated with the Word of God? That would be ever so convenient. Wishful thinking. Luther said the Word of God was like a passing thunderstorm that bursts at one moment here and then was gone. The epistle encourages us to remain in the faith. I must ask: What is the basis for our faith? Is it worth continuing in? And I feel compelled to suggest that no one ought simply to continue in what one has been taught unless and until one critically examines it. The strongest faith is the examined faith! As a boy I learned a little song in Sunday School that included the line that "every promise in the book is mine, every chapter, every verse, every line!" Not all the promises in the book are mine or yours, they were not intended for you and I and some of them I would not wish to be mine! We must ask not simply is Scripture authoritative but in what sense is it so?

Then in the gospel text (Luke 18:1-18), Luke has Jesus encouraging his friends to pray and not to lose heart in that enterprise. That principle seems to me to be perfectly sound. But to illustrate the point, Jesus tells something of an odd story. A woman who bugs a judge so long and so forcefully that he gives her what she wants just to be rid of her. Will that work for you and me in terms of prayer? Wishful thinking. The story appears to make the claim that if you harangue, badger, beg enough, and browbeat God you'll get what you want. If that's the case then it is just plain bad theology. It undergirds the "name it and claim it," "grab it and blab it" prosperity doctrines that seem so popular these days. I do not believe that prayer changes God. C.S. Lewis said he prayed because he couldn't help himself. Lewis said: Prayer changes me. Why should we pray? It's not about petitions, it's not about always asking for what we want. "God this, God that, and God the other thing. Good God, said God, I've got my work cut out." Instead, prayer is about communication with God.

I can appreciate the desire for certainty in our often unpredictable and dangerous world: Something dependable, something we can rely upon, something to cling to in our worst moments. Perhaps a relationship, an idea, an institution (like the church) or the Bible. At first blush, I could not see that our texts provided us with that kind of certainty. Much of our human struggle has nothing to do with God. Not really. Life is hard. Harder than dying. Too often the church says it is giving people hope. Sometimes I think when we fail to confront the harsh realities of life and avoid the difficulties of the text hope is taken away. Surely we all know there is no pot of gold at the end of the rainbow. Why set people up for crushing despair? Why pretend that things are other than they really are? We hear Biblical narratives piously read each week in church. Do we carefully reflect upon them? Since I am a preacher from time to time I can say this. There is sometimes too much preaching that is pedantic, insulting to intelligence, irrelevant, insipid, boring, and worst of all, sometimes dishonest. It is fair to say that the church historically has manipulated people, and has itself been manipulated. All too often in our times the church has limited usefulness. Many people turn to the church only for the convenience of hatching, matching and dispatching. What a predicament!

I think it would be quite wrong to draw from these texts that God has planned everything out for us or that every struggle is monumental or somehow connected to God. I do not think that we should assume that "supernatural" intervention will occur. The Bible is not a handy "how-to" manual for life (it can and it should be critically assessed), I find no comfort in the admonition to simply embrace the Bible. Pray until your voice fails, your knees are sore, and your eyes are skinned staring at the skies – none of that, in my experience, will change reality. This is the disturbing pattern in each of these texts. We must tell the truth about the tragedies, the bitterness, the sufferings of life. The ambiguities of the human condition. We must speak truth rather than what we think is acceptable. Grapple with the reality of suffering and the legitimacy of doubt. But – **Part Two!** – it is not the only message we can find therein.

There is another theme: It is a focus on God. An encouragement to seek for God. And to find in God strength for today and hope for tomorrow. God does not love people because of who they are but instead because of who God is.

No matter what the circumstances may be, try to never give up. If you are going through hell, keep going. Don't expect to find God waiting for you on the other side of your hell. Instead, consider that God is right there with you in your hell, every step of the way. And if you can believe that, then there is enough strength to never give up. The wrestling matches continue. The pilgrim lifts up his or her eyes to the hills. He or she knows there are dangers up there. Evil lurks. Feet may slip and slide. Uncertainty may prevail. But there can be courage to never give up. I say these things wishfully and with great hope.

And so another reading of these texts presents us with a different point of view: Don't retire from the struggle, do lift your eyes up above your circumstances, fulfil your ministry fully, and persevere. Never give up. And more concretely, the strength of the community of the faithful is real, the body of Christ metaphor is useful. Be faithful and diligent in what you know to be good, right and true. Cultivate wishful thinking. There is hope. There can be trust. There is the possibility of grace. Luther once advised one of his closest friends: "Sin boldly but believe in Christ more boldly still." Yes! Boldly expect grace! Even when it is least expected.

In the name of the one who sustains our wishful thinking, we dare to say these things. Amen.

JESUS AND THE BITCH OF TYRE

The gospel reading for this Sunday comes from the Gospel of Mark. Before we consider the Gospel of Mark, let us turn to the gospel of John.

> Imagine there's no heaven / It's easy if you try / No hell below us / Above us only sky / Imagine all the people / Living for today / Imagine there's no countries / It isn't hard to do / Nothing to kill or die for / And no religion too /Imagine all the people / Living life in peace / Imagine no possessions / I wonder if you can / No need for greed or hunger / A brotherhood of man / Imagine all the people / Sharing all the world / You may say I'm a dreamer / But I'm not the only one / I hope someday you'll join us /And the world will live as one.

The gospel of John Lennon. What may seem an odd juxtaposition – a Biblical text and a 1971 ex-Beatles song – may in fact be more closely related than it seems at first blush.

The story is set with Jesus on a journey away from home. He goes to Tyre. Today, Tyre is a city on the southern coast of Lebanon, on the Mediterranean. The first-century Jewish historian Josephus described the people of Tyre as "notoriously our bitterest enemies." The setting of this story comes right on the heels of two narratives dealing with defilement (7:1-13; 14-23). Arguably, this is among the most difficult of Gospel texts. It suggests quite clearly that Jesus (or at least Mark) subscribed to the parochialism of Judaism that not only assumed but promoted notions of priority, meaning the Jews were first in the divine scheme of things, and also the idea of choice, that Jews were God's chosen people. Right away this presents problems. Jesus leaves Jewish territory in the story and enters foreign or pagan territory. What follows is an extraordinary encounter with the "other," those people Josephus identified as bitter enemies.

The main character is the narrative is an anonymous female. Who is this woman? From the text we learn she was a Syrian from the Phoenician coast. In the Gospel of Matthew, she is called a Canaanite. Mark refers to her as a Syro-Phoenician. In Matthew, Jesus attempts to ignore her. In that account the disciples beg Jesus to get rid of her, because she is badgering them and making a plain nuisance of herself. This nameless woman must be desperate. Who is at home with the girl? Where is the father, the husband, or relatives? We simply do not know. All we can be reasonably sure of is that the woman had a little daughter in some distress, she was Syro-Phoenician, was Greek in language and social position, meaning she occupied a place in the higher middle class, and that she was pagan. In the ancient world it was considered improper for any woman to directly address a man. But this woman breaks social convention and addresses Jesus. The rest must be left to speculation.

Turning to Jesus, it is challenging to consider what we know about him and to ponder what evidence exists to support our view. Commenting on the idea that Jesus is just like you and I except without sin, the late writer Madeleine L'Engle noted dryly that he was then not just like her. I agree. Assumptions. We seldom probe them too deeply. Why not? I recall a student I taught years ago in a certain seminary who objected strenuously to my requirement that we use gender-inclusive language even when referring to God. During a pointed discussion the student burst out saying: "I don't think God is a man, he's a spirit!" No sooner were the words spoken when the student realized he had to rethink his assumptions and language. Former Anglican Bishop of Durham and New Testament scholar N.T. Wright refers to the "portrait gallery" of Jesus and this passage clearly provides us with a glimpse of a seldom contemplated image.

What Wright refers to is the shocking response of Jesus to this nameless woman. Jesus is not welcoming, he is hostile. He is not kind, he is harsh. Jesus is verbally abusive. One might say that Jesus' reply to the woman is crude. He calls her a dog which seems rather pugnacious. In light of the circumstances, Jesus seems rather heartless. After all, the woman has a daughter in some need and distress. The woman has fallen to her knees, humiliated herself, begging for intervention and Jesus is neither receptive nor sympathetic. It is difficult to see something other than a calloused attitude on the part of Jesus. Does he not in his rejoinder violate the second commandment? It is almost as though he ignores his own words elsewhere when he notes that a parent does not give a child a snake when asked for a fish or a stone when bread is needed. Morna Hooker, the former Lady Margaret Professor of Divinity at Cambridge University admonishes scholars for attempting to soften Jesus' harsh expression and sidestep his shocking words. Frankly, his refusal to offer his healing power to a desperate woman and her ailing daughter, and comparing them to dogs, with all the definite connotations of impurity, is morally indefensible. And what about those dogs?

In this context, the reference to dogs constitutes a term of abuse if there ever was one. Dogs are defiled animals (Exodus 22:31), the term is used as an insult (I Samuel 17:43 and 2 Kings 8:13). Dogs are used as a term of demarcation (Matthew 7:6) and Jews in the time of Jesus called Gentiles "dogs." There is considerable evidence in the Jewish tradition for describing Gentiles as dogs and consistently in the pejorative sense. References to dogs in the Bible are usually contemptuous. Dogs are almost always held in low esteem. In Revelation 22:15 the word "dogs" is used to describe people who are not allowed to enter the holy city. This means these people are filthy, unclean and impure. Dogs in that culture are like rats in ours. And the son of God, the man who usually speaks of inclusivity has just applied this term to a woman on her knees begging. Verse 27 uses the Greek word *kynaria* (the diminutive form) which literally means "little dogs." It is not truly possible to follow the suggestion of some people who think that Jesus might have been referring to pets and therefore try to moderate Jesus. "Doggies or puppies?" No! Jesus rejected this person not on the basis of gender but because she was a dog! In our parlance, calling a woman a "little bitch" is really no better than the epithet "bitch." It is a harsh and unkind word and finding it on the lips of Jesus makes it even more reprehensible.

Scholars have offered a variety of explanations to try and explain the narrative. There are several possible readings. First, Jesus is on vacation. After all he has gone to a coastal city in a foreign country and does not want to be disturbed. He needs a holiday. Second, perhaps Jesus is not quite serious. N.T. Wright and other scholars tell us the whole thing was friendly or teasing banter! Perhaps. But there is no evidence in the text to plausibly suggest this. Third, another explanation is this idea of the priority of Israel. In the Matthean version Jesus tells the woman he has time only for the "lost sheep of the house of Israel." Other explanations are that Jesus was simply, fourth, a sexist pig, or fifth, a proper bigot. Sixth, that Jesus does eventually do what he is asked (v.31) because he lost a debate, a verbal repartee. Regardless of how one views Winston Churchill, even his detractors note he was quite witty. Once at a party Churchill had a few drinks and a woman who did not particularly like him said disdainfully: "Winston, you're drunk!" He fired back: "Lydia, you're ugly. And in the morning I'll be sober and you'll still be ugly!" Not to be deterred she retorted: "Winston, if you were my husband, I'd put poison in your tea." To this he replied: "Lydia, if you were my wife, I'd drink it!" Churchill was witty. The Syro-Phoenician was also clever. Jesus is hiding out, perhaps a variation on Mark's "messianic secret." He went into a house, did not want anyone to know he was there. But it was impossible to keep his presence a secret (v.24). The woman found him. Jesus flat out refuses the woman's plea for help and rejected her because of who/what she was: An outsider, the "Other," a dog. The parallel in Matthew 15 has Jesus agreeing to attend to the daughter on account of the woman's extraordinary faith. In Mark, he just says: "Ok, you win." Seventh, others appear to believe that Jesus simply wanted to test her faith. I believe such explanations are little more than pious longings.

Eighth, perhaps the narrative is an example of literary irony. Instead of reflecting Jesus' own views, it highlights the extreme difference between his perspective and that of the religious authorities on this matter. The reader would expect this type of rejection to come from a Pharisee, but not from Jesus, especially as it follows his statements of inclusiveness in Mark 7:1-23! By playing the part of the religious authorities, Jesus actually highlights the absurdity of exclusion based on superficial issues that include ethnicity and gender. God's kingdom breaks down such outward barriers and judges persons based on their hearts. This story, then, is a prime example of Jesus' subversion of exclusive boundaries based on surface issues and is an outworking of those views that he had previously espoused in Mark 7:1-23. This new community of his is an inclusive one where a Gentile woman can fully experience the blessings of God.

The woman does not ask for food, but begs Jesus to help as an exorcist. Jesus' response (or in Mark's version thereof) creates an immediate exegetical challenge (strawberries, or any excuse will do), as well as a moral problem. In terms of the former, it reminds me of a story I once heard about a wealthy businessman who was asked to contribute to some cause. He replied: "No thank you, I don't like strawberries." Concluding the man had misheard, the query was repeated to which the fellow replied: "I heard you the first time, but when you don't want to do something any excuse will do." On the latter issue, it is all about those dogs. The *Jesus Seminar* says the whole thing is a made-up story! I think the tale is so bizarre and un-Jesus like not to be true. Can we be as banal to say that Jesus was probably just tired and said something he shouldn't have? But the woman on her knees set him straight. She wasn't mean, she did not return a harsh response to his offensive barb, but she stood her ground. She did not take no for an answer. The anonymous woman gives Jesus his deserved comeuppance. Many will be disturbed by such explanation for it strikes at the root of their assumptions about Jesus. Perhaps that in itself is part of the dilemma.

If we cannot arrive at a certain explanation, perhaps we can determine a useful application of the gospel tale. The story is about healing and deliverance, though this is a minor theme. It seems to have more to do with prejudice and boundaries that too often separate people from each other and by extension from God. Are we Christians, or just secular people who happen to go to church on Sundays? This is a query each of us must consider personally and carefully. I sometimes worry that I am a secular man who has come each Sunday for several years to St. Anne's. If there is any truth in that worry, what am I prepared to do about it? I am confident there is no more God in this building than there is God in our hearts. For God dwells nowhere else.

I think the text challenges us to especially think about how do we treat the "Gentiles" of our own times? Those who are different by virtue of choice, or by origin, gender, race, ethnicity, social standing, sexual orientation, theological or political persuasion? Do the "others" get a fair share? Or do they just get the crumbs after we've had our fill? The epistle lesson in James 2:1-10 addresses this. To put it another way: Have we moved beyond the notion that some people are dogs and the "children" should be fed first? Let us hope so. For the Episcopalians shall not be first in the Kingdom of God and Israel is not the chosen people. The Jewish prerogative existed at the time of Jesus and it is not removed in this story. But the development of Christian theology even in the New Testament confirms that as a concept, it was on the way out. It is high time to give Marcion (that second-century heretic) some place on the stage of Christian history and theology.

The second-century church father Irenaeus relates a story about the apostle John who was on the way to bathe at Ephesus, and learning that Cerinthus (another outsider and suspicious character) was in there, rushed out of the bath-house without bathing, exclaiming: "Let's go, because the bath-house might fall down, because Cerinthus, the enemy of the truth, is inside." And Polycarp, an early Christian martyr himself replied to Marcion, who met him on one occasion, and said: "Do you

know me?" replied: "I do know you, you're the first-born of Satan."
What's the matter, John? Is the Father, the Son, and the Holy Ghost,
not enough for you? It is a bad idea to run out of the bathhouses. What's
the problem Polycarp? Is the power of God insufficient to protect you
from the men and women who scare you? Do you have fewer brothers
and sisters than God has sons and daughters? The Syro-Phoenician
woman on the Lebanese coast was part of the mass of the unwashed and
unholy. Historically, Jews at the time of Jesus were quite obsessed with
avoiding ritual uncleanness. A few years ago, the *Associated Press* ran a
story detailing the production of glasses (spectacles) in Jerusalem that
intentionally blur vision. Why? So that orthodox Jewish men, for the
low affordable price of $6, can better avoid seeing women! Poor souls.
It is not new. Seventeen hundred years ago, we read a similar tale. One
of the desert monks ran into a group of nuns and seeing them left the
road to put as wide a berth between himself and them. The abbess (the
head of a female religious community) said to him: "If you were a
perfect monk you would not have looked close enough to see that we
were women." Indeed!

At the end of the story Jesus proclaimed that the demon has been
exorcised from the afflicted girl. But perhaps more importantly the
demon of prejudice so active between the differences of the human
family had also been driven out. That is what we learn from this text.
That is what is needed today in our churches, in our societies. The
kingdom of God will last forever, the American Empire is doomed. Do
we risk the challenges of difference in refusing to be shackled to
traditionalism? The lesson from the Gospel of Mark teaches us two
important lessons. First, we should rethink our assumptions about Jesus
and secondly, we need to address the problem of fences. Moving those
fences helps to alleviate the torment caused by the sins that put them
there in the first place.

The reign of God is where people come together in such a way that all
the differences and barriers are obliterated: All theological differences,

political differences; religious differences; economic differences; social differences; gender differences; cultural differences; ethnic differences; racial differences; intellectual differences and so on. It calls us to think about those fences, walls and barriers we have put up and insist upon maintaining. Such fences produce the sins of intolerance; prejudice; bigotry; back-biting; self-righteousness; criticism; bitterness; anger; fault-finding; attitudes; hatred; dogmatism; theological arrogance and a hundred more sins. What do we do then? I can find no better vision than that offered by Albert Schweitzer at the end of his monumental book, *Quest of the Historical Jesus*, written more than 100 years ago. "He comes to us as one unknown, without a name, as of old, by the lakeside he came to those men who knew him not. He speaks to us the same words, follow me, and sets us to the tasks which he has to fulfill for our time. He commands. And to those who obey him, he will reveal himself, in the toils, the struggles, the conflicts which they shall pass through in his fellowship. And as an inexpressible mystery they shall learn in their own experience who he is."

In the name of the one who calls us to imagine, who moves fences, and who comes to us in our own experiences, we dare to say these things. Amen.

AND THE WINNER IS...GOD!

An elderly lady was painstakingly manoeuvring her battered old car into place in a parking lot intent on parking the vehicle. All at once a young man in a brand new hot-rod sports car zips in front of her and slides his shiny red car into the very spot she was about to pull into. Leaning out the window she protested: "Sorry, but I was trying to park there." The young fellow smiled, shrugged, and answered: "Well, that's speed for you." The lady glared at him for a moment and then put her car into reverse and ploughed right into the sparkling new sports car. Shocked, the young man complained: "You hit my car." The lady grinned: "Well, that's money for you."

Much of western theology has taught for a very long time that at the end of life, or at the end of human history, all people will wind up either in heaven or hell. These states or places – heaven and hell – are eternal and presented as everlasting realities. St. Augustine one of the great thinkers of the early Christian centuries defended most vigorously the idea of literal eternal punishment. Others were quite graphic in their portrayal. Tertullian wrote at length that among the joys of heaven would be the opportunity to watch the agonies of the damned in the everlasting fires of hell. The view "excites my admiration," it "gives me joy" and "arouses me to exultation," Tertullian writes, watching so many bad people "groaning in the lowest darkness." He giddily describes the scene as more entertaining than the circus, the theatre and the race course. Such sentiment has a parallel in more recent times among those who wish to witness first-hand the lethal injections, electrocutions, hangings and gas chamber twitches of the criminally damned.

Not everyone agreed with Tertullian. There was a fellow named Origen who lived most of his life in the early third century. When his father was martyred, young Origen wished to join him but his quick-thinking mother wisely hid his clothes thus preventing him from rushing to an early death. Later, after perusing Matthew's Gospel where it reads that some make themselves eunuchs for the kingdom of heaven, Origen, apparently seized with a sudden inspiration, took a knife and castrated himself. It is said that later in life Origen came to regret his youthful enthusiasm. Once he healed from his wounds, he became a famous theologian first at Alexandria and later at Caesarea. For all his brilliance, Origen held some rather odd ideas. Among his controversial views were the ideas that the will of God cannot be thwarted forever and an eternal hell did just that. Therefore, hell could not truly be eternal. Origen also taught that there was no soul so hopelessly wicked that it could not be cleansed from evil and redeemed. He went one step farther and boldly declared that even Satan would, in the end, be saved. Had Tertullian still been alive when all this came out there should be little doubt he would have been shocked at the thought of the heavenly entertainment program being cut so drastically. Tertullian was dead but St. Jerome was alive and he appears to have had an absolute fit over this and seems to have suffered nightmares over the thought that the Devil might end up saved! Profoundly offended at such thinking and greatly shocked he offered a rebuttal. As far as he was concerned, Origen was the root and father of all heresies. The man was filled with foolish and insane ideas! Jerome counselled his readers to flee from Origen as one would from a poisonous snake. The castrated scholar's theology was sheer madness and his books filled with blasphemous passages. Thus far Jerome.

Theological opinion soon came to side with Jerome and Augustine against the opinions of Origen. In the year 543 the idea of universal salvation was formally condemned and the second ecumenical council of Constantinople in 553 upheld this condemnation and also passed legislation against Origen and his followers. The ruling went something like this: If anyone says or *even thinks* that the punishments of hell are not eternal and might one day end, or that wicked people and devils might be restored to God, let such a person be damned. There was no equivocation in that sentence. The church declared: We must have hell.

The idea of the restitution of all things has always seemed particularly abhorrent to most theologians. After all, the Devil was the Devil and he, she, or it (whatever the Devil was), ought to be locked up tightly and forever in a lake of fire. The Devil certainly did not deserve a chance for salvation. That's why the Devil is the Devil. Moreover, all men and women who sinned and did not repent likewise deserved everlasting punishment in hell. Origen was not the only one to dissent from this sort of thinking. There were plenty of others in those early centuries of the Christian Church: Ephraem the Syrian, Gregory of Nazianzus, Didymus the Blind, Gregory of Nyssa, Diodore of Tarsus, Theodore of Mopsuestia, Evagrius of Pontus, and possibly Clement of Alexandria and John Chrysostom. Even one of the greatest enemies of this notion, Augustine, reported that there were many who believed in universal salvation. During the Middle Ages there was very little theological reflection that followed Origen. John Scotus Erigena in the ninth century would be a notable exception. The firm efforts of Augustine and the decision at Constantinople had put the lid on ideas like universal salvation. Wicked sinners would just have to go to hell after all and stay there forever and that's all there was to it. Erasmus may well have commented that the quality of mind belonged much more to Origen than to Augustine but the latter was a saint; the former a heretic.

In the twentieth century the influential theologian Karl Barth seems to have come very close to affirming the truthfulness of Origen's position. Barth's ruminations on the subject are revealing but in the end he too reverted to traditional theological reflection and submitted to the influence of John Calvin. But if Barth hesitated a bit, the same cannot be said for the Russian theologian Nicholas Berdyaev who commented that the existence of an actual eternal hell was unacceptable and utterly "incomprehensible, inadmissible and revolting."

> It is impossible to be reconciled to the thought that God could have
> created the world and man if he foresaw hell, that he could have
> predetermined it for the sake of justice, or that he tolerates it as a special
> diabolical realm of being side by side with his own kingdom. From the
> divine point of view it means that creation is a failure. The idea is
> altogether unthinkable and, indeed, incompatible with faith in God. A
> God who deliberately allows the existence of eternal torments is not a
> God at all but is more like the devil. Hell is a fairy tale; there is not a
> shadow of reality about it; it is borrowed from our everyday existence
> with its rewards and punishments. The idea of an eternal hell is one of
> the most hideous and contemptible products of the triumphant
> herdmind. From the point of view of God, there cannot be any hell. To
> admit hell would be to deny God.

Such words strike conservative Christians as shocking. Agreeing with
that theological perspective cost American pastor Carlton Pearson his
6,000 member church in Tulsa, Oklahoma amid heresy accusations in
2004. Still, if God is love, how can hell, evil and sin persist for eternity?
If God is all-powerful why does God not do something about the
situation? Much of western theology has been deterministic; that is,
God causes people to sin and then punishes them when they do. That
appears to suggest that God has some rather strange hobbies. An entire
stream of Christian thinking adopts the view that before either time or
creation began, God appointed some to heaven and others to hell and
both parties wound up where they did to the glory of the Almighty. The
conclusion seems inescapable: God causes sin. God hates sin. God is
very upset with sin, very annoyed with sinning in general and more or
less on the outs with sinners. Therefore God created hell to deal with
the whole bother. This is the way the world is designed and there is no
escape for "sinners in the hands of an angry God." Jonathan Edwards,
who once preached a sermon with that title, said that God held people
over hell as one might torture a helpless spider or some other hapless
insect. God sees sinners as worthy only of the fire. As harsh as it may
sound, most Christian theology does not admit that God wills or desires
all, or even most, people to be saved.

In colonial New England, prospective Calvinist ministers presented for ordination were asked if they were willing to be damned for the glory of God. If they answered "no" or appeared to hesitate they remained unconsecrated and were effectively told to seek alternative employment elsewhere. That said, there is no avoiding the problem of irreconcilable Scriptures on this matter. Romans 5 and 11 and I Corinthians 15 seem very explicit in terms of the restitution of all things. There are other passages in each of the four canonical gospels and elsewhere in the New Testament (at least a dozen of them) that seem to declare the same thing. On the other hand, one does read of a fire that never goes out, of punishment that seems eternal, and the separation of the wicked from the righteous. It has been argued that God's sovereign will prevents God from saving all people. That sounds like God truly wants to save but is prevented from doing so by Godself. It also tends to suggest that God might be suffering either from a split-personality syndrome or have multiple-personality disorder. If that be the case, we should all feel rather sorry for poor old God and be equally concerned about ourselves and the fate of all creation. Or, one might hope that through the aeons of time God has managed to work through some of these knotty issues.

Of course there is the human element in all of this as well. All theology – whether that be Augustinian, Calvinist, Origenist, Thomist, eastern or western – truly amounts to human attempts to understand God. The tendency to inject human thinking into the nature of God is well nigh unavoidable. A system of rewards and punishments is how our culture operates. Is God subject to human reasoning? God wanted Jonah to go and preach to the city of Ninevah. Curiously, Jonah did not want God's mercy to extend to the Ninevites. He did go, rather grudgingly holding his nose – but not before he pulled an unsuccessful disappearing act on God and went AWOL, booking a maritime holiday in faraway Tarsus – and preached that judgment day was coming soon. Having reluctantly fulfilled his calling and duty, he retired a safe distance, like Tertullian, to watch the fireworks. To his surprise and dismay, the city repented en masse and turned from evil. God changed plans and decided not to wipe out the entire city of Ninevah. Jonah was very upset about this since he thought that every last Ninevite clearly deserved to be exterminated. The afternoon matinee entertainment cancelled, he protested bitterly to God who paid no heed to the angry complaints of the grieved prophet. When Paul preached in Jerusalem and told his hearers that God wanted the gospel proclaimed to the Gentiles, the crowd went absolutely berserk and began raving that Paul ought to be executed since clearly he was unfit to live. Why would Jonah begrudge salvation to a city with a population of 120,000 people? Why were the Jews so insanely jealous that God might turn to the Gentiles in mercy? The answer is possibly the same one to explain why so much Christian theology revels in the idea of an eternal hell.

It has been argued for centuries that God possesses true and complete justice on one hand and true and complete mercy on the other. These attributes have been viewed more or less as absolutely separate. But are they? Was the cross at Golgotha an expression of divine love and grace or a sword to execute the wicked? Does God who is love, truly take pleasure or find satisfaction in the destruction or eternal punishment, of aspects of God's creation? What exactly is the point of an eternal hell? What good does it do, what function does it accomplish? Does it exist so God can make a point? If so, what exactly is that point? Has it been conceived to provide eternal entertainment for the likes of Tertullian and his sadistic cronies? Does God win by locking men, women and devils up in a lake of fire where the torment lasts forever?

It is also worth posing the query about what crime or sin merits eternal hell. Even if one lived a hundred years and sinned mightily every day, is eternal torment a just and fitting punishment? If so, by whose standard and according to which law? The Scriptures claim that humankind was originally created in the image of God. If one is rotten to the core, what has become of that divine image? Unless theologians are prepared to admit that the image of God has been entirely destroyed in certain contemptible scoundrels – Adolf Hitler, Joseph Stalin, Mao Zedong,

Pol Pot, Idi Amin, Nicolae Ceaușescu, Charles Manson as examples –
then part of God goes to hell with each of the damned. Is God in hell?
Can God be damned? Can humankind destroy the image of God? If so,
how? What does it mean to be God-damned, if not to lose in the greatest
encounter of the cosmos? Is there some chance that well-intentioned
theologians have utterly botched God's plans for humankind? Have we
unwittingly deprived God, theologically, of God's ultimate triumph by
banishing Origen and proclaiming Augustine? What purpose has been
served in condemning Didymus the Blind and praising Jerome?

It makes me wonder if it is truly possible to be damned by theology or
theological mistakes? I was taught as a youngster (by church ministers
though not by my father who knew better) that holding certain views of
God would almost certainly send one to hell. The idea was reinforced
time and time again that if one was not baptised in the proper way, that
is using the right formula and proper mode, then salvation was quite
impossible. I thought it odd that God seemed so prickly and that
salvation appeared to have been left in the hands of ordinary people
who by most theological accounts were pathologically prone to sinning.
I also heard repeatedly that if one failed to attain to a particular level of
spirituality and have certain experiences then salvation and heaven were
very much in doubt. There is absolutely nothing modern in this view.
The ancient Athanasian Creed is similarly unambiguous. Whoever fails
to adhere to proper doctrine will be damned to an eternal hell where the
fires burn forever and the torments never cease. It would appear that
the Gnostics do win after all. One is saved by what one believes and by
what one knows. If you've got the formula you're in; if not, well, thank
you very much for playing but I am afraid it's hell for you. In this
schema, God becomes the lord of technicalities and the mission of Jesus
to Golgotha entirely perfunctory for in the end proper formulas, correct
theologies and insider information is all it really takes.

Martin Luther wrote in his commentary on the book of Jonah in 1526
his doubts about an eternal hell: "Whatever hell might be in the end, I

do not really know. But I do not think that it is some special place where the souls of the damned are kept." Later he confessed: "Everyone carries their own hell with them wherever they are and this lasts as long as that person feels and fears the final necessity of death and the wrath of God." If sin persists then the cross winds up, somehow and rather tragically, as a failure. If men and women go to an eternal hell then God's love is not all-powerful. If God wills that there be a hell for the everlasting torture of the sinner then the Kingdom of God cannot truly be realized. If the Devil successfully resists the grace of God then at best God's triumph is a split-decision. On the other hand, if sin is swallowed up in love then the cross becomes a cosmic triumph. If men and women do not sink forever in the bowels of hell then God's love is unchallenged as the most powerful force in the universe. If God does not and cannot tolerate a literal, eternal hell, then the Kingdom of God truly fills the universe. If the Devil is redeemed then God's victory is complete and in the end the winner is ... God.

As far as Luther was concerned, sin was inevitable in this world for righteousness could not truly prevail but we must look for a new heaven and a new earth in which righteousness does reign. Through the riches of God's glory one can know that the Lamb of God takes away the sins of the world. Therefore, Luther wrote, no sin can separate us from the Lamb, not even if we commit awful sins a thousand times every day. The Lamb has triumphed, the Lamb will triumph, and every authority and power shall be destroyed. Death will be destroyed and everything put under the feet of Christ. When everything has been brought into subjection to Christ, then the kingdom will be turned over to God so that God may be all in all. That is theological rhetoric. It sounds good. It sounds proper. It sounds orthodox. But what exactly does it mean to say that God shall be all in all?

It stands to reason that God can be everything only when sin, hell and Satan are no more and have either been annihilated or transformed. Having won the war and brought about their defeat, God could simply destroy sin, hell and the Devil through annihilation. There might be good arguments for this course of action. But what greater victory could there be then the reconciliation of all things to God?

After the long, dark, Christmas-less winter in the land of Narnia, Aslan is reported to again be on the move. Spring comes. Ice melts. Snow disappears. New life appears. When the *Star Wars* are lost and won the terrible Darth Vader is unmasked and restored. Sin is horrible, but not eternal. The victory of Golgotha is timeless for Christ will see to that and as Julian of Norwich declared: "All shall be well and all manner of things shall be well." To annihilate sin is one thing. To metamorphose that same sin into righteousness would be unexpected and magnificent transformation. To execute Satan might seem like fitting justice. To restore the old boy in grace, love and mercy would spell the end forever to the darkness and would be a miracle of the highest order. Then the light of the Lamb will have consumed everything and the uncontested winner, in absolutely every way, will be God and God alone.

Silver Star Mountain, Washington

Remembering Laura

It has been thirty years since I met Laura. Almost a lifetime ago. Laura was young, attractive, full of life, energetic. She wrote poetry, played the guitar. She was almost perfect: pure loveliness, fit, witty, smart, a winning personality, wonderful sense of humor, excited, creative, kind, tender, generous, well read, curious, up for a good challenge, open and honest, exciting, gentle, interested in all manner of new ideas, excellent at communicating, heart-warming smile, capable of both stimulating and sustaining conversation, loved the outdoors, respectful, positive, and a person of deep faith. She filled empty spaces with warmth. She especially loved animals, music, art, poetry, photography, literature, and children. Backstage at a concert once, Paul McCartney told her she looked like the actress Annette Benning. He was right. She told me once in a letter: "You are the deepest friend I have ever had." Years after I met her I thought she could have made me a better man.

Over the years we enjoyed visits, had many phone calls and breathlessly exciting conversations. There were even more emails. She loved books and regularly introduced me to authors and writings and came up with some of the most amazing things I'd never heard of. There was a poem she especially wanted me to know. The words of "Summons" by Robert Francis were written out on a napkin I have kept through the years.

Keep me from going to sleep too soon
Or if I go to sleep too soon
Come wake me up. Come any hour
Of night. Come whistling up the road.
Stomp on the porch. Bang on the door.
Make me get out of bed and come
And let you in and light a light.
Tell me the northern lights are on
And make me look. Or tell me clouds
Are doing something to the moon
They never did before, and show me.
See that I see. Talk to me till

I'm half as wide awake as you
And start to dress wondering why
I ever went to bed at all.
Tell me the walking is superb.
Not only tell me but persuade me.
You know I'm not too hard persuaded.

I wish I could have kept Laura from going to sleep and now that she has fallen asleep I wish with all my heart I could waken her. Unfortunately, her last years were overtaken by grim darkness. A life of extraordinary promise was interrupted by cruelty, pain, disappointment, and sadness. There was not enough grace or mercy and vagaries that can neither be numbered nor accounted. On New Years' Eve, 2019 her journey came to a sudden end. There was no warning. The news hit me like a freight train. I had the awful misfortune of lacking the gift of time. I wish with all my heart I'd had the opportunity to tell her how much I cared. I may even have been bold enough to look into her lovely blue eyes and tell her I had always loved her. I cannot describe the emotion that swept over me when I learned those same eyes had been given to a transplant services center. In consequence, a blind man recovered his sight and is now able to see the world through Laura's eyes. An empty box filled.

Laura left us far too soon. I still cannot imagine she is gone. I still cannot conceive of the world without her in it. I watched a video memorializing her life and the many images filled me with gratitude but also with unspeakable grief. Writing this reflection, I am again overcome by the memory of her and my heart aches for the girl I knew so long ago and so far away who was so brightly endowed with the sunshine of love, life and goodness. I have not grieved for someone as much as I have grieved for Laura. Her mother told me she liked to think of Laura now as seeing unimaginable beauty, having no problems to escape, enjoying good health, and receiving lots of love from her creator.

Our lives are like fireplaces where the fire seems to have gone out. But if one stoops and blows gently on the coals, sometimes a flicker of a flame appears. The fire has not been extinguished entirely. Laura may have been surprised to know that she blew on the coals of my heart and made me realize there was still some light and warmth remaining. That was Laura's gift to me. Just one gift in one empty box. There were many others.

A few years ago, I found myself home: Saint John, New Brunswick, Canada. Up the road a quarter mile from the old family house is Fernhill Cemetery. Founded in 1848, it is a lovely place and one where I often walked as a boy. My ancestors are buried there, grandparents, aunts, uncles, cousins, and more recently my own father. Three or four years ago I learned there is room for me. This means when I arrive at the end of the road I have a reserved spot just in case I have nowhere else to go. In Fernhill Cemetery, one summer evening, I came across a grave stone inscription for a little girl untimely deceased. It's from a poem by Ellen Brenneman: "No one that is loved, is ever lost, and no one who has ever touched a heart can really pass away, because some beauty lingers on in each memory of which they've been a part." How true this is of Laura. She lingers in so many happy and wonderful memories. This book is for her. I will always love her.

Young pilgrims, May 1965

ABOUT THE AUTHOR

Thomas A. Fudge was born in Maritime Canada and in addition to the "Great White North" has also resided in the United States, England, the Czech Republic, New Zealand and Australia. He holds a Bachelor of Arts degree in Religion *summa cum laude* from Warner Pacific College in Portland, Oregon, a Master of Divinity degree *summa cum laude* from the Iliff School of Theology (seminary) in Denver, Colorado, a Doctor of Philosophy degree in History from the University of Cambridge in England, and latterly a Doctor of Philosophy degree in Theology from Otago University in Dunedin, New Zealand. He has served parishes in Oregon, Washington, and Colorado holding various church leadership capacities as director of adult education, associate pastor and pastor and has had association with Lutheran, Evangelical Covenant, Pentecostal, Baptist, United Methodist, Anglican and Episcopal, along with non-denominational traditions. He is formerly an Assistant Professor of Religion at Warner Pacific College and Senior Lecturer in History at the University of Canterbury in Christchurch, New Zealand. He has also taught college-level courses in the Texas prison system. He is the author of at least seventeen scholarly books along with about seventy articles in academic journals and monographs. He is an occasional poet, enjoys hiking, spelunking, watching films, listening to music and fresh corn. He is a retired mountaineer and certified scuba-diver. He considers himself a pilgrim, not a settler, identifies as a traveller, celebrates questions and sees life as an adventurous journey. For the past ten years he has been the Professor of Medieval History at the University of New England in Armidale, Australia.

English Channel, off the coast of Dover

Lightning Source UK Ltd.
Milton Keynes UK
UKHW020221100522
402745UK00014B/77/J